THE
COSMOPOLITAN
TRADITION

THE
COSMOPOLITAN
TRADITION

A NOBLE BUT
FLAWED IDEAL

MARTHA C. NUSSBAUM

THE BELKNAP PRESS OF HARVARD UNIVERSITY PRESS
CAMBRIDGE, MASSACHUSETTS
LONDON, ENGLAND
2019

First printing

Library of Congress Cataloging-in-Publication Data

Names: Nussbaum, Martha Craven, 1947– author.
Title: The cosmopolitan tradition : a noble but flawed ideal / Martha C. Nussbaum.
Description: Cambridge, Massachusetts : The Belknap Press of Harvard University
    Press, 2019. | Includes bibliographical references and index.
Identifiers: LCCN 2018057772 | ISBN 9780674052499 (alk. paper)
Subjects: LCSH: Cosmopolitanism—Philosophy.
Classification: LCC JZ1308 .N87 2019 | DDC 306—dc23
LC record available at https://lccn.loc.gov/2018057772

For Miriam Griffin (1935–2018)
With admiration, affection, and love

CONTENTS

THE
COSMOPOLITAN
TRADITION

ONE

World Citizens

I. Citizens of the Kosmos

Asked where he came from, Diogenes the Cynic answered with a single word: *kosmopolitês*, meaning, "a citizen of the world" (Diog. Laert. VI.63). This moment, however fictive, might be said to inaugurate a long tradition of cosmopolitan political thought in the Western tradition. A Greek male refuses the invitation to define himself by lineage, city, social class, even free birth, even gender. He insists on defining himself in terms of a characteristic that he shares with all other human beings, male and female, Greek and non-Greek, slave and free. And by calling himself not simply a dweller in the world but a citizen of the world, Diogenes suggests, as well, the possibility of a politics, or a moral approach to politics, that focuses on the humanity we share rather than the marks of local origin, status, class, and gender that divide us. It is a first step on the road that leads to Kant's resonant idea of the "kingdom of ends," a virtual polity of moral aspiration that unites all rational beings (although Diogenes, more inclusive, does not limit the community to the "rational"), and to Kant's vision of a cosmopolitan politics that will join all humanity under laws given not by convention and class but by free moral choice. Diogenes, they say, "used to make fun of good birth and distinctions of rank and all that sort of thing, calling them decorations of vice. The only correct political order was, he said, that in the world *(kosmos)* as a whole" (VI.72).

Cynic / Stoic cosmopolitanism urges us to recognize the equal, and unconditional, worth of all human beings, a worth grounded in moral choice-capacity (or perhaps even this is too restrictive?), rather than on traits that depend on fortuitous natural or social arrangements. The insight that politics ought to treat human beings both as equal and as having a worth beyond price is one of the deepest and most influential insights of Western thought; it is responsible for much that is fine in the modern Western political imagination. One day, Alexander the Great came and stood over Diogenes, as he was sunning himself in the marketplace. "Ask me for anything you want," Alexander said. He said, "Get out of my light" (VI.38). This image of the dignity of humanity, which can shine forth in its nakedness unless shadowed by the false claims of rank and kingship, a dignity that needs only the removal of that shadow to be vigorous and free, is one endpoint of a line that leads to the modern human rights movement.

In the tradition I shall describe, dignity is non-hierarchical. It belongs—and in equal measure—to all who have some basic threshold level of capacity for moral learning and choice. The tradition explicitly and pointedly excludes non-human animals, and I shall return to this problem in Chapter 7, rejecting that judgment; in some versions, though not that of Diogenes, it also excludes, though less explicitly, humans with severe cognitive disabilities. These shortcomings must be addressed in any contemporary version of the idea.[1] The idea of dignity is not, however, inherently hierarchical or based on the idea of a rank-ordered society. In the medieval and early modern era, versions of the idea of dignity did crop up that were hierarchical and suited to a feudal society. I do not study these ideas here, or the traditions they ground. It is important to emphasize the egalitarian heart of this Stoic type of cosmopolitanism, since some scholars writing about dignity recently have supposed that the entire history of that concept derives from ideas of rank and status in hierarchical societies.[2]

Taken by itself, this vision need not involve politics: it is a moral ideal. In the thought of many of the tradition's exemplars, however, the idea of equal human dignity does ground a distinctive set of obligations for international and national politics. The idea of respect for humanity has been at the root of much of the international human rights movement, and it has played a formative role in many national legal and constitutional traditions.

Nor is the idea of equal human dignity peculiar to the philosophical traditions of the West, although those traditions will be my focus in the present book. In an India riven by hierarchical ideas of caste and of occupations assigned at birth, Buddhism has long brought a different idea, the idea of human equality. Although Gandhi reinterpreted the Hindu tradition in a more egalitarian manner than was conventional, the Buddhist antecedents of the new nation's founding principle of

3

equal citizenship were dramatized by Gandhi, Nehru, and the other national founders by placing the Buddhist wheel of law at the center of the flag. The main architect of India's constitution, B. R. Ambedkar, one of the great legal minds of the twentieth century, converted to Buddhism late in his life and remained entranced by it throughout his life. An "untouchable" (now *dalit*), he insisted on framing the constitution in ways that put the idea of equal human dignity front and center.[3] He wrote an entire book on the Buddha, published in 1957, shortly after his death, in order to make clear that tradition's idea of human equality.[4]

Similarly, the freedom movement in South Africa made respect for human dignity the center of a revolutionary politics. In this case, Stoic doctrines did play a role—alongside traditional African ideas of *ubuntu*. Philosopher Kwame Anthony Appiah has emphasized the formative role of Cicero's idea of world citizenship in the life and work of his father, Joe Appiah, founder of the modern nation of Ghana,[5] discussing the ubiquity of Cicero's ideas in at least all the Anglophone parts of Africa. But recently it has emerged that Nelson Mandela—who later titled a book of interviews and letters *Conversations with Myself,* alluding explicitly to the influence of the Stoic philosopher Marcus Aurelius, had access to the *Meditations* already as a prisoner on Robben Island.[6] When South Africa's constitution was written, it contained these ideas. Whatever the role of Stoic ideas in the founding document, at least they dovetailed with ideas Mandela had already derived from his own traditions and his experience.

When the Universal Declaration of Human Rights was framed, its framers included representatives of many world traditions, including those of Egypt, China, and Europe. As French philosopher Jacques Maritain relates, they explicitly avoided language that was the sectarian property of a particular tradition—for example, the Christian language of "the soul." The language of equal human dignity, however, as an ethical notion attached to no particular metaphysics, was something they felt they could use and make central.[7]

The ideas of the cosmopolitan tradition have, then, been immensely fertile, and they have also intersected with related ideas from other traditions. But the founders of this Western tradition also introduce a problem with which the tradition has been wrestling ever since. For they think that, in order to treat people as having a dignity that life's accidents cannot erode, they must scoff at money, rank, and power, saying that they are unnecessary for human flourishing. The dignity of moral capacity is complete in itself. Diogenes doesn't need to ask Alexander for a decent living, citizenship, health care: all he needs to say is, "Get out of my light." Moral personality is complete, and completely beautiful, without any external aids. Cosmopolitan politics appears to the framers to impose stringent duties of respect, including an end to aggressive war, support for people who have been unjustly attacked, and a ban on crimes against humanity, including genocide and torture. But it imposes no duties of material aid—on the grounds that human beings do not really need the goods of fortune. Without such aid, human dignity is still inviolate.

This bifurcation of duties is problematic for several reasons. First, material inequality is an evident fact of human life, too glaring in its effects to be overlooked. A child born this year in the United States has a life expectancy of 79.1 years.[8] A child born in Swaziland can expect to live 49.0 years. Most adults in the United States and Europe are literate, although marginal literacy remains a disturbing problem, correlated with poverty. Some developing countries attain nearly this overall rate of literacy: Costa Rica, for example, has 97.4 percent adult literacy, Sri Lanka 91.2 percent, the Philippines 95.1 percent, Peru

93.8 percent, Colombia 93.6 percent, Jordan 97.9 percent, Thailand 96.4 percent, Botswana 86.7 percent. In many nations, however, a person's chance of learning to read (and, hence, to qualify for most well-paying jobs) is far lower. In India, only 62.9 percent of the population is literate, in Pakistan 54.7 percent, in Bangladesh 58.8 percent, in Nigeria 51.1 percent, in Ethiopia 39.0 percent, in Niger 15.5 percent. (These figures of course are averages that conceal gender gaps, rural-urban gaps, and, often, gaps between ethnic or racial groups.) Clean water, health services, sanitation, maternal health and safety, adequate nutrition—all these basic human goods are distributed very unevenly around the world. The accident of being born in one country rather than another pervasively shapes the life chances of every child who is born. Being female, being lower-class, living in a rural area, membership in an ethnic or racial or religious minority—these also affect life chances within every nation. Material inequality, then, is internal to every nation; but at present the gap between nations outstrips the internal gaps.[9]

The first and largest problem with the bifurcation of duties is, then, that it neglects a fact of staggering importance. The ancient Greeks and Romans did not have our data, and very likely their world contained fewer inequalities between nations, perhaps even smaller internal inequalities, than does our world. Still, the differences were large enough, and philosophers such as Cicero, Seneca, and Marcus, well-traveled and busily engaged in projects of imperial expansion, should not have neglected them.

A second problem with the bifurcation of duties is that it involves the pretense that fulfilling the duties of justice does not require material expenditure, something that is empirically false, if we include among the duties of justice duties to protect people from aggressive war, from torture, from slavery, and from other crimes against humanity. Indeed, the cost of a defensive war may vastly exceed the costs involved in alleviating hunger. Once we see this, we should grant that the distinction is one of degree rather than of kind, and perhaps not even one of degree, so far as spending our resources is concerned.

But there is a deeper incoherence. The tradition appears to hold that material possessions make no difference to the exercise of our capacities for choice and other aspects of our dignity. If one really believes that human dignity is totally immune to the accidents of fortune, then slavery, torture, and unjust war do not damage it, any more than hunger and disease. But this seems false: people who are ill-nourished, who have no clean water, and who have no access to resources connected to health, education, and other "material" goods are not equally able to cultivate their capacities for choice or to express their basic human dignity. (To put this in terms of the modern human rights movement, the "first-generation rights," such as religious freedom and political liberty, require the "second-generation rights," the economic and social rights.) The mind and soul are aspects of a living body that needs nutrition, health care, and other material goods. The Stoic position appears internally incoherent, granting that in some ways the world makes a difference to human dignity and that in other (very similar?) ways it does not.

Incoherent or not, the bifurcation of duties between duties of justice and duties of material aid has exercised a decisive influence on the course of international politics and on the developing human rights movement.[10] We have a fairly well worked-out set of doctrines about duties of justice, which command wide assent and have become the basis for widely agreed accounts of "first-generation rights." We have no equally worked-out doctrines on the other duties, those in the "second generation," and we do not seem even to know where to begin, once we step outside of national boundaries.

The essays in this book investigate the attractive ideas inherent in the cosmopolitan tradition, but also its intellectual and practical problems. Some of the material was based on my Castle Lectures, delivered at Yale University in 2000, but new essays on Grotius and Smith have been added, and an essay on Kant has been deleted on the grounds that Kant's contributions are well known and much studied, and, furthermore, that Grotius and Smith move the tradition forward, in the area of material aid, in a way that Kant does not.

This is unabashedly a book of connected essays, not a continuous historical narrative. There would be little philosophical point in attempting to mention every figure in the tradition, although from the historical viewpoint many figures merit attention. The list is long, including many fascinating and little-known medieval and early modern thinkers.[11] But that is not my project. Instead, I select examples that follow a particular logical trajectory, starting from Cicero (not a Stoic in all areas, but extremely close to the Stoics in ethics) and the orthodox Stoics, and probing and revising those doctrines. (This means that my primary modern figures, Grotius and Smith, exemplify a Protestant cosmopolitan tradition, rather than the Catholic tradition that begins from Aristotle and develops in rather different ways.) Because I think that the work of each of these thinkers, all major philosophers, deserves to be treated as a complex whole, rather than as bits and pieces, each essay is substantially independent, and multi-faceted as is the thinker on whom it focuses in each case. Connections, however, are always evident.

My basic story describes the origins of the bifurcation and traces a series of gradual steps away from it, in the direction of a more capacious sense of transnational, and also national, obligation—culminating, ultimately, in the contemporary "Capabilities Approach" (at least my version of it). I begin, in Chapter 2, with Cicero's *De Officiis* (44 BCE), one of the most valuable and influential works of political thought in the Western tradition, and one that has influenced most subsequent attempts to think about the moral underpinnings of international relations. Cicero develops the picture of a world where justice in some manner governs all human relations, and in an attractive way he describes those duties of justice and what they require of nations and individuals. In his treatment of proper occasions for war *(ius ad bellum)* and proper conduct in war *(ius in bello)*, he lays the foundations for all subsequent Western attempts to work out the law of just war. But at the same time, Cicero begins our puzzling bifurcation, treating the duties of material aid very differently from the way in which he treats the duties of justice. The essay critically scrutinizes that bifurcation. But I also note that as soon as Cicero announces the bifurcation, he already begins the move away from it with his fascinating insistence on a doctrine of negative responsibility: we are culpable not just for wrongs that we actively do, but also for many wrongs that we fail to prevent.

The cosmopolitan tradition has another deep problem, which lies in the realm of human psychology. Chapter 3 presents and confronts that issue, beginning earlier than Cicero's time with the Greek Cynics and Stoics, but focusing on the second-century CE Stoic emperor Marcus Aurelius and his convoluted negotiations with the notion of dignity. His work poses some questions relevant to the bifurcation of duties, asking us to ponder what type of treatment human dignity requires, if it is, as the Stoics hold, inalienable. What damage is done by slavery, for example, if the dignity of the slave is never affected by it? I ponder these questions about dignity, showing that Stoicism needs, but does not yet have, a distinction between levels of "capability," which I shall ultimately attempt to supply through my Capabilities Approach (different in some key respects from Amartya Sen's). Meanwhile, Marcus's cosmopolitanism also reveals aspects of the motivational and emotional underpinning of cosmopolitanism that make our worries deepen. Can a cosmopolitan politics provide real people with a basis for emotions toward one another sufficient to motivate altruistic conduct, without losing a sense of personal meaning? Surely some statements by Marcus, asking us to renounce close personal ties to family, city, and group, seem to threaten deep concern and the very sources of our motivation to act. They appear to leave us with a barren life in which nothing is worth loving or doing.

To get a sense of how we ought to solve this problem, I return to Cicero at the end of the chapter. A committed Roman patriot, Cicero lost his life to assassination shortly after writing De Officiis, while carrying out a last-ditch effort to save the Roman Republic. In the work itself he makes it clear that, although all human beings are bound to all other human beings by ties of recognition and concern, the motivational tie to one's own republic has a special salience for the organization of one's entire moral and political life. At the same time, he shows that the right type of cosmopolitanism can make a large place for friendship and family ties. In the contemporaneous works De Amicitia (On friendship) and De Senectute (On old age), and above all in his correspondence with his best friend, Atticus, he shows the enormous importance of these bonds of love in a life dedicated to others.[12] More persuasively by far than the Stoics, Cicero balances the near and the distant, pointing the way to a reasonable moral psychology for today's world. He argues that these bonds are not just motivationally and instrumentally, but also intrinsically valuable. I allude to this contribution briefly in Chapter 2, but develop it much further in Chapter 3.

With Chapter 4, we enter the modern era, turning to Hugo Grotius (1583–1645), whose *On the Law of War and Peace* (1625) set the agenda for the modern law of war, and also made a more general contribution to the articulation of an international order suffused with moral norms. Grotius is deeply indebted to Cicero and the Stoics; he views his enterprise as a continuation of theirs. Famously, and shockingly, and even while professing himself a devout Christian, he denies that politics needs a theistic Christian foundation. Grotius argues against a proto-Hobbesian position on international politics that holds that no moral relations obtain between states. He supports the Ciceronian-Stoic idea that international relations should be grounded in moral norms of respect for humanity. I study those arguments, and the picture of nations and international morality that emerges. Grotius, like Cicero, gives moral importance to the nation, but he also argues that nations and their citizens have moral obligations to people in other nations. (Throughout this book we must remember that recognizing the moral centrality of the nation in the way that Grotius and I recommend does not entail, and indeed positively forbids, a type of me-first tub-thumping nationalism that is all too familiar in our time.) Grotius's nuanced and conflicted doctrine of humanitarian intervention gives useful guidance to us, as we grapple with the claims of humanity and national sovereignty. Further, he takes a decisive step away from the Ciceronian bifurcation of duties, admitting transnational duties of material aid in some circumstances alongside duties of justice. Grotius's writings provide an attractive and highly influential basis for much of international law, as is widely acknowledged; but this material-aid aspect of his thought has been neglected. This side of his thought also includes a valuable account of duties to admit needy migrants. Furthermore, he articulates a promising basis for thinking that all nations share some duties to protect the natural environment. Finally, as does Cicero, Grotius also makes a start toward resolving Marcus's motivational problem, by imagining the world community as a society in which each of us participates, while at the same time cherishing our own nations as sources and vehicles of human autonomy and human connection.

Adam Smith (1723–1790) is often misrepresented as a champion of the unfettered free market, although a new wave of Smith scholarship has begun to undo these misreadings. In fact it is Smith, among all of my interlocutors, who makes the most useful contributions toward undoing the bifurcation, emphasizing the importance of national commitment to material redistribution. Smith, who often lectured on Cicero and the Stoics, is steeped in their writings, quoting effortlessly and without even footnotes, since he presupposes similar familiarity on the part of his readers. But in *The Wealth of Nations* (1776) he goes much further even than Grotius in undoing one of Cicero's mistakes, by arguing that the claims of humanity generate stringent duties of material aid in the domestic context, particularly in the areas of health and education. These duties are to some extent extended to the entire world, although Smith focuses on a critique of colonial domination and the economic damage it does to colonized nations. Smith also makes progress in moral psychology, following Cicero in defending particular attachments to family and friends, and he articulates a positive albeit critical notion of patriotism.

On material duties and moral psychology, then, Smith makes decisive progress. At the same time, however, his ideas about both duty and motivation, particularly in the various editions of his *Theory of Moral Sentiments* (first edition 1759, sixth edition 1790) are internally vexed by a persistent fascination with the Stoic sage, who asserts his dignity by showing that he really doesn't need the goods of fortune. These complexities in Smith's thought are valuable to study, because they show us something about the ways in which strongly gendered images of masculine self-sufficiency deform political psychology, as much in our own day as in his.

These four essays leave us with achievements, but also with problems to solve. My two concluding chapters move us from cosmopolitanism to the contemporary normative view that I call the Capabilities Approach. In Chapter 6, I investigate five issues that the tradition simply does not talk enough about, but which must figure in any decent international politics today. The first is the issue of moral psychology, where I argue that Cicero provides a promising way forward, which we can further develop. Just as we can defend the intrinsic and motivational importance of ties to family and friends without denying that we owe something to all our fellow citizens (which a just tax system would presumably arrange), it is possible to cultivate (through moral and civic education) a type of patriotism that is, on the one hand, compatible with strong familial, friendly, and personal love, and, on the other hand, builds ties of recognition and concern with people outside our national borders. This has often been done, and great political leaders including Lincoln, Nehru, F.D.R., and Martin Luther King, Jr. have succeeded, at least for periods of time, in cultivating that type of mixed concern in their nations.

Second, I confront a problem posed by people's plural "comprehensive doctrines," that is, their views, whether religious or secular, of what the best human life is. Cosmopolitans tended to believe that just one normative view is correct, and that people could be governed in accordance with that correct view. Contemporaries of Grotius and, even more, of Smith, however, were already thinking differently: religious freedom and non-establishment are, they thought, key elements of any decent national order. But cosmopolitanism needs to change in recognition of this idea. I discuss, and defend, the generalized form of this idea of non-establishment that John Rawls has called "political liberalism": the idea that political principles should not be built on any single comprehensive doctrine, but should avoid sectarianism as far as possible, while still espousing some core moral doctrines that may be able to command an "overlapping consensus" among the holders of all the reasonable comprehensive doctrines. I then try to show what this idea looks like in the larger world between nations, and what sort of international society it supports. On this issue, cosmopolitanism needs major amendment, but much of its content can still be preserved, as the international human rights movement—already in the thought of Maritain a form of political liberalism—shows.

Our next two problems are thornier. They are both set in motion by the recognition that the nation is a unit of both practical and normative importance. It is normatively central, as Grotius argues, because it is the largest unit that is an effective vehicle of human autonomy, and accountable to people's voices. And it is of great practical importance because its institutions have great power in today's world as places where both duties of justice and duties of material aid are made real. If the nation were not normatively central, we could wish to supplant it in its practical role; but its normative importance ought to curb such ambitions.

Given the nation's two roles, our third problem is the longstanding weakness and inefficacy of international human rights law. I argue that this weakness is not just descriptively true, it is normatively desirable, given the fundamental moral role of the nation. But it is still problematic: if we care about the welfare of people everywhere, what structures should we endorse to make progress? Focusing on the specific case of women's human rights, I argue that the role of international agreements is moral and expressive more than legal, but that nonetheless it can give an impetus to legal traditions inside each nation. International law does not, and probably should not, change domestic law directly. But that does not mean that international movements and laws are impotent to effect real change. Above all, international human rights law helps political movements organize to fight injustice and to change things within their own nations. *Pace* many human rights thinkers, we should not wish things to be otherwise, given the strong endorsement I have given to the moral status of the nation and national sovereignty.

My fourth problem is similar: what to do about material aid given the role of nations. This issue, too, is both normative and practical. We can produce a very good moral argument to the effect that morality requires richer nations and their citizens to provide a good deal more aid than they currently do to poorer nations. That's what the bifurcation denied, and undoing the bifurcation is what my argument has been all about. Such aid could be normatively problematic if disbursed in a paternalistic way: so the first question is how aid can be given consistently with people's right to make their own laws. But now we are learning that there is another problem of a practical sort that greets us even if we solve the normative problem. There is mounting evidence, most compellingly argued by economist Angus Deaton, but supported by many scholars of economics and international politics, that foreign aid is basically useless and often counterproductive, in that the dependency on money from abroad erodes the political will to manage health, education, and so on well and stably within a nation. If we are morally required to do something, but we can't see what we could possibly do that would make things better, what then? I try to give a cautious but not utterly despairing answer to this question.

Finally, fifth, we must confront the problem of migration: both refugees seeking asylum from persecution and war, and migrants seeking a better way of life. (Given my insistence on the importance of material conditions for the exercise of our human powers, these two reasons for migrating are not always sharply distinct.) This problem was ignored by most members of the cosmopolitan tradition, although the Romans made a large start on it in practical terms, extending Roman citizenship to most parts of the empire, and although Smith mordantly observed that the problem of unequal wealth between nations is in large part created by colonial plunder. Whatever the origins of the desperation with which people flee their homelands, we need to have something to say about it if we are to assess the contemporary viability of the cosmopolitan project. This is a huge philosophical issue. It deserves a book of its own, and it has received some excellent philosophical analyses. Here I simply attempt to sketch the approach that the type of account I am developing ought to take, compatibly with my defense of the role of the nation and national identity.

It will be obvious that I have so far been silent about one of the largest problems with the cosmopolitan tradition: its disdain for non-human animals and the world of nature. Typically the tradition grounds our duties in the worth and dignity of moral / rational agency. This is not even a very good approach for the human kind, since it excludes humans with severe cognitive disabilities, who are certainly our fellow citizens and ought to be viewed as equal in worth. And it certainly excludes non-human animals: the tradition often argues for human worth precisely through a pejorative contrast with the "brute beasts." We need an international politics that is truly cosmopolitan, and such a politics, I argue, must be grounded in the worth and dignity of sentient bodies, not that of reason alone. That extension may already have been made by Diogenes the Cynic at the start of the tradition: he was unashamed of his animal body, and did not seem drawn to a hierarchy of faculties. But subsequent thinkers have failed to cultivate his insight, which was too radical for them. Because recovering that insight is a large part of my current work on the Capabilities Approach, I take up this deep issue in Chapter 7.

My concluding Chapter 7, "From Cosmopolitanism to the Capabilities Approach," describes where we are: with a version of my Capabilities Approach that extends to all nations and all people, but that gives a special place to the nation. I ask how we ought to think about the relative claims of the nation and the world, and about the prospects of the moral emotions in a newly complex world. As for the bifurcation, how should we think of economic and social rights as national duties? And is there any useful way of extending those duties to the world, given the problems the previous chapter has raised? I end by defending the general approach of the tradition, if not its detail: moral duties do not stop at national boundaries, and we are all bound to all others by ties of recognition and concern.

I end Chapter 7 with the largest challenge of all: extending the cosmopolitan tradition to non-human animals and the world of nature. The Stoics, among the ancient Greek philosophical schools, were the least interested in the moral claims of non-human animals. Treating them as brute beasts, they refused all evidence of their complex capacities and showed indifference even to their sentience.[13] We must and can do better.

TWO

Duties of Justice, Duties of Material Aid

Cicero's Problematic Legacy

I. The Statesmen's Bible

For many years the international community has been working with an account of some transnational duties that commands a wide consensus. These include duties of nations and their agents in time of war and duties of all nations to uphold (some) human rights, those that are standardly called "civil and political." While there is much debate about when and how nations are permitted to interfere in the affairs of other nations (a topic I shall take up in Chapter 4), there is general agreement that the community of nations must work to secure and protect (some) human rights for all the world's people. Theories of the proper conduct of war, and of proper conduct toward the enemy during war; theories about torture and cruelty to persons; theories even about the rape of women and other transnational atrocities; theories about aggressive acts of various other sorts toward foreign nationals, whether on our soil or abroad; even theories about our duties to support other first-generation human rights, such as the freedom of speech and association—all these things nations have seen fit to work out in some detail, and our theories of international justice have been dealing with them at least from the first century BCE, when Cicero described the "duties of justice" in his work *De Officiis* (On duties), perhaps the most influential book in the Western tradition of political philosophy. Cicero's ideas were further developed in the Middle Ages by thinkers such as Aquinas, Suarez, and Gentili; they were the basis for Grotius's account of just and unjust war, for many aspects of the thought of Wolff and Pufendorf, and for Kant's thinking about cosmopolitan obligation in *Perpetual Peace*.[1] By now we understand many nuances of this topic and have a rich array of subtly different views—for example, on such questions as whether it is permissible to lie to the enemy in wartime, a subject concerning which Cicero and Kant are the rigorists, and Grotius takes a more indulgent line.

The rights that are standardly called "social and economic rights," however, have as yet received no clear transnational analysis. Material inequalities across national boundaries are a glaring fact of twenty-first-century life. But our philosophical theories of international law and morality have relatively little to say about what obligations, if any, flow from these inequalities. We have quite a few accounts of personal duties of aid at a distance,[2] and in recent years theorists of global justice have begun to work out the foundations for a theory of material transfers between nations, but we have virtually no consensus on this question, and some of our major theories of justice are virtually silent about it, simply starting from the nation-state as their basic unit.³ Nor has international law progressed far in this direction. Although many international documents by now do concern themselves with what are known as second-generation rights (economic and social rights) in addition to the standard political and civil rights, they typically do so in a nation-state-based way, portraying certain material entitlements as what all citizens have a right to demand from the state in which they live.

This is an uneasy position, to put it mildly. It is obvious that human lives are deformed by poverty and by the lack of social and economic goods, such as health care and education, just as much as they are deformed by the absence of political liberties, and that these deprivations are in multiple ways interconnected. Moreover, it is pretty obvious that the so-called first-generation rights cannot be protected without money, so the distinction between the two types cannot plausibly be that the former are free of cost. Most of us, if pressed, would admit that we are members of a larger world community and bear some type of obligation to give material aid to poorer members of that community. But we have no clear picture of what those obligations are, of what entity (the person, the state) is the bearer of them, and of how they ought to be fulfilled.

I shall argue here that not only our insights into the "duties of justice," but also our primitive thinking about the duties of material aid—and about the material component involved in fulfilling duties of justice—can be laid at the door of Cicero. In *De Officiis* he elaborates a distinction between these two types of duties that, like everything he wrote in that book, has had enormous influence on the course of political thought since. The general line he takes is that duties of justice are very strict and require high moral standards of all actors in their conduct across national boundaries. Duties of material aid, however, allow much elasticity, and give us a lot of room to prefer the near and dear. Indeed, Cicero thinks that we positively ought to prefer the near and dear, giving material aid to those outside our borders only when that can be done without any sacrifice to ourselves. In *De Officiis*, he cites a famous poem of Ennius to make this point:

> *A man who graciously shows the way to a someone who is lost*
> *kindles, so to speak, a light from his own light.*
> *For his own shines no less because he has lit another's.* (I.51)[4]

That is how Cicero wants us to think about duties of material aid across national boundaries: we undertake them only when it really is like giving directions on the road or lighting someone's torch from your own: that is, when no significant material loss ensues. And, as we all know, that is how many of us have come to think of such duties.

It is important to understand just how central Cicero's work was to the education of both philosophers and statesmen for many centuries. For both Grotius and Pufendorf, who quote Cicero with remarkable frequency,[5] it was the obvious starting point, because its arguments could be expected to be known to the audience for whom they were writing. The same is true of Kant in the political writings: he shows his familiarity with Cicero in many ways. Adam Smith, who usually footnotes with care the Greek and Roman philosophical texts he cites, simply assumes his audience's familiarity with Cicero's *De Officiis*, feeling that he doesn't even need to tell them when he is quoting huge chunks verbatim. Thus, in *A Theory of Moral Sentiments*, we find a sizable chunk of book III simply introduced into Smith's own prose without any mention of the author, the way we might do with Shakespeare or the Bible, feeling that to mention the source would be to insult the learning of the audience.[6] English gentlemen typically had "Tully's *Offices*" on their desks to get them through a difficult situation, or at least to display their rectitude. And they took Cicero with them when they went "visiting" (as Kant notes, a favorite euphemism for colonial conquest[7]). African philosopher Kwame Anthony Appiah records that his father, Joe Appiah, one of the founding political leaders of the Ghanaian nation, kept two books on his bedside table: the Bible and Cicero's *De Officiis*.[8] The book really was a kind of biblical text for the makers of public policy round the world. What I shall argue here is that in one important respect this Bible was more like the serpent in the garden.

I believe that Cicero, while extremely insightful concerning one important part of his topic, was a pernicious influence on another part, also important. But I also think that even his most dubious arguments are of considerable interest—worth studying not only to discover how we went wrong, but also to think better about what we want to say. We usually take on Cicero's conclusions without remembering, hence without criticizing, the arguments that led to them, and so we lack self-understanding about a very fundamental part of our own current situation. I propose to begin here to supply such a critical account; and I shall suggest that Cicero himself provides us with some of the most important resources for such critical argument. He also gives us, along with many inadequate arguments for his distinction, some much more plausible arguments that we might use to defend a moderate asymmetry between the two types of duties—but without endorsing the strong anti-cosmopolitan consequences that he believes he has defended.

I begin by outlining Cicero's distinction between the two types of duties, and asking what explicit arguments Cicero uses to support the distinction. Then I suggest that the resulting position is regarded as acceptable by Cicero and his audience in large part because of a shared view that derives from Stoicism, concerning the irrelevance of material goods for human flourishing. I then argue that his distinction does not cohere internally, even if one should accept this Stoic doctrine; and, second, that in any case we should not accept it. We then have to ask which Ciceronian arguments remain standing, and whether they give us any good ways of defending the distinction between the two types of duties.

There is one more reason for focusing on what Cicero says about this question. Cicero, more than any other philosopher who discussed this question, was immersed in it in a practical way. The *De Officiis* was written in 44 BCE, while Cicero was hiding out in the country, trying to escape assassination at the hands of the henchmen of Marc Antony and the other triumvirs—who succeeded, just several months after the completion of the work. The work, dedicated to his son who is studying philosophy at Athens, argues that philosophy is essential for public life, and that philosophers have a duty to serve the public good. It is extremely moving to read the tribute this republican statesman pays to philosophy and its role in the guidance of the state, when one remembers that he was in the midst of a desperate last-ditch attempt to save republican institutions at Rome through the composition of the *Second Philippic*, his major attack on Antony's tyrannical aims. Whatever one may think of Cicero's political judgments, one cannot help feeling respect for this statesman who was struggling to write philosophical advice while fighting for his life, and for this philosopher who was putting his life on the line for the republic.

One important note, before we begin the argument. I shall focus here on duties we or our institutions may have to other nations and their people. This single-minded emphasis produces distortion. It suggests that there is a "we" that is powerful and rich, and a "they" who are needy. But of course, in reality the "we" in each nation is composed of privileged and oppressed groups. Distinctions of class, religion, race, ethnicity, sex, and sexual orientation influence pervasively the life chances of every person in every nation. Being born in a certain region is one determinant of one's rights and opportunities; being female (for example) is another; and these two dimensions (if we focus only on these two) interact in complicated ways. Thus any really good attempt to think about international obligation will need to take other differences, and associated injustices, into account, asking, for example, what duties we may have to address hierarchies of sex or race or religion in other nations (as well as our own), and whether there may be particularly urgent duties to use our resources in that way. I neglect all of these complexities here, but return to them in Chapter 7.

II. Duties of Justice

We must begin with some summarizing, to get the relevant pieces of Cicero's argument onto the table for inspection. Cicero opens his account by mentioning that justice and beneficence, *iustitia* and *beneficentia,* are two aspects of one and the same virtue (I.20). In fact, in his taxonomy of the four cardinal virtues they do figure as a single virtue, whose name is simply *iustitia* (the other three being wisdom, moderation, and courage). We are therefore led to expect that his account of the two parts of *iustitia* (the genus) will link them closely together. This expectation will be disappointed.

Cicero's general account of the duties of *iustitia* (the species) has two parts. Justice requires, first, not doing any harm to anyone, unless provoked by a wrongful act.[9] This is the most basic way in which Cicero thinks about justice and injustice, and it proves fundamental to everything he says in what follows.

Second, justice requires "using common things as common, private possessions as one's own." The idea that it is a fundamental violation of justice to take property that is owned by someone else goes very deep in Cicero's thought, in a way that is explained by, but also explains, his fierce opposition to Julius Caesar's populist policies of land redistribution. Here he says that any taking of property "violates the law of human fellowship" (I.21). The account of the relevant property rights and their origin is remarkable for its obscurity and arbitrariness:

> Nothing is private by nature, but either by longstanding occupation (as when some people at some point came into an empty place), or by conquest (as when people acquired something through war), or by law or treaty or by agreement or by lot. Hence it comes about that the Arpine land is called that "of the Arpinates," the land of Tusculanum "that of the Tusculans." The account of private property is of a similar kind. Hence, because, among the things that were common by nature, each one has become someone's, therefore let each person hold onto what falls to his lot (*quod cuique obtigit, id quisque teneat*). If someone tries to get something away for himself,[10] he violates the law of human fellowship. (I.21)

Cicero clearly thinks that a taking of private property is a serious injustice, analogous to an assault. But nothing in this passage explains why he should think this, or why he should think that there is any close relation between existing distributions and the property rights that justice would assign. The argument distinguishes several different ways in which nature's common stock could be appropriated. They look morally different, and yet Cicero makes no moral distinction among them. It seems as if he is saying that since they are all rather arbitrary anyhow, then each person may as well start with his own share, and we'll define property rights from that point, rather than looking back to the mode of acquisition. But once he has distinguished between agreement and conquest in war, between law and mere chance or lot, we cannot help noticing that he has not said nearly enough to explain his strong preference for existing distributions. I shall return to this issue in section VI.

Having introduced the two types of injustice, Cicero now observes that the failure to prevent an injustice is itself a type of injustice; this important passage will concern us in section V. Describing the causes of both types of injustice, he remarks that people are frequently led into immoral aggression by fear (I.24), by greed (I.25), and by the desire for glory and empire (I.26). The last, he notes, is the most disturbing, since it frequently coexists with great talent and force of character; he gives Julius Caesar as a case in point.

Cicero is very clear that justice requires us to engage our adversaries with respect and honesty. Trickery of any sort is to be avoided (I.33). Furthermore, even those who have wronged you must be treated morally. For there is a limit to vengeance and punishment (I.34). Punishment seems to Cicero sufficient if the wrongdoer is brought to repentance and other potential wrongdoers are deterred. Anything that goes beyond this is excessive.

Cicero now turns from these general observations to the conduct of warfare. From now on he does not distinguish assault from property crime: and of course war standardly mingles the two subcategories of injustice. About the waging of war, he insists, first, that negotiated settlement is always preferable to war, since the former involves behaving humanly (and treating the other party as human), whereas the latter belongs to beasts (I.34). So war should be a last resort when all negotiation has failed. Cicero offers as a good example the ancient Roman fetial law, which insists that all warfare be preceded by a formal demand for restitution (I.37). And of course war is justified, in his view, only when one has been grievously wronged by the other party first. In general, war should always be limited to what will make it possible to live in peace without wrongful acts (I.35). After conflict has ended, the vanquished should be given fair treatment, and even received into citizenship in one's own nation where that is possible (I.35).

During conflict, the foe is to be treated mercifully: for example, Cicero would permit an army to surrender unharmed even after the battering ram has touched their walls (I.35); in this he is more lenient than traditional Roman practice. Promises made to the enemy must be faithfully kept: Cicero cites with honor the example of Regulus, who returned to a terrible punishment because he had promised the Carthaginians he would return (I.39).[11] Even a powerful and egregiously unjust enemy leader should not be murdered by stealth (I.40). Cicero ends this section by reminding his readers that the duties of justice are to be observed even in dealing with slaves (I.41).

In general, Ciceronian duties of justice involve an idea of respect for humanity, of treating a human being like an end rather than a means. (That is the reason that Kant was so deeply influenced by this account.) To assault someone aggressively is to treat them as a tool of one's desire for wealth or power or pleasure. To take their property is, in Cicero's eyes, to treat them, again, as simply tools of one's own convenience. This underlying idea explains why Cicero prefers the injustice of force *(vis)* to the injustice of deception *(fraus)*. The former is the act of a lion, the latter of a fox (I.41): "both are most foreign to the human being, but deception is more worthy of hatred"—presumably because it more designedly exploits and uses people.

In book III, Cicero returns to the duties of justice, elaborating on his claim that they are the basis for a truly transnational law of humanity. Since the useful frequently conflicts with the honorable, he writes, we need a rule *(formula)* to follow. The rule is that of never using violence or theft against any other human being for our own advantage. This passage, more rhetorical than the book I account, is the text that most deeply influenced Grotius, Smith, and Kant:

> Then for someone to take anything away from another and for a human being to augment his own advantage at the cost of a human being's disadvantage, is more contrary to nature than death, than poverty, than pain, than all the other things that can happen to his body or his external possessions.[12] For to begin with it removes human fellowship and social life. For if we are so disposed to one another that anyone will plunder or assault another for the sake of his own profit, it is necessary that the fellowship of the human kind, which is most of all in accordance with nature, will be torn apart. Just as, if each limb had the idea that it could be strong if it took the strength of the adjacent limb away for itself, the whole body would necessarily weaken and perish, so too, if each one of us should take the advantages of others and should snatch away whatever he could for the sake of his own profit, the fellowship and common life of human beings must necessarily be overturned. (III.21–22)

The point is, presumably, that the universal law condemns any violation that, should it be general, would undermine human fellowship. Klaus Reich has found in this passage the origins of Kant's formula of universal law.[13] Whether this is right or wrong, we certainly should see a strong similarity between Cicero's argument and Kant's idea.

Cicero now calls this principle a part of "nature, that is the law of peoples," and also "nature's reason, which is divine and human law." He notes that it is also widely recognized in the laws of individual states. We should all devote ourselves to the upholding of this principle—as Hercules did, protecting the weak from assault, a humanitarian act for which he was made into a god. In general:

> If nature prescribes that a human being should consider the interests of a human being, no matter who he is, just because he is human, it is necessary that according to nature what is useful for all is something in common. And if this is so, then we are all embraced by one and the same law of nature, and if that is so, then it is clear that the law of nature forbids us to do violence to *(violare)* anyone else. But the first claim is true, so the last is true also. (III.27)

Cicero remarks that it is absurd for us to hold to this principle when our family or friends are concerned, but to deny that it holds of all relations among citizens. But then, it is equally absurd to hold to it for citizens and deny it to foreigners. People who make such a distinction "tear apart the common fellowship of the human kind" (III.28). (Hercules, his salient example of nature's law, was a cosmopolitan in his aid to the weak.[14])

This section makes it very clear that Cicero's duties of justice are fully global. National boundaries are morally irrelevant, and Cicero sternly reproves those who think them relevant. At the core of Cicero's argument is an idea of not doing violence to human dignity—and, when we add in the distinction from book I (and the Hercules example), of not allowing people to be violated when you can help them. *Violare* includes physical assault, sexual assault, cruel punishments, tortures, and also takings of property. Cicero now links to that idea of humanity as an end the idea of a universal law of nature: conduct is to be tested by asking whether it could be made into such a law. Cicero clearly wants the world citizen to be Hercules-like in his determination to create a world where such violations of humanity do not occur, a world that accords with nature's moral law. The law of nature is not actual positive law, but it is morally binding on our actions, even when we are outside the realm of positive law.

This is the material in Cicero that became the foundation for much of modern international law, including both the law of war and human rights law. Grotius's *De Iure Belli ac Pacis* is, we might say, a commentary on these passages. Kant's *Perpetual Peace* also follows them very closely.[15] Particularly influential was Cicero's moral rigor, his insistence that all promises be preserved: in the form of the Grotian maxim *pacta sunt servanda,* this is the basis for modern conceptions of treaty obligation—although of modern thinkers only Kant follows Cicero all the way to his praise of Regulus.

III. Duties of Material Aid

Duties of justice are fully universal, and impose strict, exceptionless obligations. Regulus had to return to his death; it is wrong to poison even the foulest of tyrants. Very different is Cicero's next group of duties, the duties involved in giving material aid to others. Cicero begins by saying that these duties, too, are basic to human nature, but there are many constraints. We have to make sure our gifts do not do harm; we have to make sure we don't impoverish ourselves; and we have to make sure the gift suits the status of the recipient. Distinctions that we may legitimately take into account under the last rubric include the recipient's character; his attitude toward us; benefits previously given to us; and the degree of our association and fellowship (I.45). Duties are strongest when all of these intersect; but throughout there is a role for judgment as to what seems weightier (I.45). If other things are equal, we should help the most needy (I.49).

As if introducing an independent consideration—which he never clearly ranks against the preceding—Cicero now says that human fellowship will be best served if the people to whom one has the closest ties (ut quisque erit coniunctissimus) should get the most benefit. He now enumerates the various degrees of association, beginning with the species as a whole, and the ties of reason and speech that link all humans together. This all-embracing tie, he now says, citing Ennius, justifies only a type of material aid that can be given without personal diminution (sine detrimento). Examples are: allowing a foreigner to have access to running water and fire; giving advice to anyone who asks. But, he says, since there exist an infinite number of people in the world (infinita multitudo) who might possibly ask us for something, we have to draw the line at the point Ennius mentions.

Cicero then discusses other bonds that do in his view justify some substantial giving: the bond of nation and language; of the same state; of one's relatives; of various degrees of familial propinquity; and, finally, of one's own residence. In no case, it's important to note, does his argument for the closeness of the connection rest simply on biology or heredity; at least one relevant feature, and usually the central one, is some aspect of shared human practices. Citizens are said to share "a forum, temples, porticoes, roads, laws, rights, courts, elections." Families are held together by blood, but also by the shared task of producing citizens, and by "goodwill and love: for it is a great thing to have the same tombs of ancestors, to use the same religious rites, to have common burial places" (I.54–55). (It is of considerable practical importance to Cicero to show that family ties are not merely blood ties, because adoption, remarriage, and other common features of Roman life had made family lines look quite different from bloodlines.) Cicero does not make it clear whether our duties are greater to those who are closer to us in these various shared observances.

Cicero now praises friendship as an especially powerful source of duties of aid, for friendships are more likely to be cemented by the bonds of virtue and shared aspiration than are family relations. His highest praise, however, is reserved for shared political institutions:

> But when you look at everything with your reason and mind, of all the forms of fellowship none is weightier, none more dear, than that which each of us has with the republic. Parents are dear, children relatives acquaintances are dear; but the republic embraces all these loves of all of us together, and what good person would hesitate to die for her if it would help her? How much more detestable, then, is the monstrosity of those men who have cut up their country with every type of crime, and have been, and are still, engaged in her utter destruction! (I.57)

Although we cannot be certain, and the hasty character of the writing in this passage makes the whole course of the argument rather unclear, Cicero here appears to distinguish our affiliation with the republic from the shared association he previously mentioned, that of fellow citizens who share a forum, temples, and so forth. The affiliation praised here is with the republican institutions themselves, which make it possible for us to live a fully human life.

Cicero now turns to the question of ranking these duties. First, he says, are duties to the republic and our parents, because we are obligated to both by strong duties of gratitude, for their benefits to us in the past (I.58). Next are our children and our household, because they "look to us alone, and have no other available refuge." Next our relatives, who are congenial to us, and with whom we generally share our fortunes. But at the same time, we must look to need as well, and to what anyone would or would not be able to attain without our help. Different circumstances suggest different orderings: for example, one should aid a neighbor in preference to a brother in gathering the harvest; but in a lawsuit one should defend a relative or friend rather than a neighbor.

In short, then, Cicero proposes a flexible account that recognizes many criteria as pertinent to duties of aid: gratitude, need and dependency, thick association—but also preserves a role for flexible judgment in adjudicating the claims when they might conflict. Individuals are given a great deal of latitude in considering the cases.[16] What is clear, however, is that people outside our own nation always lose out. They are just that *infinita multitudo* who would drain off all our resources if we let their demand be heard at all. Fire and water for the alien are not nothing: they can be refused. But they are exemplary, for Cicero, of that which can be granted without diminution of our own stock.

IV. A Lurking View about the Good

Why is it at all acceptable to Cicero that this asymmetry should hold? He thinks it so terrible to contemplate a human being assaulting or stealing from another human being. Even a lie to the enemy seems to him the gravest desecration of the very concept of human fellowship. And yet if the same people are starving and my nation has a surplus, it seems to him just fine. There are many things that help explain these attitudes, including (as we'll see further in what follows) Cicero's strong and utterly unjustified account of property rights. But we must now mention another piece of the picture.

In *De Officiis*, Cicero's view lies somewhat closer to orthodox Stoicism than in most of his other works. Perhaps because he is writing at such speed, basing his work on several Stoic texts, perhaps because these are topics on which he has in any case fewer disagreements than usual with the Stoics, he tends to sympathize with the Stoic doctrine about the badness of the passions and the beliefs about external goods that are their ground. Both here and in the roughly contemporaneous *Tusculan Disputations* he takes the Stoic line that one should never have grief, or fear, or anger—and he goes even further, denying in *Tusculan* book IV that one should even have the approved variety of Stoic *erôs*.[17] In *De Officiis*, the same view is evident. Right after the passage on justice and material aid, we find courage defined as a lofty attitude of mind that rises above the passions and is able to look down serenely on the vicissitudes of fortune (I.61–68).

But of course the Stoic thesis about the passions is inseparable from the Stoics' view that external things, the gifts of chance, are irrelevant for the truly well-lived life or *eudaimonia*, human flourishing. The wise person scorns all such things and considers them small. He does not get upset at the loss of a fortune, or health, or reputation and honor, because all that is trivial stuff anyway.

This view Cicero accordingly endorses: the courageous person is "great and lofty in soul, despising human things" (I.61). Again, "a brave and great mind" is revealed "in the despising of external things, given that he is persuaded that a human being should wonder at and wish for and seek nothing but what is morally good and appropriate, nor should he yield to any human being or any disturbance of mind or any fortune" (I.66). In short then: we can afford not to worry about the evenhandedness of our beneficence, because the really strong person—and that is any of us at our best—does not need these things. In *De Finibus*, where Cicero goes into more detail about his ethical theory, his own "New Academic" view differs from Stoicism only in that it admits degrees of eudaimonia. External goods are not necessary for eudaimonia, but their presence can give people a higher degree of it.

The Stoic thesis typically makes it very difficult for any Stoic to motivate and defend beneficence. The Greek Stoics seem to have turned at this point to their view of Providence: Zeus asks us to concern ourselves with the distribution of material goods, even though, strictly speaking, such things have no real importance. In general, these things are "preferred," their opposites "dispreferred"; it is therefore appropriate to pursue them, though not to grieve when one cannot attain them. Cicero, unable to take up Stoic teleology because of his own epistemic skepticism, takes a line more like that of Roman Stoics such as Seneca and Marcus Aurelius: if people are really good they don't mind the loss of externals, so, by implication, if they do mind them that shows they are morally defective.[18] That does not mean that we should not aid them—but it does color our sense of why that aid is needed, and what its limits might be.

V. Does the Distinction Stand Up?

It is now time to ask some questions. First, we need to try to understand whether Cicero's distinction of duties is coherent, even to one who accepts the Stoic doctrine. Three arguments suggest that it is not.

A. Justice and Respectful Treatment Are External Goods

The first objection we might make is that if we are really thorough-going Stoics, we should not care about just or respectful treatment any more than about material aid. All these things are externals, in the hands of chance. To a person who is truly free within, slavery, torture, and rape are no worse than poverty. Stoics were quite explicit on this point. The wise person is free, even though he may be a slave. The sage on the rack is happy. The person who sees things aright will not care about the contempt and abuse of society: Seneca tells a story of Cato's undisturbed demeanor when someone spat at him in the forum (*Ir.* III.38). Even political freedom, a goal dear to many Stoic statesmen both before and after Cicero, is not, strictly speaking, important for true well-being. (At one point Seneca, describing Cato's struggles for political freedom, feels it necessary to remind his readers that Cato did not really think it important for himself, but only for his followers—who, presumably, were still morally defective, too dependent on the gifts of fortune.)

If this is so, then one rationale for the distinction between the two types of duties disappears. If humanity is owed certain types of treatment from the world, it would seem that it is owed good material treatment as well as respect and non-cruelty. If the world's treatment *doesn't* matter to humanity, then it would seem that torture, rape, and disrespect are no more damaging, no more important, than poverty. (And aren't they material anyway? Stoics were physicalists, so they themselves thought so.) It is incoherent to salve one's conscience on the duties of material aid by thinking about their non-necessity for true flourishing, and at the same time to insist so strictly on the absolute inviolability of the duties of justice, which are just other ways of supplying human beings with the external things they need.

To see how fascinating this Stoic incoherence can be, let us consider Seneca's letter on slavery,[19] which is rightly regarded as one of the formative progressive documents on this topic. Its general argument is that slaves have human worth and dignity, and therefore are due certain sorts of treatment suited to that human worth and dignity. Seneca's imaginary interlocutor keeps saying, "He is a slave" ("Servus est"). Seneca keeps on replying, "No, he is a human being" ("Immo homo est"). But to what, precisely, does Seneca think humanity entitles this human being? Both a lot and a little. A lot, in the sense that Seneca is prepared to make quite radical changes in customs of the use of slaves. Slaves are to be reasoned with and made partners in the planning of the household. They are to sit at our table and eat with us. All cruelty and physical abuse is absolutely banned. Especially radical is an equally absolute ban on using the slave as a sexual object: for intercourse with slaves was such an accepted part of the conduct of life, where male owners are concerned, that it was not defined as adultery under law,[20] and the only other person we know who objected to it was the Stoic philosopher Musonius Rufus.[21]

What, however, about the material conditions of slaves—their lack of self-ownership, their inability to own material goods, in short, the institution of slavery? This, it seems, Seneca never thinks to question. And his rationale for this quietism is what we might by now expect: slavery does no harm, because the only important goods are the goods of the soul. The interlocutor utters his scornful "He is a slave" one last time, toward the end of the letter. But this time Seneca does not reply that the person is human and had therefore to be treated thus and so:

> "He is a slave." But maybe he has a free soul. "He is a slave." Will this do him any harm? *(hoc illi nocebit?)* Show me anyone who is not a slave: one person is a slave to lust, another to greed, another to ambition, all to hope, all to fear. (*Ep.* 47.17)

But this tack confounds the person who had just been thinking that the treatment of people *does* matter, who had just been agreeing with Seneca that it is entirely wrong to use a human being the way one uses a beast of burden (47.5). For how can it be wrong to neglect or fondle or terrorize or even beat a slave, if all that matters is the free soul within and that cannot be touched by any contingency? How can it be wrong to treat a slave like a beast, if it's a matter of indifference whether one is a slave or a freeman? Seneca would like to say that humanity requires respectful treatment, and yet that it doesn't: for obviously enough, the entire institution is an insult to humanity, because it treats a free soul as an unfree possession. This was well known to Seneca and to his contemporaries. There was no coherent Stoic defense of the institution available to him, although in fact most Stoic philosophers did support it.[22] Seneca therefore falls back, at this juncture, on the familiar point about the external goods, and the familiar paradox that only virtue makes one truly free. But that maneuver does too much work if it does any at all. For it negates the importance of everything that has been argued up to this point. If it is really true that the only important form of slavery is internal slavery to passion, and if we accept the Stoic thesis that these passions are always in our control, then there is no reason to think that the lot of the abused and insulted slave is any worse than the lot of the slave who sits down with Seneca at the dinner table.

I believe that much modern thought about duties suffers from this same incoherence.[23] People have long held that there are certain things that are so bad, so deforming of humanity, that we must go to great lengths to prevent them. Thus, with Cicero and Seneca, they hold that torture is an insult to humanity; and we now go further, rejecting slavery itself. But to deny people material aid seems to such people not in the same category at all. They do not feel that people are torturing or raping people when they deny them the things that they need in order to live—presumably because they do not think that these goods are in the same class. Humanity can shine out in a poor dwelling, and it can appear that human dignity has not been offended by the poverty itself. Poverty is just an external: it doesn't cut to the core of humanity.

But of course it does. First of all, certain living conditions are an offense to humanity whether the person is inwardly altered by them or not. And, second, there is a considerable likelihood that the person will be affected by them. The human being is not like a block or a rock, but a body of flesh and blood that is made each day by its living conditions. Hope, desire, expectation, will—all these things are shaped by material surroundings. People can wonderfully rise above their conditions, but that does not mean that the conditions themselves are not important, shaping what they are able to do and to be.

I believe that the Stoic idea of the invulnerability of the will to contingencies—and related Christian ideas about the soul—lie behind these confused judgments. I shall pursue these issues in Chapter 3.

B. Interdependence and Interweaving

Even if we should convince ourselves that the presence of humanity imposes duties of justice but no duties of material aid, we would still have a problem on our hands: for the duties of justice cost money. To promote justice requires material aid. Any political and legal order that is going to protect people against torture, rape, and cruelty will need material support. There will need to be lawyers, courts, police, other administrative officers, and these will need to be supported, presumably, by a system of taxation. Where internal budgetary discussions are concerned, Americans very often miss this point, thinking that money spent on welfare and relief of poverty is money spent, but that somehow the police, the courts, the fire department—everything that is required to maintain a system of contract, property rights, and personal safety—are all free of cost.[24] Similarly, political liberty is not free: once again, tax money supports the institutional structures that make liberties of speech, association, and conscience more than words on paper.

Such issues become vivid when one visits a nation that has a weak tax structure. Where the central government is weak, relatively few citizens pay taxes. This means that the infrastructure is in disarray, jeopardizing freedom of travel and public safety; that the legal system has huge multi-year delays, jeopardizing other rights and liberties; that personal security is not protected by effective law enforcement; and so on. In short, people are not free to do as they wish in matters touched on by the duties of justice unless material resources have been distributed—and, in most cases, redistributed—to deal with the problem.

Such problems internal to each nation already put the Ciceronian project in trouble, for it begins to look as if we are not going to be able to protect the rights of all world citizens in many areas of basic liberty without redistribution from richer to poorer nations. Humanity is being violated daily, not only because of evildoers, but also because of the sheer inability of nations to maintain public order and public safety. If we really care about the duties of justice, in short, this already requires us to think about material aid. But the problem is magnified when we think about what an effective system of international justice requires. Maintaining a system of global justice that would be at all effective in dealing with torture, cruelty, unjust war, and so forth involves massive expenses on both the military side (NATO, for example), and on such international institutions and exchanges that we believe important to that task. Meeting these expenses requires redistribution of resources from richer to poorer nations, whether in the form of military aid or in some other form. Caring about basic human rights means spending money, not just talking fine talk.

But then the difference between the two types of duties becomes a matter of degree only, and it is not at all clear which set of duties will cost more. Military preparedness to defend one's own citizens from unjust attack, an important part of the duties of justice, is extremely expensive, even before we get to the protection of allies. Probably ending hunger around the world is a more finite and doable goal.

In fact, when we look into the matter seriously, we will probably find that the enormous price of protecting citizens from torture, securing effective police protection, and protecting basic security of the person and of property is quite comparable to, and likely exceeds, the cost of providing basic material necessities.[25] So we should conclude that if people say they are for the duties of justice in the world as a whole and yet are unwilling to redistribute money across national borders, they are actually halfhearted about the duties of justice.

C. Positive and Negative

The duties of justice look different from the duties of material aid because they do not involve doing anything, or anything much. They mainly involve refraining from certain acts: aggressive war, torture, rape, and so on. Duties of material aid, by contrast, look like they require us to do a great deal for others. That intuitive idea is very central in our thinking when we suppose that the recognition of duties of material aid would impose a great burden on our nation, while the recognition of duties of justice would not. I have already cast doubt on the positive / negative distinction by pointing out that real protection of people against violations of justice is very expensive: if we really are serious about protecting people in other parts of the world against wrongdoing, we will have to spend a lot of money on the institutions that do the protecting. But someone may now say, if we decide not to spend this money, violations may occur, but at least the violators won't be us. We can consistently draw a line, if not precisely where the old line between justice and material aid went, at least between acting and refraining. If we refrain from cruelty and torture, and so on, then we are doing no wrong, even if we are unwilling to spend our money on people at a distance, even where justice issues themselves are in play. Some understandings of Kant's ethical position take this line.

To this argument the best reply was given by Cicero himself. In this very section of book I of the *De Officiis,* he wrote:

> There are two types of injustice: one committed by people who inflict a wrong, another by those who fail to ward it off from those on whom it is being inflicted, although it is in their power to do so. For a person who unjustly attacks

another under the influence of anger or some other disturbance seems to be laying hands, so to speak, upon a colleague;
but the person who does not provide a defense or oppose the
injustice, if he can, is just as blameworthy as if he had deserted
his parents or his friends or his country.

The more active sort of injustice, he continues, is usually motivated by
fear, or greed, or the love of honor and glory. (Julius Caesar is, as elsewhere, his salient example of the last bad motive.) Cicero now turns to
the second type, considering his own profession in the process:

As for neglecting the defense of others and deserting one's
duty, there are many causes of that. Sometimes people are
reluctant to incur enmities or hard work or expenses. Sometimes they are impeded by lack of concern or laziness or
inactivity or by some pursuits or business of their own, to
such an extent that they allow those whom they should protect to be abandoned. We must therefore watch out lest
Plato's statements about philosophers prove to be insufficient: that because they are occupied in the pursuit of truth,
and because they scorn and despise the things that most
people intensely seek and for which they are in the habit of
murdering one another, therefore they are just. For they
attain one type of justice, not wronging anyone by the
infliction of a wrong, but they fall into the other type of
injustice. For impeded by their zeal for learning, they desert
those whom they ought to protect. Thus he thought they
would not even help the republic unless compelled. But it
would have been fairer that this be done willingly; for a

right action is only just if it is done willingly. There are also some people who either because of keenness to protect their estates or through some hatred of human beings say that they mind their own business and don't seem to be doing anyone any harm. They are free from one type of injustice, but they run into the other; for they abandon the fellowship of life, inasmuch as they do not expend on it any zeal or effort or resources. (I.28–29)

Cicero makes an important contribution in this fascinating section. He grants that in a certain sense the active-passive distinction makes sense. There is a morally relevant distinction between actively doing a wrong oneself and simply sitting by while a wrong takes place. But this distinction, while morally relevant, does not entail that no wrong is done by the person who sits by. Making unjust war is one bad thing, but not protecting your fellows (and the reference to "so to speak, colleagues" seems to mean fellow human beings) when you have the resources to do so is another.[26] We readily see this when we think of families, he suggests: for Cicero knows that the average Roman will think that the failure to defend one's family members from attack is a paradigm of bad behavior.[27] But the same is true for larger groupings of our fellow human beings: standing idly by while they get attacked is itself a wrong. There are many reasons why people behave like this: they don't want hard work, they don't want to make enemies, they are simply lazy. But none of these excuses the bad behavior or makes it the blameless innocence it represents itself as being.

Cicero's argument is not wholly satisfactory, because it relies on an antecedent analysis of when a wrong has taken place, or what help from others people have a right to expect. Cicero does not make that background account explicit. And yet he clearly believes that any acceptable such account would entail that failing to prevent a grave harm when one can is itself a wrong, comparable to an active assault. As I have suggested, he relies on a moral tradition in which the failure to defend friends and family is a paradigmatic moral failing. What he does is to extend that account to areas in which people do not usually think such thoughts.

Especially fascinating is Cicero's attack on his own philosophical colleagues. They love what they are doing, and they don't like the idea of getting messed up in politics. So, as Plato imagines, they will have to be forced to take part in the affairs of state. Cicero replies that they do wrong if they do not take part of their own choice. Like misanthropes and obsessive money-makers, they do harm to humanity by failing to aid it. This theme is of urgent significance to Cicero, who is about to be murdered for having made a different choice, and he returns to it later, saying that such a life of retirement has been chosen by "the noblest and most distinguished philosophers, and also certain strict and serious men who could not bear the conduct of the people or their leaders" (I.69). What they were after is clearly appealing: "They wanted the same thing kings do: to need nothing, to obey nobody, to enjoy their liberty, which is defined as doing as you like." Cicero is even prepared to concede that sometimes that choice may perhaps be blameless—if people have retired because of ill health or "some other very serious reason," and, he now adds, if they have extremely fine minds and are devoting themselves to learning. (Here he seems to go back on what he said about Platonic philosophers, albeit in an uncertain and half-hearted way.[28]) But anyone other than these is surely in the wrong to pursue a life that does not involve service to others through political action.

How does Cicero see the relevance of these observations to his own argument? Clearly he means to blame people who will not serve their own nation, and to defend the life of committed public service. In the earlier passage, he also pretty clearly says that nations (or their citizens) should not stand by when wrong is going on somewhere else. Not to help someone who is being attacked is like deserting your family or friends. Perhaps there is an implicit restriction to co-nationals and important allies, but I don't think so: the active sort of injustice is defined fully generally, as assault "against anyone" *(in quempiam)*, and the ensuing account of the passive sort seems equally broad in its application: when that same anyone is getting attacked, it is unjust to stand by.

Cicero certainly does not elaborate on the duties imposed by the requirement to avoid passive injustice. To whom do these duties belong? In the first instance to nations? To their citizens? To both? How widely do they extend? What is meant by "if you can" *(si potest)*? Does it mean only "If you can without any sacrifice to yourself"? But this reading seems ruled out by his attack on the motives of people who will not help because they do not want to incur expense or hard work. Presumably, then, he thinks that people are in the wrong unless they are willing to incur enmity and expense and hard work in order to protect their fellow human beings.

Although Cicero's distinction between duties of justice and duties of material aid is in many ways the origin of modern philosophy's distinction between perfect and imperfect duties, this section shows that the relationship is complicated. Perfect duties are duties to assignable individuals that admit of no flexibility: they must be completely fulfilled. Imperfect duties allow considerable latitude about how far and to whom they may be fulfilled. Clearly Cicero treats duties of beneficence as imperfect: but duties of justice, insofar as they require spending finite money in a complicated world, look different from perfect duties. Nations are obliged to aid other nations in their struggles against injustice, but it is likely that they will need to make decisions about how much money to spend and where to spend it. Cicero does not elaborate on how these difficult decisions would go, but he makes it clear that they are difficult because of the outlay of money they require. His rejection of the active / passive distinction makes all duties have some of the characteristics of imperfect duties.

By placing this discussion inside the section on the duties of justice, and by characterizing active injustice as some sort of assault or aggression, Cicero seems to limit the passive sort to warding off actual attacks or assaults. Clearly he does not think that hunger and poverty are the type of assaults against which one has duties to protect one's fellows, or else he would have to rewrite completely the section on beneficence. But why not? It seems quite unconvincing to treat the two types of harm asymmetrically. Furthermore, even Cicero's limited point has implications for the topic of beneficence, which he does not notice. For even to protect our neighbors from assault will surely require, as I have argued, massive uses of our own material resources, of a type that he seems to oppose in that later section.

At this point, then, we must part company with Cicero, viewing the discussion of passive injustice as highly suggestive, but underdeveloped. Clearly Cicero did not see its importance for his later discussion of beneficence. This is perhaps not surprising, given the speed at which he was writing, with death looming ahead of him, and given his intense focus on justifying the philosopher's choice to serve the public realm.

The important point is that Cicero is right. It is no good to say "I have done no wrong" if, in fact, what one has done is to sit by when one might have saved fellow human beings. That is true of assault, and it is true of material aid. Failures to aid when one can deserve the same charges that Cicero addresses to those who fail to defend: laziness, self-preoccupation, lack of concern. Cicero has let in a consideration that is fatal to his own argument, and to its modern descendants.

One more rescue attempt will now be attempted. Cicero, it will be said, is perfectly consistent when he applies his doctrine of passive injustice only to the sphere covered by the "duties of justice." This is so because passive injustice is a failure to ward off *an assault or aggression*. But lack of material goods is not an assault or aggression. Nothing Cicero has said commits him to the view that it is also passive injustice not to supply things that people need in order to live. And indeed, it seems likely that some such intuitive idea lies behind Cicero's way of arguing here. Moreover, this same intuitive idea is in many modern people's minds when they think of what justifies humanitarian intervention.

Of course, as I have already insisted, even to protect people against assaults takes money. So this distinction cannot really help us defend Cicero's original bifurcation of duties. But let us see whether there is even a limited coherence in Cicero's doctrine, so understood. We may think of assault or aggression in two ways. In one way, assault is something that hits people from outside, through no fault of their own. But in this way of thinking, many natural events look like assaults: floods, famines, depredations of many kinds from animals and the natural world.[29] Cicero lets himself in for this extension by his reliance on the example of Hercules: for obviously enough, Hercules primarily helped people who were assailed by catastrophes of non-human origin: the Nemean lion, the Stymphalian birds, the Hydra, the boar. These are still monsters who commit human-like assaults, but they remind us that many of the invasions of our well-being that we most fear have a non-human origin. And Hercules' monsters obviously have, as well, a mythic significance that makes them emblematic of the way in which ills such as disease and hunger stalk humanity: indeed, the Hydra is an apt metaphor for the ever-renewing nature of bodily need.[30] Some of Hercules' labors, furthermore, for example the descent to the Underworld, have this more general significance directly: he faced death itself, for humanity's sake. In short, Cicero's use of Hercules betrays the fact that he has no clear way of drawing the line between human and non-human assaults, or even between assaults by animals and assaults by other malign aspects of the natural world.

Cicero himself is aware of this larger significance of the figure of Hercules. Indeed, he seems quite fascinated with this character, who, having endured risk to save humanity from various dangers, then found his body devoured by unendurable pain. In *Tusculan Disputations* (II.20–22), discussing the question whether pain is the greatest of evils (a question on which he ultimately defends the Stoic line that pain is not an evil), Cicero takes time to translate into elegant Latin verse of his own the passage of Sophocles's *Trachiniai* in which Hercules depicts the assaults of the fatal poison on his organs. This is among the most graphic passages in all of Greek literature in its depiction of bodily pain; the pain is seen as an invasion, akin to an assault. The poison "clinging bites and tears my vital organs, and pressing heavily drains the breath from my lungs; now it has drunk up all my discolored blood. My body, used up by this terrible conflict, dwindles away."[31] The passage makes it clear that the assaults of monsters were nothing compared to this one. It seems fair for us to remind Cicero of this passage, given his evident fascination with it.

Suppose, however, we think of assault as *iniuria*, another person's wrongful act. The text suggests this, clearly. Then we may be able to let Cicero off the hook concerning animals and natural catastrophes—though it is still not terribly clear why, from the victim's viewpoint, such a line should be considered salient. Have we now given him a consistent way of maintaining that there is no passive injustice when people are hungry and impoverished, and so on? I believe not. For obviously enough, we cannot assume that their hunger and poverty are not caused by the wrongful act of another person or persons. Given that hunger is typically caused not so much by food shortage as by lack of entitlement to food, it is a thoroughly human business, in which the arrangements of society are profoundly implicated.[32] With poverty, this is even more clear. Just because it is difficult to decide whom to blame, that does not mean that no wrongful act has occurred and that no response need be made. Most nations have the capacity to feed all their people, if they had a just system of entitlements. Where war is concerned, we sometimes understand that we can judge a wrong has taken place without being exactly clear on who did it: we don't always require that there be an easily recognizable singular "bad guy" such as Hitler or Milosevic before we undertake an act of humanitarian intervention, or declare war on a nation that has wronged another (though clearly the presence of such a "bad guy" gets Americans going more easily—witness the failure to intervene in Rwanda).

Moreover, we should at least consider that some of the wrongdoers may be ourselves. Through aid, we can feed all the world's people; we just don't. Of course, in the context of the present argument it would be question-begging to assert that the failure to give material aid across national borders is *iniuria.* So too, however, would be the assertion that our failure to aid involves no *iniuria.* At the very least, we should concede that the question of our own moral rectitude has not been resolved.

On any understanding of the distinction between aggression and non-aggression, then, Cicero's refusal to extend his analysis of "passive injustice" to failures to give material aid looks unconvincing. If aggression is catastrophe, there are many natural and social catastrophes that have no clear "bad guy"; if aggression is wrongful action, there is almost certain to be wrongful action afoot when people are starving and in deep poverty, even though we cannot easily say whose wrongful action it is. And yet, most of us do continue to think in something like Cicero's way, feeling that it is incumbent on us (maybe) to save people from thugs and bad guys, but not incumbent on us to save them from the equally aggressive depredations of hunger, poverty, and disease. Hercules knew better.

I have argued that Cicero's distinction is not fully coherent, even to one who accepts the Stoic doctrine. And yet it also gets a lot of mileage from that doctrine, because Stoic moral theory permits us to salve our conscience about our failure to aid our distant fellows, telling ourselves that no serious harm has befallen them. Let us therefore, turn our attention to that doctrine.

D. The Falsity of the Stoic Doctrine

The Stoic view about external goods has been lurking around, providing a motivation for some of Cicero's arguments, a consolation in connection with others. But insofar as Cicero, or his modern descendants, would be disposed to reply by appealing to the Stoic doctrine that external goods are unnecessary for the good human life, we must now say that this doctrine is false. People do indeed have amazing powers of resistance, and a dignity that can frequently surmount the blows of fortune. But this does not mean that these blows are unimportant. The dignity of human beings deserves support and respect; miserable conditions insult it. Moreover, such conditions profoundly affect the very parts of the person that are of greatest interest to the Stoics: mentality, moral power, the power to form confirming associations with other human beings. The Stoic position seems to be: either these things are external blows, in which case they don't touch what really matters, or they are the result of some moral weakness in the person, in which case they do matter but the person herself is to blame. But this is a false dichotomy: the fact that moral character can sometimes survive the blows of fortune unaffected does not show that the blows of fortune do not deeply affect it, or that any such effect is the result of weak or bad character. Moreover, such a survivor is very likely to have had the goods of fortune in at least some measure at some time: a good enough home in childhood, parents who nourished self-regard, and good enough nutrition when crucial faculties are developing.

Do we need to say this? Is there any danger that our modern Ciceronians will avail themselves of such a self-evidently false doctrine? I fear that there is, and we will see the bad influence of this doctrine on Adam Smith, despite his many valuable insights about the damages of poverty. And, equally important, many contemporary Americans believe that poverty doesn't really affect the will, and that, when we see the will affected, it must consequently be the result of personal weakness or failure. This is the Stoics' false dichotomy: either unimportant or in the control of will. Thus, as we know too well, poverty is often treated as a moral failing, even by people who would not so treat the damages done to a person by rape or torture or even racial discrimination. In the area of the duties of material aid, Stoicism lives on.

When differences between nations are at issue, differences that really do seem too large to be a matter of indifference, such modern Stoics can't quite bring themselves to blame each and every individual citizen of those nations for being shiftless and lazy. But then a substitute is quickly found: blame of the nation, or the people, for sluggishness or bad planning, or stupid management of their economy. Insisting on the falsity of Stoic doctrine is a first necessary step to placing these important issues on the table.

The Stoic false dichotomy has deep roots, and is not so easy to evade. For we do not want to treat human beings as simply the passive recipients of whatever nature dishes out. We want to say, with Kant and the Stoics, that there is a dignity that shines out even when nature has done its worst. Indeed, if we do not say this we are in danger of losing the very basis for claims of aid: for if there is no longer a human being there, but simply a substance that has been pushed around in various ways by life, we no longer know why we have stringent duties to support that substance. I believe that the Stoics get into difficulty on this point precisely because they are so determined to insist that the basis for moral duties is never effaced by life's contingencies and hierarchies. Like their predecessors the Cynics, they want to say that wealth, rank, birth, freeborn status, ethnicity, nationality, and even gender are all morally irrelevant, in the sense that they do not create differences in fundamental human worth. But, like the Cynics, they think that maintaining this requires maintaining, as well, that free status, citizenship, wealth, and so forth don't matter at all for the things that are most important in life. They seem to be afraid that if they did admit the importance of external goods they would be in danger, once again, of creating plural races of human beings, with different degrees of dignity. Because they are determined to insist that all humanity is equal, they refuse to acknowledge the depth at which humanity can be deformed by circumstances.

There is no easy solution to this dilemma, and I shall address it in the following chapter. Meanwhile, we can see that the Stoic view is no easily dismissed absurdity; nor has modern moral thought come to a satisfactory consensus on how to handle the issue.

VI. What Is Left?

We have removed some of the main props for Cicero's distinction of duties into two kinds, one strict and one less strict. Let us now consider his remaining arguments.

A great advantage of Cicero's discussion is that it does not simply assume that national boundaries are of obvious moral relevance; nor does he rely on mysterious ideas of blood and belonging that frequently substitute for argument in these matters. Instead, he believes that we need to point to some feature or features of our fellow citizens that can justify differential treatment. Indeed, even in the case of family he does not fall back on an allegedly obvious relevance of consanguinity: perhaps the prevalence of adoption of heirs in the Roman middle and upper classes helped him avoid a pitfall of some modern discussions. So while I shall be critical of some of his specific arguments, I think we should applaud their general direction: nationality in and of itself supplies no sufficient moral argument for a difference of duties. Consanguinity, and indeed family, are proxies for other morally significant characteristics.[33] But once we make this step, the door is wide open to asking whether these features really do coincide with shared ethnic or family membership; other people situated elsewhere may possibly share with our co-nationals the relevant features. Thus most of my criticisms of Cicero in this section take advantage of an avenue of debate opened up by Cicero himself.

I. PROPERTY RIGHTS. Cicero will insist that there is a fundamental part of justice itself that has implications for material redistribution. For, as we recall, he defined justice partly in terms of respect for property rights, understood as justified by the luck of existing distributions. He argued that once property is appropriated, no matter how, taking it away is the gravest kind of violation. Clearly it is his purpose to use that argument to oppose any state-mandated redistributive policies, such as Caesar's attempts at land reform. But this argument has implications for the entire issue of beneficence: for if I have a right to something, and it is egregiously bad for someone to take it away from me, then it would seem peculiar to say that I have a strict *moral* duty to give it away to someone else.

Thus modern Ciceronians might grant everything I have said about the unfortunate problems in Cicero's distinction of duties and yet hold that property rights are so extremely important that by themselves they justify making the duties of beneficence at best imperfect duties. I believe that some libertarian thinkers would take this line.

Yet any such thinker who starts off from Cicero is bound to notice the thinness and arbitrariness of his account of these rights. Why should it actually be the case that "each should hold what falls to the share of each, and if anyone takes anything from this he violates the law of human association"? Why not say, instead, that such claims to ownership are always provisional, to be adjudicated along with claims of need? By emphasizing need himself, as a legitimate source of moral claims, Cicero has left himself wide open to this objection.

Here's where we should say that Cicero's highly partisan politicking distorts his philosophy. His Stoic forebears, as he well knows, thought all property should be held in common;[34] he himself has staked his entire career on an opposition to any redistributive takings. So it's no accident that he skates rather rapidly over the whole issue of how property rights come into being, and neglects to consider alternative accounts. But the modern reader needs to pause. By now in the history of philosophy, we have too many different competing accounts of property rights to be at all satisfied by the thin account that Cicero hands us, unless some compelling argument is given as to why we should prefer that account to others that are available.[35]

Moreover, this argument proves too much, if anything at all: for it would also prevent governments from appropriating citizens' money to support the fulfillment of the duties of justice.

2. GRATITUDE FOR NURTURE. A stronger and more interesting argument is Cicero's contention that citizens owe gratitude for their nurture to parents, relatives, and especially the republic. This gives them reasons to give their resources to those who have expended resources on them. This argument offers a good justification for at least some asymmetry in our duties of material aid. It seems unlikely, however, that it justifies Cicero's conclusion that we have duties to people at a distance only when it costs us absolutely nothing—a conclusion that modern Ciceronians eagerly embrace.

3. NEED AND DEPENDENCY. Another good argument Cicero makes is that some people depend on us in a very personal way. Our own children, for example, have needs that only we are likely to be able to meet well. In addition to those intimate needs, I think he is saying, they

also have expectations of material aid that only we are likely to meet, and in that way if we let them down they are likely to suffer greatly.

Several things in this argument seem right. It seems right that some duties to children can be met only in a context of intimacy; something similar probably holds of fellow citizens, whose knowledge of one another's history and goals helps them relate well in political life. But it seems questionable whether the duties of material aid are like this. Of course giving money is often done obtusely, and money, to be wisely used, needs to be used with knowledge of local circumstances. But that is a different point. The *need* for money can in principle be met by getting resources from abroad, so long as the actual user is intelligent about the local scene. Perhaps parents should give love and attention to their own children, but a lot of their money to international welfare agencies, and similarly to fellow citizens.

As to Cicero's point that the children rely on our material aid and would be bereft without it, we can say that this is an artifact of current arrangements, and can hardly be used to justify those arrangements. It seems likely that a good way of organizing the care of children will involve a certain measure of parental responsibility and parental control over resources; similarly, a good way of organizing citizenship will almost surely involve various forms of local responsibility and local control. But as to how much, and whether this is at all incompatible with strong duties of transnational redistribution, Cicero has said nothing.

We might even grant to Cicero that families are usually the best performers of duties to children, and that nations, similarly, are the best protectors of various interests of citizens—without treating these duties as special duties in any deep or fundamental way. That is, we may see the so-called special duties as good ways of channeling the general duties we have to other humans worldwide. This seems to have been the position of the original Greek Stoics; it is also Adam Smith's position in at least some very important passages.[36] Whether this is the correct position about either nations or families requires further argument. My point is that Cicero has said nothing here to rule it out.

4. THICK FELLOWSHIP. Cicero's most interesting claim for the republic is that our participation in it makes claims on our human faculties that other more distant associations do not. We share in speech and reason in a variety of ways when we associate with our fellow citizens, thus confirming and developing our humanity in relation to them. This is not the case with the foreign national, unless that person is a guest on our soil. For this reason, Cicero thinks, we owe the republic more material aid than we do to foreign nations and nationals. The idea is presumably that we have reasons to make sure that the institutions that support and confirm our humanity prosper.

One might complain, first, that Cicero's point was already of dubious validity in his own time, since already Rome had complex civic and political ties with many parts of the world, and non-Italians were not yet, though some of them later became, Roman citizens. His son is off studying philosophy in Greece; his philosophical descendant Seneca was soon to be born in Spain. North Africa, Gaul, and Germany, though often crudely caricatured in imperialist writings,[37] were known to be the homes of people with whom Romans had many forms of cultural and human exchange. So citizenship and fellowship were not coextensive even then.

In our day, when we develop and exercise our human powers, we are increasingly associating with people elsewhere. Networks such as the international women's movement may supply people with some of their most fundamental confirming associations. So even if Cicero had made a good argument for the restriction of our duties, it would be less weighty today than formerly.

But thinking about international networks today shows us some reasons why we should doubt Cicero's argument. That is, why should it be the case that only those people who have already managed to join an international network have duties of material aid to people in other nations? Ignorance and neglect are, it would appear, their own justification. If, like all too many Americans, I manage my life in such a way that I have minimal knowledge of and contact with any other part of the world, I am thereby absolved of any duties to that world. This cannot be right.

Nor does the argument seem persuasive in any case as an argument about material resources. It might be that the networks I am in claim a larger proportion of my time, or my attention, or my work. But my money? Why should the fact that I share forms of life with my fellow citizens mean that I should deprive some child in India of a chance to live? The connections are too undeveloped for Cicero's argument to persuade.

Cicero is on the track of something extremely important about national belonging, something that Grotius will ultimately develop into a compelling argument. But he does not say enough: what, precisely, is special about co-nationality and shared institutions? We may make progress if we read into Cicero's text a point that he does not make explicitly.

5. ACCOUNTABILITY. We might read Cicero's previous argument to make, as well, the following point: our own republic is ours. One of the forms of association that we share, in that fine institution of the

republic that Cicero is struggling to preserve, is mutual accountability, and accountability of public policy to citizens. The republic is an expression of a fundamental human need to give ourselves laws of our own choosing, a feature that the world community does not possess. This is a very important point, indeed, a decisive one. I'll develop it further in Chapter 4, studying Grotius's important argument on this point. How far would it help Cicero here?

Accountability might give us reasons to use our money on a form of government that had this desirable feature. Does it give us reasons to support republican government all over the world, or does it give us special reasons to focus our material aid on our own? Here we might combine the accountability point with the points about need, dependency, and gratitude, and say that our own has an especially strong claim on our resources, and is entitled to them for support of the institutions in which we participate. We might also make an additional point about well-meaning paternalism: we have no right to tell the people of other nations what to do. Foreign aid given in order to prompt regime change would be especially suspect.

Still, suppose we have residual funds not taken by taxes for a specific purpose: discretionary funds. (Or suppose our citizens vote for taxation to support foreign aid.) At least some of the residual, and all the funds voted on as such, might be used in supporting other instances of republican governments already in place that request our aid (for example, through aid to education and other structures crucial to republican government). Its main point is that institutions of a certain type are good protectors of people, because of their responsiveness to people's voices: this makes them good ways of channeling duties of aid. But once again, this is compatible with the duties themselves being fully general.[38] We will see that there are other reasons to be skeptical of such aid, but they are pragmatic only, if we are talking about aid given to existing republics that ask for aid. Certainly the argument does not get us anywhere near Cicero's strong conclusion that no aid outside the nation is morally required if that will be even minimally costly.

Of course there is a further reason that Cicero's argument fails: it is that the Roman Republic was not accountable to more than a fraction of its citizens; it was an oligarchy in which plebeian voices were only sometimes heard. That historical limitation, however, is not my primary concern here.

In short, Cicero has some decent arguments that justify a partial asymmetry in our material duties: the arguments from gratitude, need, association, and accountability all do at least some work. But none justifies his radical confinement of duties to the interior of the republic. Another consideration, both in his day and now, is surely playing a part.

6. THE DIFFICULTY OF ASSIGNING THE DUTIES. Implicit in Cicero's argument is a consideration he never fully develops: it is just too difficult to assign the relevant duties, once we get beyond the boundaries of the republic. Within the compass of the republic, we have a pretty good understanding of who owes what to whom, because the institutional structure supports itself through taxation, and budgets are passed by an accountable political body. But once we start thinking internationally, it all seems quite bewildering and even hopeless. There are too many needy recipients, and there are all the many different levels of both giver and receiver: persons, groups, non-governmental organizations, governments. As Cicero remarks: "the resources of individuals are limited, and the needy are an unlimited horde *(infinita multitudo)*."

How can either individuals or nations possibly say to whom we owe the finite resources we have, unless we do draw the line at our friends and fellow nationals?

This problem is not recognized in the context of the duties of justice because we imagine we can give respect and truthfulness and non-rape and non-torture and non-aggression to everyone, and there is no difficult distributional problem (until we start thinking of really supporting these policies with money!). Justice looks as if it can be universally distributed without cash; material aid obviously cannot. We have seen that this is a false asymmetry if we accept Cicero's point about negative duties: we still have to choose whom to protect, if our resources are finite, as they always are. Neither set of duties is correctly understood as "perfect duties," if that means that there is no selection problem. But neither set is correctly conceived as "imperfect," if that means it is always morally okay if people elsewhere do badly. If we attack the asymmetry, however, we are left with the problem of assigning the relevant duties for all transnational duties, and thus we have made things harder and not easier.

To answer these questions well requires working out theories of institutional versus individual responsibility, and theories of just transfer between nations.[39] We don't yet have such theories, although we have good accounts of many aspects of them. We also will need to get clearer about what those duties should be aiming at: Equality? A Rawlsian difference principle? A substantial threshold level of basic capabilities? Again, we have refined alternatives before us in the domestic case, but only sketches at the transnational level.[40]

Furthermore, the role of the nation, rightly stressed by Cicero, raises difficulties both normative and practical that are as yet imperfectly understood. How can aid be given without compromising national sovereignty, if we agree that nations channel their citizens' autonomy? And, on the practical side, is such aid even effective?

This much is clear, however: the difficulty of these problems does not mean that we should fall back on the Ciceronian doctrine, with its multiple evasions. It means that we should continue our work.

In Chapters 6 and 7, addressing the contributions and liabilities of the tradition, I will offer some directions for that work. But I will also delve into the problems, both normative and practical, that lie in the way of making this work effective.

THREE

The Worth of Human Dignity

Two Tensions in Stoic Cosmopolitanism

I. Cosmopolitans

We have begun to see the fruits of the tradition inaugurated by Diogenes the Cynic in Cicero's promising, though flawed, approach to transnational duties. Now we need to dig in and understand more fully the conceptual foundations of the tradition itself. What is world citizenship? What grounds it? What attitudes are appropriate to it? What types of damage can it encounter, and to what duties do these vulnerabilities give rise?

Cynic / Stoic cosmopolitanism urges us to recognize the equal, and unconditional, worth of all human beings, a worth that the Stoics grounded in (practical) reason and moral capacity. Yet the founders of this tradition also introduce a problem with which the tradition has been wrestling ever since. For they think that, in order to treat people as having a dignity that life's accidents cannot erode, they must scoff at money, rank, and power, saying that they are unnecessary for human flourishing. The dignity of moral capacity is complete in itself. Diogenes doesn't need to ask Alexander for a decent living, citizenship, health care: all he needs to say is, "Get out of my light." Moral personality is complete, and completely beautiful, without any external aids.

I have cast doubt on this idea, suggesting that human dignity requires support from the world in two different ways. First, dignity, even if unaffected by bad conditions, is insulted by them: the worth of human dignity demands something better, something like equal respect from both people and institutions. Second, in many respects the inner life of hope, emotion, and will can be affected by conditions beyond people's control. To recognize this is essential if we want to appreciate the full importance of worldly conditions to human flourishing.

But then what of dignity? Is it inalienable or is it not?

First, I shall characterize the moral core of Cynic and Stoic cosmopolitanism, focusing on those features that most strongly influenced modern thinkers such as Pufendorf, Grotius, Smith, and Kant; second, I examine the rationale for the Stoic position about the relationship between human dignity and the worth of external goods. Many subsequent thinkers simply reject the Stoic claim that externals make no contribution to the flourishing life. I shall argue that the Stoic position, while problematic, is deeper and more persuasive than it is usually taken to be; it confronts us with a problem about human dignity that is difficult to solve if we do not adopt the Stoic position on the worth of externals. Even if we do solve this problem, however, another rationale for Stoic detachment lurks in the wings, in Stoic beliefs about partiality and the moral imagination. I argue that contemporary cosmopolitans must grapple, as well, with this line of thought, crafting a moral psychology that learns from Stoicism but does not adopt its extreme detachment.

This chapter begins by returning to the Cynics, who set the cosmopolitan tradition off on a course both radical and, in some ways, profoundly problematic. When I discuss Stoic ideas, I shall focus on thinkers who are orthodox in their Stoicism, but I draw on the Roman Stoics Seneca, Epictetus, and Marcus Aurelius to supplement the scanty Greek evidence.[1] By now we know how important it is not to treat these Roman figures simply as sources for an abstract picture of "Hellenistic philosophy." Thinkers in their own right, they are also creative participants in their political context.

II. Cynic Beginnings

The life of Diogenes the Cynic is a tissue of exemplary legends; but it is as such that they should hold our interest. What the historical figure actually said and did has, ultimately, less importance than what subsequent admirers constructed as an exemplary life. In its general outlines, however, the life reveals a historical figure who was a reflective social radical of some type, and who called his way of life philosophy. "A Socrates gone mad," was Plato's description (Diog. Laert. VI.53), and a good one. A philosophical questioner, Diogenes gained adherents through his shocking counter-cultural life, one far more unconventional than that of Socrates; like Socrates, he used his strangeness to call his society to account.

Born in 404 BCE in the Greek city of Sinope, Diogenes was exiled for defacing the city's coinage—a crime we can think of as comparable to flag-burning in its symbolic shock value.[2] In later years "defacing the coinage" became a metaphor, in the Cynic school, for their radical disdain for local belonging and wealth. ("He said that the love of money is the mother city [mêtropolin] of all evils" [VI.50].)

Arriving in Athens, Diogenes set up in the marketplace, making his home in a tub or large jar. (He said that he had learned by watching a mouse that it was not necessary to have a fancy house, and one could sleep in any corner.) He cultivated a frugal lifestyle: "One day he saw a child drinking out of its hands. He hurled away the cup from his purse, saying, 'A little child has beaten me in simplicity of life'" (VI.37). He connected this life with dignity and independence. One day Diogenes was washing some lettuce. Plato came up to him and said quietly, "if you had paid court to Dionysius [the childish and immoral tyrant of Syracuse, whom Plato tried to teach], you would not have been washing lettuce." Diogenes replied, just as quietly, "If you had washed lettuce, you would not have been paying court to Dionysius" (VI.58).

Especially notorious was Diogenes's deliberately shocking assault on conventional propriety. By evoking outrage and even disgust, he challenged observers to ask what is truly good or bad, and what is thought good or bad on the basis of habit only. Diogenes spat in a rich man's house, mocked religious rituals that have no relation to virtue, and defied conventional norms about eating and sexual behavior. "He used to do everything in public," reports the biographer, "the acts of both Demeter and Aphrodite" (VI.69). The appellation "doggy" was given to Diogenes and his followers because they ate in public, tearing at their food like animals. ("He even attempted to eat meat raw, but he could not digest it" [VI.34].) Today most people eat constantly in public, so we do not readily understand what the fuss was about. This, of course, proves Diogenes's point: we are dealing with a mere habit, unconnected to anything deep about character or virtue. "Reproached for eating in the marketplace, he said, 'Well, it was in the marketplace that I felt hungry'" (VI.58). As for sex, his followers Crates and Hipparchia famously had sex in the public square. Diogenes pursued a more radical self-sufficiency: "And while he was masturbating in public he would continually say, 'I wish it were possible to relieve hunger by rubbing one's guts'" (VI.69). (Masturbating was generally frowned on as a sign that one had no access to sexual partners, so this is shocking for that reason, too.)

Is all this simply childish acting out? And where is there anything in it that we might call philosophy? Because no Cynic treatises survive, it is difficult to know what the positive content of their thought was, but it seems likely that the movement was not solely critical and negative.[3] Behind the shock tactics lay, interpreters often say, a conviction that the worth of a human being consists in rational and moral capacity, and that human flourishing consists in the development of those capacities toward virtue. Diogenes famously spent his life in search of a virtuous man; this positive search was the counterpart to his denunciation of rank and wealth. "Asked where in Greece he saw good men, he said . . . that men compete in digging and kicking to outdo one another, but nobody competes over virtue and excellence" (VI.27). Another passage tells us that Diogenes believed education was of two kinds, mental and bodily. Both types are important, but bodily fitness is important only as a prerequisite for the development of the virtues (VI.70–72). So we may see the negative shock tactics as, indeed, a mad kind of Socratism, a kind that spits on the false images of goodness in order to draw attention to what is truly fine within. Diogenes clearly believes that all human beings contain something fine within, and that this potential is a deep source of human equality.

What is this something? Throughout the later Cynic / Stoic tradition it is imagined as a set of capacities for practical reasoning and choice, capacities that all humans possess to a sufficient degree, and that no non-human creature possesses to any appreciable degree. That binary understanding of nature is profoundly problematic, and I shall return to this problem in Chapter 7, asking whether any tradition founded on it can possibly hold our allegiance today. Maybe reform is possible, maybe not. But it is noteworthy that Diogenes does not really say this, so far as we can see. He scoffs at the "external goods," but with what does he contrast them? Usually he is read through a Stoic lens; but we could also read him as more similar to the Epicureans, who thought the good condition of the bodily organism is itself valuable and that reason's role is primarily or even only instrumental. Let's, then, not overread Diogenes. Our evidence is scanty. It seems compatible with a reading that could be more promising for modern purposes than the Stoicizing reading. So let us leave the space open.

I now must ask you to put this very grave worry aside, in order to understand the positive features of the tradition more deeply. Humans are imagined as having within themselves something worthy of respect and even awe. This basic potentiality may vary in degree in different people; the tradition neither affirms nor denies this. But any such variation is regarded as basically irrelevant, given that the bare possession of moral and rational nature (in the Stoicizing reading) or of vital human-animal nature (in my imaginary alternative)—up, presumably, to some threshold level—is sufficient to make the being in whom this potential dwells a precious being, equal to every other such being. The idea is like that of turning on a very bright light. Bright lights vary, but any one of them eclipses the darkness, and any one of them suffices to chart our course in a world of uncertainty.

Shall we call this source of light human "dignity"? That is what a long tradition stemming from the Cynics and especially Stoics, prominently including Kant, has called it. But the adherents of the tradition do not favor any particular single term. "The god within," "reason," and "soul" are all used in addition to Latin *dignitas*—a term that, after all, just means "worth," and can designate worth of many types, depending on the views of the speaker. Sometimes the term refers to a "worth" connected to status or rank; sometimes, as here, to a worth that is internal and independent of rank. In what follows I shall often use the word "dignity" as a placeholder for the human powers to which the tradition alludes, because Kant and the modern human rights tradition so use it. What is important to me is not the term but the content to which it refers. And the content is, clearly, profoundly egalitarian. It has nothing to do with rank or status, and indeed is accompanied by the most vehement repudiation of rank and status as key moral and political values. All humans are equal with regard to what matters, and the ways in which humans are conventionally ranked and ordered are, in consequence, wrong-headed and pernicious.[4] Thus later thinkers who use *dignitas* to allude to relative status or social class are not following this same tradition but departing from it in a way that the tradition would find most objectionable.

Moreover, it is this tradition, in one form or another, that has grounded the use of "human dignity" in the modern human rights movement, not any more hierarchical or monarchical tradition. When Jacques Maritain proposed "dignity" as a way of capturing, in secular ethical terms, what he as a Christian would mean by "soul," he was expressing the core values of the Cynic / Stoic tradition, which strongly influenced the Christian tradition, and which he correctly saw as egalitarian and unhierarchical. More on this in Chapters 6 and 7. At this point, what is important is the idea of a threshold property that is shared by all human beings in a way that renders them all equal for moral purposes, a property to which the correct response is (equal) respect and awe.

We now see the Cynic starting point, and the Cynics already capture in defiant terms the egalitarianism of this moral core. Already in these Cynic anecdotes, however, we see a problem to which Chapter 2 has alerted us. Why should the cosmopolitan life, so construed, also be a poor life, a life that proudly displays its homelessness and its lack of possessions? Shouldn't cosmopolitans be concerned about getting people the material things they need in order to live well?

One reason for Diogenes's dismissive attitude to material need is surely that he is more worried about the damage done to people by their excessive dependency on money and status than about the damage that can be done by hunger, illness, and exposure. He pushes people to cultivate independence from externals, in order to correct the unbalanced worship of externals he observes. Perhaps he thinks that this will leave people in about the right place, wanting only what they really need. (Epicurus thought something like this.)

There is surely truth in this account. And yet we still want to know why, in his critique of the powerful, he did not stress the importance of material redistribution. Why didn't he say to Alexander, "I want you to give all your subjects a decent minimum living standard, including adequate nutrition and basic health care?"

This imagined response, however, suggests a deeper reason for Diogenes's reticence. Picture him saying this to Alexander and you are picturing a needy man admitting that he needs what power can give. He would be saying, you have power over me, and he would be paying court to that power. We have difficulty imagining a Diogenes who behaved like that; he would not be the dignified, scornful Diogenes we know.

To put the point more generally, when someone behaves like a victim, saying, "These social arrangements damage me and I want you to rectify those damages," he seems to be saying at the same time, "I am damaged goods. I am vulnerable to what you have dished out." Maybe he does not have to say that his human dignity itself is injured—maybe he can convince you that there is a sharp distinction to be drawn between human dignity and happiness, and that his worth is untouched, though his happiness is not. Cicero's own New Academic view, which he describes in book V of *De Finibus,* attempted a related compromise: "external goods" are not necessary for eudaimonia, but they can affect the degree of one's eudaimonia. Yet there is still a problem: to the extent that the damaged thing really matters, you are admitting that you lack what really matters for human life. And you are in effect flattering power, imploring it to bind up your wounds. I think this is how the Cynics saw things. And for that reason they thought that the only way of showing that human dignity has full worth in itself, no matter what natural and social arrangements have done to it, is to show that they really don't need any of the things kings can give. So: life in a tub, marriage in the marketplace. We are already on the road to the pernicious distinction between duties of justice and duties of material aid, for Diogenes is happy to say, give me respect; and most unwilling to say, give me food and shelter. Indeed, he appears to think that he can say give me respect only if he totally refuses to lay claim to food and shelter.

"Asked what he had gotten out of philosophy, he said, 'If nothing else, at least to be prepared for every fortune'" (VI.63).

III. Stoic Independence

The Stoics, both Greek and Roman, developed the image of the *kosmopolitês,* or world citizen, much more fully. They argued that each of us dwells, in effect, in two communities—the community of our birth, and the community of human aspiration that is, in Seneca's words, "truly great and truly common, in which we look neither to this corner nor to that, but measure the boundaries of our nation by the sun."[5] The Stoics held that this community is the source of our most fundamental moral and social obligations:

> The much-admired Republic of Zeno is aimed at this one main point, that we should not organize our daily lives around the city or the deme, divided from one another by local schemes of justice, but we should regard all human beings as our fellow demesmen and fellow citizens, and there should be one way of life and one order, just as a herd that feeds together shares a common nurturance and a common law. Zeno wrote this as a dream or image of a well-ordered and philosophical community.[6]

Even in its Roman incarnation, where the empire did make it plausible to think of an actual worldwide political community, the Stoic idea of world citizenship is not focused on the goal of creating a world state.

Zeno did propose an ideal city, but we know very little about its institutional structure.[7] More important by far is the Stoic insistence on a certain way of perceiving our standing in the moral and social world. We should view ourselves as fundamentally and deeply linked to the human kind as a whole, and take thought in our deliberations, both personal and political, for the good of the whole species. This idea is compatible with local forms of political organization; but it directs political, as well as moral, thought.[8]

The basis for the cosmopolitan community, for the Stoics, is the worth of practical / moral reason in each and every human being.[9] Reason is a portion of the divine in each of us. And each and every human being, just by virtue of being rational and moral, has boundless worth. Male or female, slave or free, all are alike of boundless moral value, and the dignity of reason is worthy of respect wherever it is found. Seneca gives this idea of the moral core a beautiful expression in his *Moral Epistles* 41, in which he urges Lucilius not to bow down before the conventional images of god—and, by extension, not before conventional signs of authority or rank:

> God is near you, is with you, is inside you . . . If you have ever come on a dense wood of ancient trees that have risen to an exceptional height, shutting out all sight of the sky with one thick screen of branches upon another, the loftiness of the forest, the seclusion of the spot, your sense of wonder at finding so deep and unbroken a gloom out of doors, will persuade you of the presence of a deity . . . And if you come across a man who is not alarmed by dangers, not touched by passionate longing, happy in adversity, calm in the midst of storm . . . is it not likely that a feeling of awe

for him will find its way into your heart? . . . Praise in him
what can neither be given nor snatched away, what is peculiarly human. You ask what that is? It is his soul, and reason
perfected in the soul. For the human being is a rational
animal.

Every person's capacity for choice is infinitely precious, worthy of
wonder and awe. Seneca here depicts mature virtue, but he makes it
clear that the awe-inspiring thing, the "god within," is the potentiality
for that.

This capacity for reason makes us fellow citizens. Zeno, it would
appear, spoke of rational humanity as grounding a common idea of
law.[10] Cicero borrowed this idea in De Officiis III (his account of Stoic
ethics) to speak of a single law of nature, which commands us not to
harm anyone (III.21–22, 27). Marcus carries it further: "If reason is
common, so too is law; and if this is common, then we are fellow citizens. If this is so, we share in a kind of organized polity. And if that is
so, the world is as it were a city-state" (M. Aur. Med. IV.4).[11]

Under cosmopolitan law, all human beings are in a very deep sense
worthy of equal respect and concern. The accident of where one is born
is just that, an accident; any human being might have been born in any
nation. Recognizing this, we should not allow differences of nationality
or class or ethnic membership or even gender[12] to erect barriers
between us and our fellow human beings. We should recognize humanity wherever it occurs, and give it our first allegiance and respect.[13]
As Marcus puts it, "My city and my country, as I am Antoninus, is
Rome; as I am a human being, it is the world" (VI.44). Seneca is especially eloquent in describing the beauty of humanity, and the attitude
of quasi-religious awe with which he is inspired by his contemplation

of a human being's rational and moral purpose, which he compares to the awe with which one might contemplate the sublime beauty of nature (*Ep.* 41). Respect for humanity is a regulative ideal, against which all actual earthly politics should be measured.[14]

At this point we must zero in on a problem mentioned in Chapter 1. The Stoics ground human equality in a specific potentiality: the potentiality for moral reason. They posit that in all human beings this potentiality is present in sufficient degree and that, above this threshold, any possible differences of degree are irrelevant. Modern thinkers such as Kant and John Rawls follow this line.[15] What, then, of the dignity of a human being with profound cognitive disabilities, whether during a portion of life (for instance, a period of senile dementia) or throughout the whole of it? Here the Stoics are basically silent. One could take three positions. One might hold, first, that these humans are not of equal human dignity. Modern ethics has by and large rejected that conclusion, however, seeing in the lives of people with cognitive disabilities a profound human worth. One might hold, second, that the potentiality for moral reason is actually fully present within such people, but is simply unable to be seen or to express itself fully on account of flaws in that person's body. This position was taken by some Platonists in antiquity, and many Christian thinkers subsequently; but it is of course a fiction, and based on mere assertion.

Finally, one might revise the core of the position, saying that equal human worth need not be based on a threshold level of that specific potentiality. At this point one might go in two directions. One might say that mere human livingness is all we need for equal dignity, even if life activity is radically absent (as with a person in a persistent vegetative state); this position is taken today by many Christian thinkers. Or one might say, instead, that there is a wide disjunction of human potentialities—for emotional expression, for pleasure, for movement, for sensory experience—that is relevant to equal human dignity, and if there is some sufficient cluster of those present, then it doesn't matter that cognition has been severely impaired. We might argue, in accordance with this line, that a person in a persistent vegetative state is not fully humanly alive, and not, therefore, of equal human dignity. And yet a person who has minimal cognition but other potentialities, such as those for showing and returning affection, for delighting in music or light, is quite different, and is fully humanly alive and of equal human dignity. I am inclined to take this position, in part because it permits an easy extension of the notion of dignity to the lives of non-human animals, an issue I shall raise in Chapter 7. For now, it is enough to note the problem: the tradition reaches a morally attractive conclusion about human equality through highly questionable ideas about the superiority of reason. Let us now return to the Stoic account.

Why does respect for humanity give rise to an idea of a city or community? Why not, instead, to rules governing human beings as creatures unconnected to one another? Stoic ethics held that our moral capacities are also fundamentally social: we are born to live and work together, and our dignity is the dignity of interacting and thoroughly interconnected beings. Language is the sign of this aspect of our nature. Thus to respect human reason is also to respect human sociability.[16]

The Stoics stress that to be a world citizen one does not need to give up local identifications and affiliations. Hierocles argued that we should regard ourselves not as devoid of local affiliations, but as surrounded by a series of concentric circles. The first one is drawn around the self; the next takes in one's immediate family, then follows the extended family, then, in order, one's neighbors or local group, one's fellow city-dwellers, one's fellow countrymen. Outside all these circles is the largest one, that of humanity as a whole. Our task as citizens of the world will be to "draw the circles somehow toward the center," making all human beings more like our fellow city-dwellers, and so forth.[17] In general, we should think of nobody as a stranger, outside of our sphere of concern and obligation. Presumably the idea of concentric circles is a device of moral education: in the end, human beings have fully equal worth, and the really wise person will see this. But one way to approach that difficult idea is to think of the circles, beginning from the connections one understands from experience.[18]

In practical terms, we may give what is near to us a special degree of attention and concern. But we should always remember that these features of placement are incidental and that our most fundamental allegiance is to what is human. Special duties are just delegations from the general duty to humanity. The special measure of concern we give to our own is justified not by any intrinsic value of the local, but by the overall requirements of humanity. (The Stoics think that we usually promote the goals of humanity best by doing our duty where life has placed us—raising our own children, for example, rather than trying vainly to care for all the world's children.[19])

Seen in this way, respect for humanity has implications for social and educational reform. Thus Musonius Rufus uses Stoic cosmopolitanism to defend the equal education of boys and girls and the higher education of married women, arguing that rational and moral nature needs educational development. Marriage itself must be reformed so that it expresses mutual respect. The Cynics proposed doing away with marriage altogether: Diogenes said that anyone who persuaded the other person should have intercourse with that person, and the resulting children should be brought up communally (Diog. Laert. VI.72). Similarly, in the ideal city of the early Greek Stoics, marriage was ruled out on grounds that it would lead to jealousy and competition; a system of free consent to intercourse plus communal child-rearing was established. The Roman Stoics focused on reforming marriage rather than junking it; they proposed an equal partnership of male and female, in which both would freely exercise moral choice, albeit in different spheres. Musonius even proposed the abolition of the sexual double standard: if men expect their wives to be monogamous, they should make the same demand of themselves.[20]

So respect for humanity is not empty of consequences. But now we must turn to what is missing from the cosmic city: for, as we know, Stoic cosmopolitanism, like that of the Cynics, involves the thought that the so-called external goods are indifferent.

The Stoic account poses a profound question to its skeptics: how can we give sufficient respect to rational capacities, while still portraying both virtue and happiness as in need of external resources?

We should bear in mind that it seemed, in Chapter 2, that people could be harmed by the events of chance in two distinct ways. First, they could be stopped from doing the things they want to do. (Pointing ahead to Chapter 7, let us call this type of damage a failure in combined capabilities, meaning internal powers of mind plus worldly circumstances for their exercise.) But they can also be harmed with respect to the development of reason, desire, and will. (Let us call this type of damage a failure in internal capabilities.) They still have rational and moral potential (what I call basic capabilities), but this potential hasn't been fully developed within. To get still clearer about this distinction, let's think of two memorable images used by seventeenth-century philosopher Roger Williams, a creative and critical follower of the Stoics, when he spoke of the deprivation of religious liberty. Some types of deprivation, he said, are like "imprisonment": those are the types that allow you to believe freely but prevent you from acting on your beliefs. But some types go deeper, and he called them "soul rape," thinking of the inner damage to character and integrity caused by being forced to affirm things you don't really believe. Respect for human dignity entails contending against both forms of insult. So what do the Stoics have to say about imprisonment and soul rape?[21]

IV. Cosmopolitans on the Damages of Luck

We understand our problem better, and see its depth more clearly, if we now consider the psychology of the cosmopolitan, one of Stoicism's most fascinating topics. According to the Stoics, as we by now see, none of the passions will figure in the life of the good cosmopolitan, since all ascribe to people and things outside the agent's own moral powers an importance vis-à-vis her good that they do not really possess. To the person who sees the world aright, there is nothing to fear, because moral powers cannot be lost. There is nothing to be angry at, because the things that can be damaged by other people's malice are just externals; damage never cuts to the core.

In one way this has to look like a very attractive proposal: for we are just as aware as were the Greeks and Romans that a lot of damage is done in the world by anxieties and angers that are the result of unwise attachments to externals, such as money, power, and status. That recognition was always the strength of the tradition. When one walks out into a competitive and hierarchical world, it is not so bad to do so with the thoughts of Marcus Aurelius, as he prepares to greet the new day:

Say to yourself in the morning: I shall meet people who are interfering, ungracious, insolent, full of guile, deceitful and antisocial . . . But I, . . . who know that the nature of the wrongdoer is of one kin with mine—not indeed of the same blood or seed but sharing the same kind, the same portion of the divine—I cannot be harmed by any one of them, and no one can involve me in shame. I cannot feel anger against him who is of my kin, nor hate him. We were born to labor together, like the feet, the hands, the eyes, and the rows of upper and lower teeth. To work against one another is therefore contrary to nature, and to be angry against a man or turn one's back on him is to work against him.[22]

Marcus speaks to himself as to a person very prone to anger and resentment. Here the cosmopolitan thought of respect for humanity and sociability steps in to give him a new view of his political enemies. This humane view, in turn, permits him to cultivate his own humanity toward them, and to persist in the goals of cosmopolitanism, rather than relapsing into the faction-ridden style of politics he has sought to avoid. Cosmopolitanism supports the removal of anger, because it tells him that connectedness is important and insults are unimportant. And the removal of anger further supports cosmopolitanism. Because he sees his enemies as fellow humans, sharing purposes and ends with him, he can treat them as ends, rather than merely as obstacles in the way of his policies.

The Stoics seem right to think that if we are to produce a world in which respect for humanity governs actions and policies, we need to deploy at least some of these tactics. We can't pursue common goals well—especially when they involve personal sacrifice—if we are all the time worrying about our own standing toward external goods such as wealth and status. And they seem right to say that the radical program of detachment they propose is sufficient for removing many problems that stand between human beings and the kingdom of ends. And yet, as we reflect, we sense that the life with which detachment leaves us is not free from difficulty, even from the viewpoint of cosmopolitan goals.

First, we encounter a problem about moral development. For Stoics are deeply concerned about education, and, reformers in that area of social life, they clearly think that in giving everyone education (women, slaves, the poor), they are giving them not just a nice frill, but something they need—something, to use my terminology, that develops their basic capabilities into full-blown internal capabilities. They think that respect for humanity naturally expresses itself in the desire to educate people, as also in non-cruelty and sexual restraint. But why? Either these things are external goods or they aren't. If education is not external to virtue, but required for human flourishing, then the Stoics are just flatly inconsistent when they claim that we don't need anything beyond our power to flourish. But if it is an external good and not required for flourishing—if the Stoic idea is consistent—then it makes no sense to be upset if someone doesn't have it, any more than it makes sense to be upset if she doesn't have dinner, or a place to sleep. They are forced to admit that something politics can deliver or fail to deliver is of such great importance that it makes sense to be passionate about it. Or if they don't make this concession, they have difficulty explaining their own zeal for the broad dissemination of philosophical teaching.

Much the same problem arises when we think of incursions into people's mental life after they are educated: by sexual violence, by torture, by post-traumatic stress, by other psychological calamities for which external conditions are to blame, not failure of effort and will. Internal capabilities are damaged, and we ought to be upset. The significance of these losses gives us reasons to make international politics take a determined stance against torture, sexual violence, and other forms of mental injury. The human psyche is porous and vulnerable, even if determined and strong. The Stoics deny this at the cost of having nothing useful to say about some of the worst things in the world, which clearly pertain to their own idea of respect for humanity.

And what of "imprisonment"? Isn't that bad in itself, and something cosmopolitan politics should work to avoid, even if it doesn't damage internal capabilities but only combined capabilities? To try to figure this out, we need to dig deeper.

Let us now look more deeply at this picture of a cosmopolitan moral life held together by respect and humane concern, without the taint of divisive passions. Even where consistent, how attractive is it? What, precisely, is the nature of the Stoic's concern for his fellow human beings? What does the good cosmopolitan feel, when they are hungry or ill or burdened by aggressive warfare?

One thing that the texts make clear is that the cosmopolitan's attitude cannot be the emotion that we usually call pity or compassion, a painful emotion grounded in the belief that someone else is suffering in a serious way, and that this suffering is a bad thing—the emotion of the spectator at a tragic drama. The Stoics like compassion just as little as they like the tragic dramas that cultivate it. "For what are tragedies," writes Epictetus, "but the sufferings of people who have been wonderstruck by external things, set down and displayed in the customary meter?" (Disc. 1.4.26). Of course these wonderstruck people are just wrong, and we shouldn't weep with them. As Epictetus again says, "Look how tragedy comes about: when chance events befall fools"

(2.26.31). If the person were not a fool, he would not mind the chance event, any more than Socrates minded his death. And why should we moan and groan over the inflated sufferings of a fool?

If the attitude is not compassion, however, what is it? It is not indifference, clearly: for Stoics again and again commend their line on emotions by pointing to the way in which getting rid of emotions helps us cultivate a humane attitude of concern and benevolence toward our fellow citizens. Marcus urges the cosmopolitan to be closely and keenly concerned with the interests of his fellow humans: "Love the human kind," he writes (*Med.* VII.31), using Aristotle's word for friendly love, *phileô*. Indeed, we are to see all other people's concerns as our own: "That which is not in the interests of the hive cannot be in the interests of the bee" (VI.54).[23] This concern has to remain in a certain way provisional: for the minute a person becomes an obstacle to our concerns, we must distance ourselves from thoughts that would lead to anger. Thus, Marcus makes the following interesting suggestion:

> Looking at things one way, human beings are the closest things in the world to us, insofar as we should do them good and stick to it through difficulty. But insofar as some of them pose an obstacle to the acts that most concern us, human beings become one of the things indifferent to me, no less indifferent than the sun or the wind or a wild beast. (V.20)

We may wonder how close the closeness can really be, if it can so easily flip over into that cool detachment. Marcus is on sounder psychological ground in a later passage, when he suggests that the wrongdoer continues to be an object of intense concern, with the aim of reform and benefit:

Kindliness is immovable, if it is genuine and not a pretend smile or a theatrical performance. For what can the most violent person do to you, if you persist in being kindly to him, and, if you have a chance, gently exhort him and teach him a better way at the very time when he is trying to damage you? No, child. We were born for something other than this. I won't be harmed, but you, my child, will harm yourself. (XI.18.9)

Stoics are ambivalent, then, about how we are to regard difficult and unpredictable creatures of the human species. On balance, however, and not without vacillation, they think we should have a close and sympathetic concern, and try assiduously to benefit them, even when they are hostile. "Your only joy, and your only rest, is to pass from one action performed in the service of the human community to another action performed in the service of the human community" (VI.7).[24]

The problem I now want to raise is, how will this benefiting take place, against the background of a view that has leached all importance out of the things in life with respect to which people usually would like to be benefited? What, in short, are the point and purpose of the moral and political life? In one mood, Marcus assures us that benevolence and good works will forward the purposes of cosmopolitan humanity, and that we will be all the more free to give such benefits when we are less hung up by personal anxiety. But if they are fools, we reply, why should we encourage them in foolishness by giving them the external things they need? Listen to Marcus talk about his own military enterprise, as he tries to repel the invading Sarmatians, who threaten the safety of his people: "A spider prides itself on hunting down a fly, one man a hare, another a sardine, another wild boars, another bears, another Sarmatians" (X.10). The defense of one's own is no more truly weighty, properly regarded, than some fishing for sport, or the reflexive movements of an insect. Can such attachments sustain a cosmopolitanism grounded in the defense of human beings against both "imprisonment" and "soul rape"?

In response to this question, Stoics move in different directions. Seneca, I argue elsewhere,[25] moves, unsteadily and unclearly, toward a more passionate engagement with at least some externals, such as the struggle for liberty and the defense of one's own against a tyrant's onslaught. Marcus, by contrast, remains consistent with the Stoic program. He gives our problem the best solution it can be given within that framework. Cicero alone, and only at times, rejects the framework, restoring love of children, country, and friends to a place of prominence.[26]

Recall that in his little lecture to the evildoer he addressed him as "child." This is, in effect, his answer. "If there is a shortage of things indifferent," he writes, "do not imagine that there is any great evil present; for that is a bad habit. But still, as the old man in the play . . , gave his child back the little top, fully mindful that it was just a top, you too behave in a similar way" (V.36). This image of parental concern for the distress of a child is his image for the Stoic cosmopolitan's benevolence. Do not think, yourself, that the externals around which the drama of the moral life revolves are of deep and abiding significance. But recognize that most people do care about them very intensely, like little children who have not yet developed a sense of true value. Because you care for those children, and those children are all wrought up over trivial things, you too have to take those trivial things seriously, in a way. You give them the things they need, but you never forget that they are childish things.

This is an initially promising attempt on our problem. For we know that parents can be genuinely and very actively concerned for the well-being of their children—without sharing these children's view of what constitutes real importance. But Marcus's idea is not altogether satisfactory. First, it seems insufficient to motivate the kind of aggressive concern with the redistribution of externals that a cosmopolitan life would appear to require. Stoic children have to learn true values at some point, and why not by deprivation of worthless externals? It is not surprising that thinkers who take such an attitude should fail to pursue material aid to people at a distance, or even the abolition of slavery: for as Seneca says in his letter on the latter topic, what harm does that institution do, if the soul is free within (*Ep. 47*)? As we've already concluded, this is not adequate. Don't we need to say that such material conditions are themselves an insult to humanity, and that changing them is an essential step in a cosmopolitan politics?

Second, Marcus's attitude is condescending. Are most human beings just "fools" when they mind the loss of liberty, when they grieve over the deaths of loved ones? Stoics start from a Cynic disdain for convention, and this in some respects wise detachment moves them too far away from an immersed human relationship to value. In short, the Stoic attitude to externals bodes ill for the world of equal respect and reciprocity that they prize.

Finally, Marcus's view really leaves too little in human life to make it a life worth valuing at all. What we are left with, it would appear, is moral capacity, but nothing for which these capacities actually matter. The tendency to justice, but no urgent work for justice to accomplish. Goodness without deep love of family, children, friends. Marcus really does see life as a kind of dead procession of meaningless occurrences:

> The vain solemnity of a procession; dramas played out on
> the stage; troops of sheep or goats; fights with spears; a little

bone thrown to dogs; a chunk of bread thrown into a fish-
pond; the exhausting labor and heavy burdens under which
ants must bear up; crazed mice running for shelter; puppets
pulled by strings . . . (VII.3)[27]

Nothing stands out above anything else, and everything looks equally
devoid of value.

Nor is this a momentary lapse, or a sign of personal depression. It is of
the essence of Stoic cosmopolitanism that things should be seen this
way, denuded of their ordinary human significances, since these significances are erroneous. Marcus does not come by his strange vision of
the world naturally, or as the result of a lonely, stress-filled life. It is
through Stoic exercises that he strips the humanity from human things,
rewriting his inner discourse to bring it into consistency with the
doctrine that externals are indifferent. Consider the following extraordinary passage:

How important it is to represent to oneself, when it comes
to fancy dishes and other such foods, "This is the corpse of
a fish, this other thing the corpse of a bird or a pig." Similarly, "This Falernian wine is just some grape juice," and
"This purple vestment is some sheep's hair moistened in the
blood of some shellfish." When it comes to sexual intercourse, we must say, "This is the rubbing together of membranes, accompanied by the spasmodic ejaculation of a sticky
liquid." How important are these representations, which
reach the thing itself and penetrate right through it, so that
one can see what it is in reality. (VI.13)[28]

Well, yes. It is important to think this way, if what one wants is to escape from bondage to externals. But this detached way of viewing human events and actions, if applied to hunger, pain, and the horrors of war, will hardly prove sufficient to motivate energetic efforts of benevolence, or, indeed, to make a world humanly worth dwelling in.

Marcus suggests that we have two choices only: the world of real-life Rome, which is like a large gladiatorial contest (Sen. *Ir.* 2.8), each person striving to outdo others in a vain competition for externals, a world exploding with rage and poisoned by malice; and the world of Marcus's lonely gentle sympathy, where kindliness to one's foolish children is mingled with thoughts of the emptiness and vanity of all human endeavors.

V. Reforming the Stoic Position

Not so, we might say. We have other options of a more hopeful, a more moderate, sort. On some points, we may accept Marcus's program of revaluation. Distinctions of rank, for example, really are just silly fantasies, correctly dispelled (along with the passions to which they give rise) by a process of critical self-examination. With other goods, such as money, health, shelter, and social inclusion, we should agree with Marcus that the excessive and idolatrous pursuit of them is both ridiculous and reprehensible—and that all the inflamed passions that go with them should be eliminated. We may also repudiate retributive anger as unproductive and poisonous to the cooperation we badly need to live well. We should still insist, however, that there is a certain level of external goods that it is right to be concerned about, instrumentally, because a decent life for a human being, a life worthy of human dignity, is not possible without that; nor is it possible without political liberty, and education, and confirming and mutually respectful relations with one's fellow citizens.

Finally, with yet other externals, such as friendship and love of family, love of one's republic, one should go even further, along with Cicero: these are important intrinsic goods, although they also depend on luck to some extent. Cicero's *De Amicitia* extols the intrinsic importance of personal friendship while making clear its vulnerability to betrayal and to loss; the same evident love of friendship suffuses his letters to his best friend Atticus.[29] His love for his daughter Tullia, acknowledged often as one of the most important things in his life, leaves him vulnerable to devastating grief, as his letters reveal. He is perfectly aware that his friends, influenced strongly by Stoicism and other detachment-seeking philosophies, will think his prolonged grieving inappropriate. But he says that he can't stop grieving, and does not believe that he should. Finally, love of one's own republic and one's relationship with it, highly fragile external goods, rightly lie, for Cicero, at the core of a cosmopolitan life, and he grieves as well for the impending loss of those institutions.

Cicero's heroic efforts to save the Roman Republic, not always well conceived perhaps, but always inspired by genuine love of institutions that protect freedom and accountability, as well as by love of Rome's particular institutions and history, show us that a cosmopolitanism that turns outward toward the whole world, as in *De Officiis* (his last work) can also involve intense love for and vulnerability to some matters of chance. If one values one's own republic rightly, one understands that at least some externals should be objects of eager devotion. For that love Cicero was assassinated a very short time after writing *De Officiis*. He could have saved himself by caring less and leaving Rome sooner—

or by a full-blown detachment like that of his friend Atticus. Atticus was an Epicurean, not a Stoic; but genuine Stoic principles seem to tend in the direction of that detachment. (Brutus was a Platonist, not a Stoic, and he auditioned the conspirators to find out whether they agreed with him philosophically, in believing that tyranny was worse than civil war, something that Stoics denied.[30]) According to Plutarch, Cicero leaned forward out of his litter to meet the assassin's knife, expressing his belief that one should meet life's accidents with dignity, but hardly deny their profound significance. The subsequent cosmopolitan tradition is mixed, part Stoic, and part Ciceronian: Adam Smith reproves the Stoics for urging detachment from our family, friends, and nation. He clearly treats these not simply as local delegations from universal duties but also as having intrinsic worth.

On the question of moral capacity and our respect for it, we can adopt a two-tiered solution that is more Aristotelian than Stoic. We can insist, that is, on a distinction between "basic" or innate capacities and trained or developed capacities, which I call *internal capabilities,* and on a further distinction between trained or developed capacities and the real opportunity to express these in a flourishing life, which I call *combined capabilities.* (If we revise the conception of dignity as I suggested above, basic—that is, innate—capacities will be an open-ended disjunction of capacities for action and emotion.) A moderate cosmopolitan can hold that the source of our infinite and equal worth as persons is the capacity for some types of human living with which we come into the world. Those capacities, however, are as yet unformed. They require external support—love, health, food, shelter, education—to develop into mature human internal powers of choice, action, and emotional response. But even complete *internal capability* is not sufficient for human flourishing. Here we need externals once again: the conditions of action, citizenship, liberty, friendship—and, as before, health, food, shelter. If a person is denied that which transforms innate capacities into trained capacities, this is tragic. We cannot have for this victim of life the kind of awe we feel for Seneca's strong man who has survived nature's accidents; but we can and should still feel respect and awe for the human potentiality that has been tragically starved or deformed. If a mature developed person is denied the things of chance, then we should react as we do to the tragic hero: with respect and awe for the intact humanity that is manifest even in disaster, but also with real sorrow for the eclipse of human activity and full human flourishing.

These suggestions need further development, which they receive in Chapter 7. But they give us hope, at any rate, that we can forge a moderate cosmopolitanism based on Stoic ideas without the deforming consequences to which the Stoic rejection of externals leads them.

VI. Particularistic Passions

When we have solved this problem, however, if we have, another one awaits us. For the Stoics believe that if we reintroduce even a limited attachment to externals, and particularly any attachments to family, loved ones, and nation, those attachments are likely to be partial and uneven, binding the mind to its immediate sphere. Such attachments are also especially likely to be unstable, giving rise to vindictive anger should they be blocked. (Epictetus addresses Medea, saying: "Stop wanting your husband, and there is not one of the things you want that will fail to happen" (*Disc.* 2.17.22). They are also likely to turn attention away from the legitimate claims of human beings in other places, giving rise to aggressive war and other crimes against humanity. Even Cicero, who deplores such crimes, still advocates giving one's material aid only to the near and dear, something that ought to be highly problematic from the point of view of an impartial cosmopolitanism.[31] Thus even the most limited and reasonable reintroduction of emotional attachments—for example, Adam Smith's idea that we can have intense emotions of concern for members of our own family, provided that these are bounded by what a "judicious spectator" will feel appropriate—leaves, one might worry, too much room for both malice and partiality.

The Stoics have identified a very serious problem for any moderate cosmopolitanism. A few rare human beings may be able to have intense love and concern that is truly cosmopolitan (compatible with due respect for all human life and due attention to the just claims of all) and to live their lives with an awareness of the equal worth and the equal needs of all. But once we let the passions back in, we will discover that they are not stably supportive of these ends. They take their nourishment from the soil of intense particular attachments, and in most people they wither in the absence of such attachments. Aristotle, criticizing Plato's fantasy of intense brotherly love uniting an entire city, wrote, "There are two things that make people love and care for something: the thought that it is all theirs, and the thought that it is the only one they have. Neither of these will be present in that city" (*Pol.* 1262b22–23). Instead of intense brotherly love, Plato's city, lacking close erotic and family ties, will contain only a concern that is "watery" all round (1262b15).

Yes, Marcus will say, Aristotle is right. The roots of the strong passions are indeed particularistic. And there is no doubt that my even-handed cosmopolitan concern will, in consequence, strike some as watery. But watery evenhandedness is the only real alternative to jealousy and competitive hate—just as sex as the rubbing of membranes is the only real alternative to sex as a source of fantasied delight and divisive jealousy. There's no happy moderate in-between. Because Medea loved her husband, she was "transformed from a human being into a poisonous snake" (Epict. *Disc.* I.28.8–9).

It is thus, I believe, in the Stoics' distrust of personal attachment, and their view that all strong attachment is at root non-cosmopolitanly personal, that we should find the deepest source of their rejection of externals. It is because they think that we must ultimately choose between a self that is respectful of the dignity of all humanity and a self that is devoured by erotic longing and jealousy that they persistently deny the importance of externals for flourishing, even when externals seem required for cosmopolitan politics itself. They have concluded, in effect, that we cannot have cosmopolitan politics without remaking humanity. Marcus's first lesson from his tutor was "not to be a fan of the Greens or Blues at the races, or the light-armed or heavy-armed gladiators at the Circus" (M. Aur. *Med.* I.5). But we are all Bulls fans and Knicks fans, and our emotional life is radically partisan, revolving around the sharp imagining of the seen.

The Stoics show us a world of austere gentleness, of tender yet restrained sympathy—and they ask us to live in that world rather than in the world of tragic poetry. If we find it a barren and frightening world, as we probably will, we nonetheless have to take its challenge seriously. For their idea is supported not only by a powerful picture of dignity, but also by even deeper intuitive ideas about partisanship and the emotional conditions of world peace. If we reject the world of Marcus, we must try to say how else cosmopolitan morality, and a perpetual peace among nations, might be possible. How might we, remaining ourselves, still enter that kingdom of ends?

For Marcus, a passionate man for whom the question becomes a life-long obsession, the answer remains dark: there is no alternative. We really have to give it all up in order to be just. Only in something like death, in effect, is moral rectitude possible. And the best consolation for that bleak conclusion comes also from the thought of death. Consider this characteristic reflection on that theme, which I find both deeply moving and horribly unsatisfactory:

> Think all the time about how human beings of all sorts, and from all walks of life and all peoples, are dead . . . We must arrive at the same condition where so many clever orators have ended up, so many grave philosophers, Heraclitus, Pythagoras, Socrates; so many heroes of the old days, so many recent generals and tyrants. And besides these, Eudoxus, Hipparchus, Archimedes, other highly intelligent minds, thinkers of large thoughts, hard workers, versatile in ability, daring people, even mockers of the perishable and transitory character of human life, like Menippus. Think about all of these that they are long since in the ground . . . And what of those whose very names are forgotten? So: one thing is worth a lot, to live out one's life with truth and justice, and with kindliness toward liars and wrongdoers. (VI.47)

Because we shall die, we must recognize that everything particular about us will eventually be wiped out. Family, city, sex, children, all will pass into oblivion. So really, giving up those attachments is not such a big deal. What remain, the only things that remain, are truth and justice, the moral order of the world. In the face of the looming inevitability of our end, we should not mind being dead already. Only the true city should claim our allegiance.

If we feel that this cannot be right, that justice must be from and for the living, we cannot simply assert that Marcus is wrong. We must solve his problem, creating a convincing theory of cosmopolitan emotion and of the relationship between particular attachments and the love of humanity.

In executing this task, Cicero is, so far as this tradition goes, our best guide, showing us how friendship, family love, and love of the republic support a life devoted to cosmopolitan goals. There is tension in this life, and there is conflict. The *De Amicitia* discusses cases in which loyalty to a friend may undermine political justice. Cicero's life shows how love of a daughter may cripple a person with grief as he attempts to pursue his political duties. But for the most part the intense love of the near supports the worldwide goal, since republican institutions really are, as Cicero says, good for the world, and the love of family and friends gives depth and energy to a personality devoted to justice, an energy that Marcus's solitary life lacks. Moreover, such a life, loving the near and the far, is a life that displays the richness of human commitment that makes a life worth living. The challenges of such a life are many: for the cosmopolitan must imagine, and sustain, a love of country that does not entail rivalrous hatred of other countries; a love of friends not predicated on enmity to any other clan, group, or individual; and a love of family that is prepared to be fully fair to the opportunities of other people's children. To say the least, Roman history subsequent to Cicero's death failed to take up these challenges. Instead, the Roman Empire basically adopted a Rome-first attitude without complexity or compromise. And where family was concerned, the imperial leadership all too often pursued patronage and power to the exclusion of any type of fairness.

We must try harder.

FOUR

Grotius

A Society of States and Individuals under Moral Law

But among the traits characteristic of the human being is an impelling
desire for fellowship, that is for common life, not of just any kind,
but a peaceful life, and organized according to the measure of his
intelligence, with those who are of his kind . . . Stated as a universal
truth, therefore, the assertion that every animal is impelled by nature
to seek only its own good cannot be conceded.

—Grotius, *On the Law of War and Peace*[1]

In the twentieth century . . . there has been a retreat from the
confident assertions . . . that the members of international society
were states and nations, towards the ambiguity and imprecision on
this point that characterised the era of Grotius.

—Hedley Bull, *The Anarchical Society*

I. Bringing the Tradition into the Modern World

The Ciceronian / Stoic tradition gives the world of international relations some valuable concepts and ideals, and the general outline of a

world in which all the activities of individuals and governments should be constrained by respect for humanity. But these ideas need further development if they are to provide direction for the modern world, which in many respects has a different shape from the world the Greeks, Stoics, Cicero, and Seneca knew. The Greeks worked with the city-state as the basic unit, the Romans with the expanding reality of the Roman Empire. None dealt with the modern reality of separate nation-states.

The tradition's core idea that the world is regulated throughout by moral law, and not simply by considerations of expediency, was radical in the time of the Stoics, since previous philosophical views had suggested that we have no moral obligations to those who live outside our own city. It was radical still in the early modern world, when views of the amoral nature of international politics were already dominant, and Hobbes would soon defend the proposition that only a sovereign can put an end to the "state of war" that otherwise obtains between human beings. And it is radical today, when considerations of national security still dominate most nations' thinking about dealings with other nations and individuals. It is radical today, when neo-Hobbesian views are still dominant. How to make sense of it, then, in our time, and in our world of separate nation-states?

The tradition also leaves modern thought with some great problems, and two in particular. First, it leaves us with the puzzle of how to understand the role of the republic (or the nation) in the moral life of human beings, in relation to the duties we have to respect all humanity: should our fellow citizens take priority in our thought about justice and material aid, and, if so, how and to what extent? Second, Cicero's inadequate reflections about material distribution leave the tradition with the challenge of dealing with material and economic inequalities between nations, which threaten the very conception of a "cosmic city" regulated by universal moral law.

Hugo Grotius (1583–1645) takes up the task of bringing the Stoic tradition into the modern world. In his works on the freedom of the seas and the law of war, he draws heavily on the Stoic / Ciceronian tradition, which, for him, exemplifies the humanist ideal that he is attempting to commend to Christian nations. Although his classical learning is extensive and he quotes both classical and Christian authors of many types, it is the Stoic / Ciceronian view that, more than any other, shapes his argument, as he applies the idea of a natural law of respect for humanity to arguments about international relations in both peacetime and war. I shall argue, indeed, that understanding Grotius as the heir to the Stoic tradition gives us insight into the structure of his argument that we do not get if we see his moral outlook as a more diffuse one. In the process of extending the tradition, he makes three salient contributions.

First, Grotius systematizes the tradition, providing it with explicit arguments against an amoralist conception of international relations[2] and in favor of the idea that international relations should be seen as governed by stringent moral norms. He then goes to work showing how very general ideas of human dignity and sociability can, through intermediate principles, give rise to a determinate conception of war and peace, of property rights, and of the general elements of a world society. In this way, he makes the tradition useful and available to modern international law, whose founder he may justly be said to be.

Second, Grotius at least makes a beginning of the problem of international material inequality, developing out of traditional Stoic materials a new view of ownership that has definite implications for the issue of material aid across national boundaries.

Finally, and most important, Grotius brings the tradition into the world we now inhabit, a world of separate nation-states, each with considerable autonomy, all wrestling with issues of religious pluralism and toleration. To this world he offers a conception that subtly interweaves three elements: (1) recognition of national sovereignty as a fundamental expression of human autonomy, (2) insistence that the fundamental subject of moral and political justice is the individual, who has certain rights no matter where he or she is placed, and (3) the vision of an "international society" that goes beyond and in some ways against traditional international law (*ius gentium,* the law of nations)— that links individuals, states, and a variety of non-state groups in complicated ways—a society, suffused by moral norms, which nonetheless respects national sovereignty and self-determination. This last contribution has been said by recent thinkers to make Grotius a prescient precursor of the contemporary world, in which we need to imagine international society in a multifaceted and flexible way, aware of tension and ambiguity, and to recognize that the international realm is not constituted by the interactions of states alone, or even only by states plus traditional international law.[3]

II. States, Pluralism, Autonomy

The age of Grotius, and his own writings, may justly be said to mark the dawning of the Enlightenment, in the sense given that term by Kant: "man's emergence from his self-incurred immaturity." Although the Peace of Westphalia, which systematized the modern order of separate European states, was not signed until 1648, three years after

Grotius's death, his era marked the gradual emergence of that system out of tumultuous religious controversy and the bitter conflict of the Thirty Years' War. The Dutch people were struggling to establish independence from Spanish rule; Grotius's writings on the freedom of the seas were closely linked to Dutch politics. Later, his own life was marred by the religious strife of the times: imprisoned for his Arminian (heretical) beliefs, he had to be smuggled out of Holland in a trunk, and spent the remainder of his career at the court of Louis XIII of France.[4]

This era marked the gradual emergence of the general idea that human beings are no longer living under centralized theocratic control.[5] In the Middle Ages, whatever political divisions existed, authority was ultimately based in Rome. The Reformation brought with it the idea of the religious independence of each believer from centralized Church authority. This religious idea, in turn, gave rise, during the seventeenth century, to an idea of political autonomy, the idea that each people has a right to exist under its own self-chosen laws. The idea that diverse religious beliefs should be tolerated *within* a single state was not a part of the picture until much later, in Europe at any rate.[6] But the idea that each nation has a right to give itself laws of its own making, including laws pertaining to religion, was becoming increasingly dominant, and, with it, the idea of national sovereignty, the idea that each nation has a right to carry out these aspects of its business without external interference.

But if one holds that legitimate law is in this way made by and for human beings, that even people whom one views as heretics or infidels have the *right* to give themselves laws and to live in accordance with them, without interference, then one is also holding that human reason is to a significant degree independent of religious authority. For one is saying that even people not guided by God have the right to have their own self-imposed choices respected. And this suggests that the human mind, even without God (or the "correct" idea of God), can arrive at choices, legal and political, that are respect-worthy. When we combine this idea with the idea that in the most important matters we are all bound—or rather, we ought to bind ourselves—by a moral law to which we all have access, regardless of religion, we have many of the ingredients, at least, of the Kantian notion of autonomy, cashed out in political terms. National sovereignty and individual autonomy are kindred and mutually reinforcing ideas.

The idea of moral autonomy is not precisely new: for obviously enough the cosmopolitan tradition of the Greek and Roman world had it already, in the form of an idea of the authority of self-given reason above tradition, custom, and conventional religion.[7] At Rome, despite some persecution of Jews and Christians, there were also defenders of toleration.[8] Cicero himself appears to go rather far in this direction, in his correspondence with his friend Atticus, an Epicurean who justified his withdrawal from political life by the tenets of that sect. Cicero, of course, believes in nothing more deeply than the duty we all have to serve the republic; he connects this duty to his philosophical views. But he also respects his friend. In one remarkable letter,[9] he says, you know, you and I are so close that hardly anything divides us—except for the choice of a way or mode of life *(ratio institutae vitae)*. For me, a certain *ambitio* has motivated me to serve the republic. In your case, a perfectly plausible set of reasons *(haud reprehendenda ratio)* has led you to prefer retirement. In this way, Cicero grants that the reasoning of Atticus deserves respect, although he does not share it. Nonetheless, because religion is not the source of division and struggle at Rome that it became in Europe later, and because the major political upheavals of the day were motivated by rather different considerations, Cicero does not develop these ideas of respect and choice very far. Thus, reclaiming ideas of autonomy and associated ideas of toleration after the intervening period of religious domination becomes a new act against new opposition, requiring political forms different from those of the ancient republic.

When Grotius returns to the Ciceronian tradition, he does so, then, in a changed world, one that demands explicit doctrines of self-government and mutual respect if the right of both individuals and peoples to exit from centralized religious authority is to be secured. Moreover, it is obvious that the idea of human freedom was of central importance to Grotius in his own religious conception. The Arminian heresy, for adherence to which he risked his life and endured exile, was the assertion of human freedom against the doctrine of predestination: human beings have the power to determine their salvation by their own chosen acts. His religious treatises consistently express the importance of choice and responsibility.[10] At his trial for heresy, Grotius's heretical belief in choice was linked to his controversial political doctrines, in particular his defense of the autonomy of each province to legislate on religious affairs.[11] Thus it is not surprising that his major work on political philosophy should also give ideas of freedom and sovereignty a central place.

In the Prolegomena to BP, Grotius takes a famous and decisive step. Medieval natural lawyers had of course allowed that natural law could be apprehended by human reason without faith. Ultimately, however, it derives its validity from God and God's law. Grotius, by contrast, states: "What we have been saying would have a degree of validity even if we should concede (etiamsi daremus) that which cannot be conceded without the utmost wickedness, that there is no God, or that the affairs of men are of no concern to Him." The fact that this remark is wrapped up in a tissue of pious sentiments, and that Grotius takes utmost care throughout the work to present himself as a deeply pious man (as he probably was), did not cause these bold words to escape people's notice. Referred to simply as the *etiamsi daremus,* this argumentative move of Grotius's became the hallmark for many political thinkers as the Enlightenment dawned. For Grotius, it is not simply that heretical and infidel peoples may happen upon moral truths without being aware of a religious truth that justifies them. The moral arguments that human reason creates and assesses have validity independently of not only the believer's relation to God, but also the very existence of God. Human morality, supported by freestanding moral arguments, is self-given law.

Grotius connects this idea of validity apart from God with the idea of national sovereignty, to which he attaches great importance. Already in his early work *De Iure Praedae* (ch. 2), he asserts that separate states are a very important part of protecting and fortifying the society of all human beings. Here in *BP,* he defines sovereign power as power "whose actions are not subject to the legal control of another, so that they cannot be rendered void by the operation of another human will" (I.3.7.1). He then goes on to insist that there exist many legitimate sovereign states, each of which has the right to impose laws by its own choice:

> Just as, in fact, there are many ways of living, one being
> better than another, and out of so many ways of living each
> is free to select that which he prefers, so also a people can

select the form of government which it wishes; and the extent of its legal right in the matter is not to be measured by the superior excellence of this or that form of government, in regard to which different men hold different views, but by its free choice. (I.3.8.2)

Grotius's version of this doctrine would not satisfy modern proponents of democratic sovereignty: for he insists that a people has the right to enslave itself, and thus he defends the rights of many actual kings to the virtually unlimited power they exerted. It is impossible to know how far these parts of the work reflect the political pressures under which he lived, as a refugee given a fragile existence at the court of a foreign absolute monarch. But the crucial move is his insistence that the choice of the people is authoritative, whether right or wrong. Superior excellence does not mean a right to impose one's will on another.[12]

Grotius thus makes it explicit that the fact that a people has customs or religious practices different from one's own is not a legitimate ground for aggression. He cites Plutarch: "To wish to impose civilization upon uncivilized peoples is a pretext which may serve to conceal greed for what is another's" (II.20.41). He shortly argues explicitly that waging war on account of religious difference is illegitimate (II.20.44); even stating that infidels have sovereignty, and this sovereignty is to be respected (II.20.44–47). Addressing the contention that we may justly make war, at least, on states who refuse to accept Christianity after it is offered to them, he rejects this contention as well. In *De Iure Praedae* too (ch. 12), he insists that infidel states have property rights and rights of political sovereignty of which they cannot be justly deprived on the grounds that they are infidel, or on grounds of papal donation. He thus rejects an argument commonly used since the fifteenth century to justify expansionist war—and rejects, as well, the division that argument posits, between a world of Christian states and a world of non-Christian states.[13] Sometimes, as Grotius's own life clearly shows, violence against heretics can seem to Christians even more justified than violence against infidels. But his position similarly entails that Christian heretics cannot justly be targets of aggression (II.20.50). The one thing he does grant is that we may justly make war on states that persecute Christians cruelly for the sake of their religion alone (II.20.49)—a point to which I shall return in speaking of humanitarian intervention.

How is Grotius's view about political sovereignty connected to his general concept of human moral sovereignty? In one way, the two views are obviously of a piece, and the moral doctrine gives support to the political doctrine. For the right of a people to give itself laws, even when we may think the people heretical or infidel, gets a lot of mileage from the idea that important moral and political truths are both logically and epistemologically independent of the true religion. The conception of the human being as a source of valid norms through its own autonomous activity is deeply built into the picture of peoples, and of their sovereignty, that he presents.

Yet we can also see a tension emerging between the two strands of Grotius's interest in autonomy, and it is a tension that has been with us ever since. On the one hand, a people has a right to choose its laws. On the other hand, law-giving of this sort often oppresses human beings domestically, thus violating the autonomy of individuals. In particular, as the modern human rights movement will insist, there are important moral truths that transcend time and place, giving rise to individual rights, for example, rights of free speech and freedom of conscience. Sovereign peoples often ignore these rights, which may be extremely important to autonomous individuals. Doesn't full respect for the autonomy of our own moral reasoning require that in central cases touching on core moral values, the individual must be protected against the sovereign, but putatively immoral, actions of a people, ours or another's? In the name of individual autonomy, may we hold that the sovereignty of a nation has limits?

It is because Grotius's idea of sovereignty is a moral idea, founded on a moral doctrine of autonomy, that he has this dilemma, which ultimately produces his complex and indeterminate position on humanitarian intervention. If his doctrine of sovereignty were like that of Hobbes, then that would be that: what the sovereign imposes is imposed, and there is no right of resistance, internal or external. But for Grotius, the ultimate source of both moral autonomy, and, through it, political sovereignty, is the conscience of the individual; and the individual may often be in a position to criticize a sovereign regime and may also be victimized by it, for example in matters of religious repression. Grotius is unable and unwilling to turn away from this problem in the Hobbesian manner: international society as a whole stands under moral law, and each individual is both a giver of and subject to that law. Moral sovereignty underwrites political sovereignty, but it doesn't get altogether absorbed into it. Grotius does not courageously press forward in the defense of individual conscience, as did his seventeenth-century contemporary Roger Williams and the slightly later seventeenth-century thinker John Locke.[14] But he has all the materials of the problem at his disposal. As we wrestle today with the twin pressures of human rights and state sovereignty, so too did Grotius in his era: and the self-conscious complexity of his response may prove a valuable guide to our situation.

III. Natural Law and the World of Sovereign States

Grotius announces that he has been led to defend the claim that there is a moral law linking all nations because of the "utter ruthlessness" (Proleg. to BP 29) he observes in dealings between nations, a shameful and barbarous "lack of restraint" (28). Such behavior derives aid and comfort, he believes, from the doctrine that there are no moral laws or norms appropriate to war, and from the more general doctrine, frequently linked with it, that moral norms, in politics, stop at the national boundary: what reigns between states is simply force and self-interest. These realist doctrines, which have dominated much of our own contemporary thought about international relations, are as old as the ancient Greek world, and Grotius cites a host of classical authorities who endorse them. His own resistance to the amoralist doctrine is modeled on Stoic and Ciceronian resistance to its ancient version.[15]

Unlike most of his Stoic forebears, Grotius reflects explicitly about how one may argue for the existence of something as fundamental as the moral law (or "natural law"[16]), and for the nature of its specific requirements. He offers two distinct paths to his conclusion. The former he calls "more subtle," the latter "more familiar." We may show that something is natural law, first, a priori, that is, by showing that it has a "necessary agreement . . . with a rational and social nature" (BP I.1.12). Elsewhere he expresses this as the idea that we refer our arguments to "certain fundamental conceptions which are beyond question, so that no one can deny them without doing violence to himself" (Proleg. to BP 39). Second, we may show that the proposition in question is natural law a posteriori, by showing that it is "believed to be such among all nations, or among those that are more advanced in civilization," and that it therefore expresses the "common sense of mankind" (BP I.1.12).

This latter route, with its questionable distinction between advanced and non-advanced civilizations, is not favored by Grotius himself, although he feels free to use it, and it is never a bad thing, in his view, if this approach can give additional support to the first sort of argument. Part of using the latter route, he makes clear at many junctures, will be to cite the opinions of philosophers, poets, and other cultural authorities—since, of course, that is the only way we have access, over distances of space and time, to the "common sense of mankind."[17] This appeal to reflective people may also make his notion of "common sense" less like a mere opinion poll and more like the Aristotelian notion of *endoxa,* the reputable opinions of "the many and the wise." But it also has the problem that key ethical conclusions are supported by appeal to cultural authority.

Grotius's method of a priori argument is Socratic: he asks each reader to consider the fundamental concepts of his or her person and their relations, and to judge whether a proposed doctrine does violence to those concepts, or, by contrast, inheres in them. This sort of free-standing moral argument (whether we should really call it a priori or not) is what he very much prefers. One grave defect of the argument from "common sense" is that, as Grotius is well aware, the common sense of mankind often yields wrong conclusions, and embodies a less rigorous moral concern than the conscience of the individual, after reflection on Grotius's arguments, is expected to yield. For Grotius recognizes a very sharp distinction between the traditional *ius gentium,* the body of judgments that embody the collective wisdom of the international community over time, and the *ius naturale,* the moral law that *should* actually govern the conduct of individuals and states in their dealings with one another. In book II of *BP,* Grotius lays out in some detail the conduct in war that is and is not permitted by the traditional *ius gentium.* This standard is very permissive from the moral viewpoint:[18] it holds, for example, that one may kill noncombatants, including women and children, with impunity—although it draws the line at rape. One may pillage anything, including sacred objects. And so on. Then, in a sharp and jolting transition (ch. 10), Grotius announces that he is now going to take back a lot of what he has just said: he will retrace his steps and deprive those who wage war of privileges he seemed to grant them, but did not. He then goes on to lay out the more stringent moral standards implied by *ius naturale:* many things that may be done with impunity under current standards are morally unjustifiable. He thus reveals to the reader the fact that *ius naturale* cannot be adequately arrived at by the method of gathering up the common opinions of mankind.

Grotius clearly expects his argument to be cogent to a reader who has grown up with ordinary human understanding. In that sense, even in the *ius naturale* portion of his argument he might be said to rely on something like *endoxa* in order to persuade. But it is very important to see that sheer traditionality or widespread acceptance, though it seems weighty from the point of view of his a posteriori method, ultimately has no moral weight for him. What does is each reader's autonomous Socratic confrontation with the argument. And it is this sort of reflective confrontation that he constructs, in his crucial argument against the amoralist opponent.

Grotius points out, first of all, that human beings are not just beasts, who can and do amorally tear one another limb from limb. We are creatures of a distinctive sort, capable of governing our relations with one another by moral norms. Grotius focuses not so much on reason per se, as on the capacity for moral reasoning and for understanding and living by norms of justice. Citing the Stoics, he links this ability closely to the idea of "sociability": we are creatures who cannot flourish without interactions with other human beings—and not just any sort of interactions, but a shared life that is peaceful and reciprocal, and organized by intelligence (Proleg. to *BP* 6). The argument is not simply that we have such desires implanted in our nature. It is, apparently, the idea that these needs and desires have a salience for us when we think about who we are, and about what makes our form of life a distinctive one. We cannot ignore these aspects of our flourishing without doing violence to ourselves. Grotius, like the Stoics, thinks of *ius naturale* as taking its start from some very basic moral evaluations, and thus, as a nonderivative, or freestanding, moral conception.[19] Think of a life without moral sociability, the argument goes, and you will find that it is not only a life in which the distinctive activities of a human being are absent, but also, therefore, a life that you could not yourself endorse without doing violence to yourself.

From this very basic starting point, Grotius now proceeds to the idea of law. Let us imagine a sociable being, endowed with moral capacities, intending to live in peace with other such beings. Immediately we understand that such a being needs laws in order to construct such peaceful relations. For only rules or laws (Grotius's concept of *ius* is very broad, and at this point in the argument encompasses both positive law and binding moral norms) make it possible for beings to be sociable without all the time suffering violence or unjust deprivation at one another's hands. If we imagine a condition without laws or norms, we imagine the ubiquitous frustration of the human being's desire for mutual relations that are both moral and social. Such laws, Grotius argues, must do several basic things. They must instruct all to abstain from aggression and theft; they must arrange for restitution of what has been taken by aggression or theft, and for the punishment of the guilty parties; and they must point the way to a fair distribution of property (Proleg. to *BP* 8–10). Importantly, the law of nature enjoins that agreements are to be honored *(pacta sunt servanda):* for without such a principle, the whole edifice of law would necessarily collapse (15).

Grotius's arguments thus have a form similar to those made by Cicero and the Stoics before him and Kant after him. They ask us to see that we cherish a very basic conception of our humanity as both moral and social. They then invite us to consider a world in which some moral institution (promising the rule of law) did not exist. We see, when we consider this world, that it is no better than a bestial world, a world in which what is characteristic of our humanity will meet with continual frustration. For Grotius as for others in the tradition, this thought is supposed to give each person weighty moral reasons to support these institutions, and to abide by their demands.[20] And clearly this is a way of thinking about what it is to respect our humanity, not to use it as a mere tool of our own advantage.

Grotius now turns from the intra-state application of these ideas to the relations among states. He emphasizes that most people agree that law exists outside the borders of the state: thus we have a conventional understanding about the existence of a *ius gentium,* and of what that law involves. Nonetheless, some thinkers hold that justice and law have no proper application in this domain, which is simply a domain of force and violence. Grotius now denies this: just as the citizen who violates his country's law "breaks down that by which the advantages of himself and his posterity are for all future time assured," so the state that transgresses the law of nature and of nations cuts away also the bulwarks safeguarding its own future peace. There are thus reasons of efficiency for recognizing and obeying international law; but thinking of how the fulfillment of our sociable nature depends on the existence of stable peaceful relations between peoples gives us a more direct moral reason (18–19). If no association of human beings can be maintained without law, surely that is also true of "that association which binds together the human kind, or binds many nations *(populos complures)* together"—and this fact gives each of us reason to respect and follow the law in question (23). Again, not to do so is a way of doing violence to our own humanity.

IV. The Law of War: *Ius Gentium* and *Ius Naturale*

Grotius begins, then, with a very general conception of personhood that he believes to have deep roots in any interlocutor's way of thinking. He asks at each stage, Socratically, what institutions and practices do violence to that conception; the interlocutor is then expected to reject them, on pain of doing violence to him or herself. First, he gains acceptance for the general idea of life under law; next, for some intermediate principles, such as non-aggression, non-theft, and the sanctity of treaties and other agreements. Then he argues that these same principles must be recognized in the world outside the state. This world, he now adds, has one further intermediate principle: national sovereignty. For national sovereignty (as he argues most fully in *De Iure Praedae* ch. 2) is essential to constituting and fortifying the larger society of the human kind. As we have seen, he believes that national sovereignty is an essential expression of human autonomy, that is, in the most literal sense, the ability to give oneself laws of one's own choosing; putting this, now, into the context of his Socratic argument, we may say that the interlocutor cannot accept a world without sovereign nations, without doing violence to his own deep conception of the human being as moral and sociable.

From these principles, the highly abstract and the intermediate, Grotius proceeds to derive a normative account of conduct in war. As we have seen, the actual *ius gentium* is very permissive. But, says Grotius, the word "lawful" has two senses: it may just mean "done with impunity"; or it may mean "in accordance with moral law" (*BP* III.10.1). There is a large difference between the lawful in the first sense and the lawful in the second. Quoting Seneca, he insists that often, "What law permits, the sense of shame forbids to do," explaining that by "sense of shame" he means "not so much a regard for men and reputation as a regard for what is just and good, or at any rate for that which is more just and better" (III.10.1.2). Justice, he insists, again following Seneca, extends well beyond the current reach of positive law, and imposes more stringent requirements. For we must always recall that "national customs are not to be taken for the law of nature" (II.20.41)—both because national laws often embody particularistic religious requirements that do not apply to all, and because they may simply embody unconvincing or bad moral reasoning, including reasoning designed to feed the greed of that nation and its members (II.20.41). Not surprisingly, traditional *ius gentium* contains much that derives from national custom and that is therefore defective in one or more of these ways.

We can get a good start toward understanding these stricter requirements by thinking of what treatment is morally permissible toward a human being: as Seneca says (quoting *De Clementia* I.18), "there is something which the common law of living things forbids to be permissible against a human being." Thus, whereas the *ius gentium* permits combatants to do whatever is necessary to attain their ends (*BP* III.1.2),[21] *ius naturale* will consider the respectful treatment that is suited to a human being's moral and social nature, reminding us of our most indefeasible end, which is to live with one another in a way that befits that nature. This principle suggests the intermediate principle that even in a just war, care should be taken to moderate the killing, and to promote in this way the possibility of a peaceful reintegration after war (III.11). In war, peace and its preservation should always be kept in view, for the sake of "that greater society of states" *(maior illa gentium societas).* Throughout the ensuing chapters, references to Cicero and Seneca are especially frequent.

Grotius now goes against the *ius gentium,* in a way that has become formative for modern international law. Everything, he argues, must be done to prevent the deaths of innocent people. Children should always be spared, as should women, elderly men, prisoners, members of religious orders, farmers, merchants, and writers.[22] Those who surrender may never be killed. Even among combatants, it is wrong to kill any who fight under compulsion, such as slaves and prisoners. (This principle does not extend to conscripts, presumably because they are not captives and can leave the nation if they don't want to serve, and because nations have rights of self-defense.) Prisoners of war must be given decent treatment: no bodily mistreatment, no sexual abuse, decent nutrition and health care, tasks that are not so heavy as to cause a danger to health: in short a kind of "perpetual maintenance" (III.14).

Like Cicero, Grotius is particularly concerned with the conduct of victors. Here again, his recommendations are guided by the general thought that the goal should always be the preservation of peace for "that greater society of states" *(maior illa gentium societas,* III.25). While war is still continuing, he urges the party that has the upper hand to avoid all devastation of the enemy's land (III.12), and to avoid any assault on sacred objects and places (III.12.7). Such moderation is morally required, but it is also advantageous, because it allows the enemy to envisage a decent life afterward, and thus to avoid despair, which breeds extreme measures (III.12.8). For such reasons as well, innocent civilians are not to be deprived of property more than is absolutely necessary to pursue victory (III.13.4).

At the conclusion of war, Grotius urges victors not to press their advantage too far, but to accept peace on reasonable terms, or even terms that involve some losses (III.25). All killing must stop. Even though it is possible for the victor to assert political sovereignty over the vanquished, both morality and self-interest dictate that this should rarely be done: sovereignty is a profound expression of a people's autonomy and self-respect, and thus both respect for humanity and concern for future peace suggest that they should not be robbed of it (III.15). (Grotius predates the bulk of European colonizing, but his principles entail that virtually all of it is illegitimate.[23]) Peace is best arranged "while each has confidence in himself" (III.25.6). Holding foreign territories as colonies is not only morally problematic, but also a dangerous course, prompting strife in the future (III.15). Even when it is judged that one's own future safety requires that sovereignty be assumed over a conquered people, it is right to leave a portion of the sovereign power to the people themselves and their own rulers. In short, as much sovereignty and liberty should be left as is compatible with defending one's own nation from illegitimate aggression. It is particularly important to protect the religious liberty of the conquered people (III.15.11), although the conqueror is entitled to take steps to prevent the oppression of his own religion by that people. In general, Grotius concludes, clemency and moderation are ways of treating a people respectfully and thus building a good future. He quotes from Livy: "If you should have given to them a good peace, then you may expect it to be reliable and perpetual; if a bad one, brief." And from Cicero: "Let this be a new method of conquering, to fortify ourselves with mercy and generosity."[24]

Once made, peace must be kept with the utmost scrupulousness: here the key principle *pacta sunt servanda* returns again (III.25.7): "[P]eace, whatever the terms on which it is made, ought to be preserved absolutely, on account of the sacredness of good faith, which I have mentioned." Care should be taken not only to avoid all deceit but even to avoid causes of anger; this scrupulousness is even more important in a peace after hostilities than in an alliance.

Grotius's discussion of *ius naturale* is famously ambiguous. On the one hand, he makes a strong case that the moral law requires conduct that is not required by traditional international law or *ius gentium;* to that extent he would appear to make a case for the alteration of *ius gentium.* On the other hand, he plainly sees a role for international law as distinct from natural law: for he insists that the requirements of natural law do not change, while there is room for a realm of international law that is more time-bound, containing provisions that may reasonably be altered as conditions of life change (II.8). So how does he see his argument in book III, in its relation to traditional *ius gentium?*

If *ius gentium* is more changeable and in that sense narrower than *ius naturale,* it still ought to be consistent with it. Clearly, Grotius in book III is not merely describing a realm of moral supererogation that is not binding on actors, who are still permitted to violate moral law in ways that are currently allowed by *ius gentium.* He is talking about binding moral requirements, although he is aware that under current international law these will not be enforced. Is he suggesting that *ius gentium* ought to change so that these requirements will be enforced?

In some cases, it seems likely that this is his intention, veiled behind the tentativeness imposed by his own vulnerable situation. Thus, the requirements concerning the treatment of prisoners and noncombatants are best read as proposals for revisions in international law, and indeed most of them have been so incorporated. There are more general moral prescriptions that cannot be read in this way, however: the advice to pursue lasting peace first and foremost, and the requirement to be merciful. These cannot be translated into positive law, and remain as part of an ethical background that should inform the spirit of international law, which will likely continue to permit things that are not morally normative. There will also very likely remain cases in which international law forbids what the moral law permits: thus, the requirement not to use poison against an enemy might have a good prudential rationale in a particular era, while from the point of view of permanent moral interests a killing by poison does not look very different from any other type of killing.

Thus the world that Grotius outlines is not simple. Although he foresees an evolution in international law, he also projects a world that will continue to contain binding moral norms that are not legally enforceable—or are enforceable only when individual nations turn them into law. The relation between law and norm is intended to be contestable and complex, and Grotius gives us no easy recipe for the future of that relationship.

V. The Individual as Subject: Humanitarian Intervention

Grotius's theory ascribes considerable importance to national sovereignty, not simply as a practical force with which we must reckon.

Sovereignty also has moral importance, as an expression of human autonomy. In Grotius's view, that importance derives ultimately from the idea of the autonomy of the individual human being. For him as for the cosmopolitan tradition before him, groups are important expressions of human sociality and choice, but they are not in and of themselves loci of choice and do not as such have rights. Sovereignty is important because each person's choice of a way of life is important; for Grotius in his time, it is above all a protector of religious liberty. (It protects religious liberty, however, for the majority, not for internal minorities.)

Sovereign nations do not always protect the rights of individuals. Often they persecute people on grounds of religion, and deny them various other important prerogatives, which the law of nature would guarantee to them. (And Grotius, perhaps on account of his own delicate political position, does not say, with Roger Williams and John Locke, that natural law requires internal protection of liberty of conscience.) So a dilemma is created for international society and the nations that are its members: how far is it right to intervene in the affairs of a sovereign nation that is violating the rights of its members? Grotius's discussion of humanitarian intervention, one of the most influential in the history of the topic, and one of the most influential aspects of his book for posterity, grows out of a recognition of this dilemma.

We can appreciate Grotius's position more justly if we imagine two alternatives to it. One alternative, often associated with Kant, and perhaps rightly found in his earlier writings, though not in *Perpetual Peace*, would be to argue that individuals and their rights are the only things of real importance. Let us call this the Moral Rights position.[25] For holders of this view, national sovereignty is simply a convenient way of organizing the protection of individual rights, and the implementation of measures for upholding individual dignity. It should have no weight when nations or their leaders are violating the rights of individuals. This view would not necessarily license forcible intervention into the affairs of another state any time there are rights violations, for prudential considerations suggest that this would typically be bad for individuals in the long run. But there is no *moral* barrier to such intervention, at any rate. Such a view leads naturally in the direction of a human-rights-based world government, and a weakening of national sovereignty. It sees nations as at best conveniences; at worst, dangerous obstacles.

Another alternative to the Grotian position would be one according to which the nation-state is the only legitimate rights-protecting entity: rights are artifacts of national sovereignty, and do not reach out beyond the nation. Let us call this the State-Based-Rights view. According to this view, if an individual's rights are violated, then it is nobody's legitimate business but that of the nation in which she lives. People have rights as citizens of states, and these rights do not follow them, so to speak, into the realm of inter-state relations, which is typically imagined, by holders of this view, as a realm without rights or moral law, dominated by considerations of national security and interest. This view would not license any form of humanitarian intervention.[26]

Grotius's response to the State-Based-Rights view has two stages. First, he will argue, as he does throughout his work, that the realm of international relations is not a realm free of moral norms and binding moral requirements. But one might hold that there are binding moral requirements in the international realm (requirements about the conduct of war, for example), without holding that this realm has any legitimate business dealing with violations of individual rights within a state. One could hold, that is, that the moral norms that govern the international domain are limited to norms pertaining to the relations of one state with other states (in war especially, but also in commerce and other peaceful dealings). Most individual rights might still be envisaged as artifacts of the state, and their protection as the business of that state alone. So Grotius must then argue, further, that the same reasons that should lead us to conclude that the international realm is not in general amoral should also lead us to conclude that individual rights, as well as inter-state relations, exist outside the state and are the legitimate business of the international sphere.

Grotius makes no such explicit argument. And yet, the ideas of natural law and human sociability that are basic to his account of the law of war also clearly entail an international realm governed by a rich picture of morality whose ultimate focus is the individual person. Grotius would clearly think it absurd to accept the idea of natural law for inter-state relations and yet to deny that natural law protects the rights of individuals. The basic idea of the entire tradition within which he argues is that of the dignity of the human person, as a being both rational and social. Restrictions on inter-state conduct are ultimately justified by reference to that norm, and the associated strictures against aggression and fraud. What the law of war does, most ultimately and basically, is to protect human beings from violation. How could one coherently uphold those moral constraints on state action and yet hold that natural law does not condemn violations of individual dignity that are carried out by that person's own state? Grotius holds that human rights are prepolitical, in the sense that they are grounded in facts about the human being that preexist the state, and that do not cease to exert their claim when the state does not recognize them. So, just as natural law goes beyond the traditional *ius gentium,* so too it goes beyond the norms and actions of individual states, should those insufficiently recognize or protect human dignity. (Thus Grotius objects to the position of "Victoria, Vazques, Azor, Molina, and others" who hold that the power of punishing derives from civil jurisdiction alone, insisting that it derives from the law of nature [*BP* II.20.40.4].)

Yet Grotius clearly does not agree with the Moral Rights position. For he gives an analysis of national sovereignty according to which sovereignty itself has moral significance, as an expression of human autonomy. Human dignity and autonomy require the opportunity to live under a government that is in some way chosen by, and accountable to, the people. We may certainly feel that Grotius had too rudimentary a conception of accountability (in that he did not require anything like democratic participation, and thought that people were entitled to enslave themselves to an absolute monarch if they wanted to), and yet recognize that both consent and accountability are important features of his political conception of sovereignty and its moral weight. His picture is not conceptually incompatible with the idea that at some point the people of the world might put themselves under a world state. But his reflections on religious war suggest strong reasons why we might not move in that direction: for the foreseeable future, people will want to protect their own religious freedom by designing a state that does protect it, and this is probably most likely to be realized if there is a plurality of states. As I have mentioned, Grotius favors internal religious toleration as well as religious diversity across states; but he plainly thinks that choice of a way of life will lead to some variety, and that variety has moral significance. Its protection is a part of what it is to protect the moral rights of individuals.

Grotius's position, unlike its rivals, creates, then, a dilemma. That complexity is its strength. On the one hand, to intervene in the internal affairs of a nation is bad, a violation of the rights of human beings to choose a way of life. Moreover, in practical terms, such intervention, as Grotius repeatedly observes, is more than likely to be motivated by the desire to gain control over that territory and people. Thus to countenance it risks countenancing abuses, and, ultimately, the imposition of colonial power on a formerly self-governing people. He cites Plutarch: "To wish to impose civilization upon uncivilized peoples is a pretext which may serve to conceal greed for what is another's" (II.20.41). On the other hand, sovereignty plainly ought not to be understood as a license for some people within a nation to tyrannize over others, and thus the very rationale that supports sovereignty also supports strong protection for individual rights.

The tension in the Grotian position is thus not tragic, as it would be if he held that groups have rights in and of themselves, and those rights were in some ways on a collision course with individual rights. Because the moral significance of the nation derives from the moral significance of the individual, it is of a piece with, and coheres well in principle with, the protection of a wide range of rights for individuals. We can easily imagine a regime that is both sovereign and rights-respecting. But in the world of imperfect states that we know, it poses a practical dilemma of considerable moral delicacy. To intervene on behalf of persecuted or violated individuals seems morally required; but it also violates individuals in another way, by violating sovereignty. This is the problem Grotius now addresses in his famous and influential brief chapter on humanitarian intervention (II.20.40).

One defect of Grotius's discussion that we should note at the outset is its failure to give an adequate account of state legitimacy. His view that people may consent to enslave themselves gives him a more difficult time with the issue of intervention than he otherwise might have, because he grants legitimacy to many types of tyrannies that one might plausibly judge illegitimate.[27] Where we are dealing with such a tyranny, intervention seems morally less troublesome than when we are dealing with a regime that meets certain decent minimum standards of participation and accountability.

Another issue that he does not sufficiently consider is that of political inclusiveness. If the moral importance of sovereignty derives from human choice and autonomy, then we need to ask who gets to choose. If women, ethnic and racial minorities, and perhaps others are simply excluded from the act of choice altogether, then the appeal to violated sovereignty seems weak against an intervention that protects their human rights. Grotius devotes no consideration at all to the issue of women's non-representation, and seems to have little concern for inclusiveness in general.

Within these limitations, however, his discussion is of considerable interest. He argues that intervention is justified when a nation "excessively violates the law of nature or of nations in regard to any persons whatsoever." This right belongs to the sovereign, not to private citizens, who might otherwise excessively take the law into their own hands. (Grotius is in general opposed to all forms of private warfare.) Intervention is permissible, not (apparently) morally required in such cases, but it is praiseworthy: Grotius cites the examples of Hercules and Theseus, who assumed risks to help people in other parts of the world. (Diodorus says of Hercules, "By slaying lawless men and arrogant despots, he made the cities happy . . . He traversed the world chastising the unjust.")

Grotius cautions that national custom is not to be understood as equivalent to natural law, though people often confuse the two: thus the fact that another nation does not observe one's own national customs does not license intervention (II.20.41); nor does the fact that they do not observe one's own religion and its divine laws (II.20.42). Moreover, even when we deal with natural law, we should distinguish between general principles that are pretty obvious and incontrovertible, and particular applications, which are likely to be more controversial (II.20.43). Even if we are convinced of our own position with regard to one of these concrete matters, we can see how another nation might sincerely have reasoned differently, and we should view that case as one where ignorance of the law excuses the violator (II.20.43). Moreover, we must again remind ourselves that wars ostensibly undertaken on moral grounds may always be suspected of being really motivated by considerations of power or profit, and thus we should not undertake them "unless the crimes are very atrocious and very evident."

What are the crimes that may license humanitarian intervention? Grotius at this point has recourse to a list of remote classical examples, beginning with Alexander's punishment of the Sogdianians for impiety against their parents;[28] Grotius is euphemistic here, since the text of Plutarch to which he refers specifies that they systematically killed their parents in order not to have to take care of them in their old age. Next, he refers to the practice of cannibalism, opposed by Hercules, and to the practice of piracy. All these are described as the deeds of "barbarians, wild beasts rather than men." So this gives us a general sense of the terrain of the exception. A learned footnote expands further, mentioning Justinian's intervention with the practice of castration of male children, and the way in which "The Incas, kings of Peru, forcibly compelled the neighbouring peoples, who did not listen to a warning, to abstain from incest, from the intercourse of males with males, from the eating of human flesh, and from other crimes of that kind."

If we are inclined on first reading to think that Grotius offers too narrow an account of humanitarian intervention, especially when he omits religious persecution and other common violations of basic human rights, these fascinating examples may make us share his caution, or even think his principle too broad. For, at this distance of three and a half centuries, we see some of his examples rather as he sees them, as gross crimes against humanity, and some entirely differently, as the effect of local custom rather than as deeply rooted in core principles of morality. Thus, cannibalism, systematic murder of the elderly, and piracy (a type of terrorism) still seem very bad, and might possibly be occasions for humanitarian intervention. Incest seems highly plural and variable, and we tend to think that it is within the prerogatives of communities to define what is lawful and lawless in that sphere. (The sexual abuse of children, not mentioned by Grotius, seems the thing that ought to arouse really serious international ire, because it is a type of nonconsensual violence.) As for intercourse of male with male, there are, of course, people who do believe that this is a violation of the law of nature, though most people today do not. Nonetheless, even those people who basically agree with Grotius do not think widespread toleration of same-sex relations in a nation is an occasion for military intervention! Not surprisingly, sympathetic modern discussions of Grotius's chapter do not mention this example.

If Grotius's list is overinclusive in these obvious ways, it also seems oddly underinclusive. Even though the examples are only examples, not an exhaustive account, they oddly fail to include the most obvious cases, perhaps because Grotius is determined to cling to classical mythology in order to avoid contemporary controversy. Genocide is nowhere mentioned; the widespread rape of women, mentioned as an occasion for humanitarian intervention by Alberico Gentili in his parallel discussion, is not mentioned. And of course slavery is not mentioned because Grotius thinks that slavery does not violate the law of nature.

Religious persecution is the only one of the major concerns of today's international community that Grotius does mention as an occasion for intervention, somewhat later in the same chapter (II.20.49), but even there he permits nations to oppress internal religious minorities.[29] On the whole, then, the examples do not greatly illuminate the general thesis; indeed, by their very oddness they cast doubt on its legitimacy, by showing how very hard it is, even when one is trying one's best, to distinguish permanent moral principles from local customs.

Nonetheless, by now international reflection on these issues has arrived at a short list that commands a wide and long-lasting consensus. The international consensus focuses on the core principles of the moral law, violence and aggression: thus consensual acts such as sexual "offenses" are nowhere considered. Genocide, slavery, and the rape of women are at the core of the consensus, where the use of military force is concerned—though international human rights norms include a far longer list of basic entitlements as a persuasive matter. It would appear that Grotius's general principles survive the skepticism induced by his odd list.

Grotius's conclusion, then, is that moral respect for national sovereignty, combined with knowledge of both the greediness and the fallibility of human judgment, should make us very reluctant to intervene forcibly in the affairs of another nation. Yet in some grave and extreme instances it is both permissible and praiseworthy to come to the defense of the oppressed. The core of such cases is given by the basic principles of the moral law: the worst cases will be those that violate human dignity in some extreme and excessive way, typically through the use of violence and coercion. We may add that the reasons against intervention are weakened to the extent that the oppressed lack political rights, and to the extent that the regime generally lacks accountability.

Finally, we may add that where there is no legitimate regime in place (as in some instances of civil chaos), the restrictions would also be to that extent weakened. Despite the obvious defects of Grotius's discussion, its complexity and subtlety give it continued value, as a guide to this profoundly complicated issue.

VI. Duties of Material Aid?

From its inception, the cosmopolitan tradition has had difficulty with duties of material aid. Grotius's defense of national sovereignty might seem to compound these difficulties, suggesting that the nation is the person's proper home, and that any meaningful material redistribution ought to be carried out there. But in fact Grotius's argument provides at least a starting point for reflection about material aid and redistribution in a world containing both nation-states and individuals with moral rights. He supplies the tradition with two key notions: common goods, and claims of need.

Grotius's early writings on the seas already announce the principle that certain "common goods" of human life are the common property of all peoples and cannot be possessed by one nation as property.[30] Sea and air are the most obvious such goods, and Grotius argues vigorously for the common right of all the world's peoples to use the seas. His position on disputed matters (how to view coastal waters, channels, and so forth) shifts over time, and is shaped by the political position he played in Dutch trade negotiations. But it remains a strong defense of free access: in general neither sea nor air can be converted into private property (II.2.3). Thus even in *BP*, where he is far more guarded about coastal waters and channels, he nonetheless defends a right of passage over rivers and even lands by the route that is nearest and most convenient, and argues that the voyagers and the merchandise they transport cannot justly be taxed unless the nation through which they pass incurs expense in protecting them (II.2.11).

But in *BP* Grotius advances a much broader principle of access to material goods, based on the idea of basic needs. In time of necessity, he argues, "natural equity" requires that you first try to meet your need from your own property. But if that proves impossible, you are permitted to use the property of others (II.2.6). Thus, it is forbidden to destroy surplus food, and anyone who needs it may use it; water may similarly be used in time of need. This same right seems to him to yield a right to possess and cultivate unoccupied land (II.2.4). Even within a territory, foreigners are entitled to cultivate and take possession of uncultivated land (II.2.17). Moreover, the right to the necessities of life includes, he argues, a right to "acts required for human life," including the provision of "food, clothing, and medicines" (II.2.18). Grotius argues that there are certain "acts indispensable for the obtaining of the things without which life cannot be comfortably lived." He argues that here we do not need to show the same degree of necessity that we need to show in order to justify taking someone else's property, for here we are dealing not with a taking, but with a matter of right: even if the owner doesn't consent, that does not undermine the claim of the needy, for, given that it belongs to the needy by right, it does not belong to the owner in any case. To hinder people from getting such necessities of life is a most direct violation of the moral law. Implicit in this right is another: to buy the necessities of life at a fair price. "[T]hus in times of extreme scarcity the sale of grain is forbidden" (II.2.19).

The details of what Grotius would permit remain in some respects obscure. For example, he says that people should not be forced to sell their own belongings to others (II.2.20). So the reach of his humanitarian principle is somewhat unclear, although it would appear that in the case of extreme need his account of ownership holds that the poor person actually owns the property by right, and the holder does not. Nor is it at all clear what mechanisms of redistribution he envisages, either within nations or between nations. In any case, we can see that his principle mandates as morally required a good deal of redistribution both within nations and from richer to poorer nations. Particularly interesting is the analysis of ownership, which does not concede that current holdings settle the question, in circumstances of extreme need. Indeed, ownership is relative, not only to the welfare situation of my own fellow citizens, but also to the welfare of all world citizens. What person P owns in country A depends on facts about countries B and C: if there are hungry and suffering people there, then A does not own a certain luxury amount of goods that A would otherwise own.

What Grotius appears to be after is a set of minimal welfare rights, and in a worldwide framework: all world citizens are entitled to what they need in order to live, including food, shelter, and health care; and those things are theirs by right, even if they must come from another country. Even if there is no mechanism suggested to make these rights effective, they are said to be morally justified. Thus nations that do not meet the claims of need of people in poorer nations are violating the moral law.

Grotius is also very concerned with the situation of people who are forced by need or political circumstances to leave their own country (as he himself was). Migrants, he argues, have a right of temporary sojourn in another land (II.2.15)—which includes a right to build a temporary dwelling on land owned by that other nation and its people. If they have been driven from their homeland they have a right of permanent asylum, provided they are willing to submit themselves to the legitimate government of that nation (II.2.16). Moreover, even in a time of extreme need it is not permitted to expel foreigners who have once been admitted to a country: a common misfortune must be endured in common (II.2.19). Moreover, the right to "such acts as human life requires" includes a right to seek marriages in foreign countries, because it is repugnant to humanity to require people to live a celibate life (II.2.21). (Thus, to use a modern example, guest workers could not be forbidden to marry and establish a family in the nation into which they have migrated.) And within a nation that has admitted people from other countries, one foreign group cannot be singled out for special discrimination. Thus, if foreigners of any type are given certain rights, all law-abiding foreigners must be given those same rights (II.2.22).

Thus, despite the salience of national boundaries in Grotius's thinking, his picture of the world is highly porous, protecting a lot of the movement of peoples from nation to nation (as religious persecution frequently required), and protecting certain minimum welfare rights for all world citizens, even when the wherewithal to meet those needs must come from another nation's store. Even if all of this is highly abstract and not well connected, in some cases, to real political principles, we can see that it represents a radical departure from the Ciceronian picture. People are not required to give up bare necessities of life, but they are required to give up (or rather, told that they in fact do not own) whatever is over and above that, if other people are below the threshold of basic need. The picture of an interdependent and interacting world that the Ciceronian doctrine already realizes for issues of aggression is now realized in the area of material need as well, in a way that, if tantalizing, seems highly promising for contemporary thought about what a decent international society would require.

Sadly, Grotius never connects his doctrines concerning war and humanitarian intervention to his doctrine of material aid and ownership. Suppose there is widespread misery and acute poverty in country C, resulting from gross inequalities in material entitlements or a greedy tyranny. Is the failure to set this right a crime that excessively violates the law of nature, so that humanitarian intervention would be justified? It might appear so, for according to Grotius's analysis the rich do not actually own the over-threshold goods that they are holding onto, so his understanding of the situation is that the poor are dying because the rich are holding onto goods that rightfully belong to the poor. Perhaps these violations of the law of nature are not "excessive," but they do look like the sort of thing that undermines the very nature of human dignity and human fellowship.

Again, suppose that there is widespread misery and poverty throughout country C, because wealthy nations A and B are holding on to their surplus. They are violating the law of nature, and, according to Grotius, a portion of their holdings actually rightfully belongs to the suffering citizens in country C. Does that mean that an invasion of A and B by C would be a just war, provoked by wrongful aggression of A and B against C? If we combine Cicero's account of just war (in which property crime is sufficient aggression to justify a violent response) with Grotius's very un-Ciceronian doctrine of ownership, it would appear that this war is indeed a just war. Obviously enough, in cases of this sort C will rarely be in a position to invade A and B, because the very factors that make it poor also, very likely, make it militarily weak. But it is interesting to reflect about the fact that aggression by C may be *morally* justified, whether politically feasible or not.

Clearly, this is a point at which national sovereignty should affect the analysis. It seems perfectly justified for a sovereign nation to redistribute wealth through a system of coercive taxation. For another nation to use coercive strategies to effect a needed redistribution, even where need strongly recommends it, would mean global chaos and disorder. Moreover, there seems to be a moral wrong involved, of the sort that is involved in humanitarian intervention in all but the most egregious cases. As in that case, so here, two moral claims appear to conflict. Perhaps it is legitimate for the community of nations to exert pressure on the recalcitrant rich nation, through diplomatic pressures of various types. But to say that war is justified to effect economic redistribution seems extremely implausible, and I do not think the implausibility derives entirely from the sway of current holdings over our imaginations. Nor does it appear to derive only from prudential considerations of stability and security. The right to allocate resources seems to lie at the core of the very idea of national sovereignty, and if that idea has moral weight, it ought to limit coercive redistributions of wealth from one nation to another, absent, at least, any consent-based system at the supranational level. Grotius makes the tension clear, but in the end his analysis seems to agree with mine: we should, albeit uneasily, respect national sovereignty, but try to work through persuasion toward a consensus supporting need-based redistribution.

Even when we take its clear limits into account, however, Grotius's new moral analysis has significant implications for international debate and policy.[31] It is unfortunate that Grotius never pursues the radical implications of his ideas. But it is always open to us to do so, and the failure of international law to take up this strand in Grotius's thinking, while it has been so heavily influenced by Grotius in other respects, shows an unfortunate quietism in the face of current holdings that Grotius himself does not countenance. Scholars have often criticized *BP* as a grab-bag for its inclusion of such allegedly irrelevant topics as property rights. Grotius is ahead of them, for he sees that lasting peace in the world requires a radical rethinking of just that issue.

VII. The Idea of International Society

In the twentieth century, wrote international law scholar Hedley Bull near its close, we saw a retreat from the confident assertion that "the members of international society were states and nations, towards the ambiguity and imprecision on this point that characterised the age of Grotius."[32] We are now in a position to assess Grotius's accomplishment, and the picture of international society with which it leaves us. According to Grotius, then, the primary subject of morality, and of the moral part of political thinking, is the individual human being, seen as having dignity. That dignity gives the person a claim both to freedom from aggression and to the basic necessities of life. The person is also, however, social: the dignity of the person is to be understood as the dignity of a being who lives in complex forms of cooperation with others. So part of protecting human dignity is protecting the choices people make to band together and organize their lives in political communities.

This leads to a picture in which sovereign nations have a large place, but in which they share their power with international law, and with the more complex and indeterminate linking of all human beings in what is called "international society," the society of all human beings living under moral law. Because the source of sovereignty is the dignity of the individual, that dignity is never completely ceded to sovereign nations, who must consequently share their powers, in complicated ways and in a complicated system of claims and restrictions, with the urgent claims of individuals both inside and outside of their borders. These claims include traditional human rights claims involving aggression and violence; they also include claims to things and acts that are necessary for life. Moreover, other associations, less amply sketched by Grotius, but occasionally mentioned (conferences, trade groups) will also play a role, and frequently their operations will cross national boundary lines.

Surrounding and permeating this entire system is the moral law. But the moral law does not exert its authority directly, as in the Moral Rights position. It too has to cede some of its powers—to sovereign nations, which derive their powers from it, but also limit it in their turn. The moral law informs international law, but also goes beyond it—not only because actual states are unlikely to accept all of its stringent demands, but also because some of these demands are not the sort of thing that rightly ought to be made into positive law. The line between the coercively enforceable and the morally urgent but unenforceable is indefinite, both in Grotius's time and in ours, and it is continually shifting, as international society finds ways to make moral norms into positive law. The moral law informs the institutions of international civil society as well, since they may play an important role both in shaping international law itself and in bringing about a greater awareness of moral requirements that do not have the force of law. Finally, the moral law both limits and protects individuals, defining their entitlements and their duties.

The Grotian conception of international society is clearly superior, both descriptively and normatively, to the conception that Bull rightly describes as dominant for so long in the study of international relations: the conception of a world consisting of atomic nation-states whose relations among themselves are those of self-interest and security only. At this point in history, we can see that international relations is suffused with moral judgments of many kinds, and that nations do not limit their dealings with one another to national security interests. Nor was that ever a normatively satisfactory position, since, as Grotius plausibly argues, the very aspects of human life that give national sovereignty its deep importance also limit it, in favor of a broader multilayered consideration of international law, international morality, and individual human rights.

What are the viable alternatives to the complex Grotian picture of the world?[33] One is the idea of a world government. As Bull notes, such a government might emerge from struggle between powers, but then it would very likely be a tyranny of an obviously objectionable sort. Again, it might emerge by way of a social contract of sorts between member states, in light of ecological or other disasters: Kant and others conceive of such an eventuality. Finally, it might emerge gradually, through a broadening of the powers of a federation such as the United Nations.

In the latter two cases, there is no immediate reason to think that world government need be tyranny: its internal structure might be highly protective of human rights. But there is clearly danger in its very ubiquity and dominance: for what can check it if it begins to go awry? Even apart from this danger, there is moral difficulty in the idea. First of all, could any government this inclusive possibly be sufficiently accountable to the governed, and expressive of their wishes? It's hard enough preserving accountability in the nation-state. The global extension of power creates, obviously, huge difficulties for accountability, including the very grave question of the language(s) of the political process and, more generally, the protection of access to it. Certainly the mention of the United Nations ought to give us pause, for that institution is woefully deficient in accountability to the nations it allegedly represents. And the current crisis of the European Union indicates that people will not be satisfied by a central government perceived as distant and elite.

The mention of language raises an even deeper moral issue: for the very effacing of plurality in favor of singleness seems to violate an aspect of human sociability that Grotius rightly prizes. Even if we imagine that the world government is highly protective of the rights and liberties of religious, linguistic, and ethnic minorities, still, the very fact of its uniform structure excludes alternative structures, languages, and constitutional choices that may all be morally decent. There is not one unique right way to construct a state; instead, the moral law suggests a zone of moral permissibility, with many possible realizations. Removing this variety is itself a harm to human beings.[34]

A second alternative picture of global society is Kant's, further developed in the twentieth century by John Rawls.[35] Sovereign nations are the members of the world order, and they connect only in a compact regarding their (peaceful) international relations. This picture fails to grant that issues such as migration, asylum, the protection of the environment, and material aid rightly ground duties linking one nation to another. I have tried to show that Grotius has good reasons for questioning that approach.

There is another alternative to the world state, and that is what Bull dubs a "new medievalism."[36] In the medieval world, there were rulers, but no truly sovereign nations: each ruler "had to share authority with vassals beneath, and with the Pope and (in Germany and Italy) the Holy Roman Emperor above."[37] So too, we might imagine a kind of order, though not a theocratic order, uniting the world in the absence of a centralized world government:

> We might imagine, for example, that the government of the United Kingdom had to share its authority on the one hand with authorities in Scotland, Wales, Wessex and elsewhere, and on the other hand with a European authority in Brussels and world authorities in New York and Geneva, to such an extent that the notion of its supremacy over the territory and people of the United Kingdom had no force.[38]

This paragraph, written in 1977, seems prescient in one way: for indeed, as the "new medievalists" project, there is today a Scottish Parliament, and there is a European authority in Brussels, and with both of these the government of the United Kingdom has been sharing its authority to a certain degree—until the Brexit vote of 2016 severed the connection to Brussels in a way as yet to be determined. Nonetheless, the situation envisaged by the new medievalists has not come about: for citizenship, political participation, and economic entitlements are still in a very significant sense grounded in the nation, and it certainly is not (yet) true that the "notion of its supremacy over the territory and people . . . ha[s] no force." Economic globalization is another factor, not foreseen by Bull, that undermines national sovereignty. And yet, it seems that we are likely to live for some time in a world in which nation-states play something like the role Grotius envisaged, giving up their power to these other entities only at the margins.

What about normative issues, however? Would the "new medieval" world be in significant ways a *better* world to live in? It seems highly dubious. Nation-states are on the whole good protectors of the basic rights of their citizens, through constitution-making or its analogue, and a combination of legislative and judicial oversight. It seems unlikely that a diffuse system that leaches away powers from the nations will do better at protecting the rights of minorities, women, and the poor. Within each subgroup that sets itself up against the nation, there are likely to be differences of power, and we can already see many instances (for example, systems of religiously based personal law) in which minorities do significantly worse under the "local" authority than they would were they directly under the power of the nation. Supranational and transnational groups of many kinds may indeed play a valuable role in pushing nations toward greater recognition of human rights; and yet, if there is not to be a world state, with all its threats, it seems likely that such groups ought to remain plural, decentralized, and, in the main, focused on persuasion rather than coercion. Such entities, once again, are highly unlikely to be fully accountable to people; and, once again, they are all too likely to enforce a uniformity that the moral law does not require, precluding other permissible forms of human organization. Supranational coercion is appropriate for very grave offenses against human rights. But the current skepticism about any form of international coercion, however mild, suggests that we should ourselves remain mindful of the need for accountability, and for respect for permissible human variety.

To the extent to which the "new medievalism" is indeed emerging in our world, it is taking a form quite unlike that envisaged in the 1970s, and one that cries out urgently for Grotius's strong defense of national sovereignty. For it has taken the form of economic globalization, with multinational corporations leaching away sovereignty from the poorer nations as they pursue policies that are not exactly motivated by the moral law. This form of medievalism is a reality; but it shows the moral danger of the idea, since the global market is amoral and unaccountable. Nations, with their accountability to the lives of real human beings, continue to have the moral weight that Grotius ascribed to them, and the defense of their sovereignty seems even more important, perhaps, than it did in his time. Their connections are thicker and more complicated than those envisaged by Kant and Rawls: they go beyond questions of international relations. But the nation is still the primary locus of human self-expression and human autonomy.

I shall return to these questions in Chapter 7. But it seems fitting to end this chapter with a Stoic passage near the ending of *BP*, addressed to rulers, but suited as well to democratic subjects:

> Rightly the same Cicero says that "it is an impious act to destroy the good faith which holds life together." To use Seneca's phrase, it is "the most exalted good of the human heart." And this good faith the supreme rulers of men ought so much the more earnestly than others to maintain as they violate it with greater impunity; if good faith shall be done away with, they will be like wild beasts, whose violence all men fear . . . Violence is characteristic of wild beasts, and violence is most manifest in war; wherefore the more diligently effort should be put forth that it be tempered with humanity, lest by imitating wild beasts too much we forget to be human. (III.25.1, 2)

FIVE

"Mutilated and Deformed"

Adam Smith on the Material Basis of Human Capabilities

They were a boy and a girl. Yellow, meagre, ragged, scowling, wolfish, but prostrate, too, in their humility . . . Scrooge started back, appalled. Having them shown to him in this way, he tried to say they were fine children, but the words choked themselves, rather than be parties to a lie of such magnitude.

"Spirit! Are they yours?" Scrooge could say no more.

"They are Man's," said the Spirit, looking down upon them . . . "This boy is Ignorance. This girl is Want. Beware of them both, and all of their degree, but most of all beware this boy, for on his brow I see that written which is Doom, unless the writing be erased."

—Charles Dickens, *A Christmas Carol* (1843)

I. The Stoic Tradition and Material Need

The cosmopolitan tradition has some great strengths as an account of our ethical relationship with people outside our nation. First, unlike most non-Stoic moral positions in the Greco-Roman world, it insists that this is an *ethical* relation, not one regulated just by considerations of expediency and safety. Second, the tradition has a valuable idea about the basis of this relationship: it lies in the dignity that every human being has just by virtue of being human. Unclear though this idea frequently is, it is powerful and fertile. But so far, the tradition also has some difficulties. One obvious problem, which I shall postpone to Chapter 7, is a problem of inclusion. The tradition's focus on the exclusively human and, within the human, on capacities for moral development and choice, makes it unable to think well about the value of other species and of humans with severe cognitive disabilities. Other traditions in the ancient world did better at mapping our ethical responsibilities to other species.[1]

Two other problems, however, are gradually confronted. First is the motivational problem diagnosed in Chapter 3. The unfolding tradition gradually comes to the conclusion that strong attachments to one's own family, friends, and republic are both intrinsically valuable and central in constructing a personality capable of rising above egoism and greed to face a larger world. Cicero and Grotius both contribute in different ways to this refashioning.

Another problem involved the Stoic idea that "external goods" are not necessary for the flourishing life. Cicero's bifurcation of duties into strict duties of justice and elastic duties of material aid was unconvincing, as Grotius acknowledges. But what should replace it— compatibly with the recognition of an inalienable equal dignity? Chapter 3 suggested that one key is a recognition of basic innate powers that suffice for dignity whether or not they receive the support that they need. The presence of those powers, in turn, is a demand: without development, human dignity has been short-changed.

Adam Smith makes decisive progress on these problems. Smith is deeply immersed in the cosmopolitan tradition. Throughout his career, and certainly in his two central works, *The Theory of Moral Sentiments (TMS)*[2] and *The Wealth of Nations (WN)*,[3] Stoic ideas are of central importance as both a source and, less often, a foil for his own. His engagement with Stoicism is not cosmetic, but detailed and scholarly: he knows not only Cicero and Seneca, but also Epictetus and Marcus Aurelius. The sixth edition of *TMS*, published shortly after his death, offers a detailed account of Stoicism as one of the primary traditions in moral philosophy. More important, he clearly has a deep affinity with Stoicism; his key concept of self-command is thoroughly Stoic.

But Smith also has a keen understanding of the reality of working-class life. He sees clearly what a difference habit and education make to human abilities, and he sees that circumstances of life may, if propitious, cause basic human abilities to flourish or, if malign, to be starved and deformed. He sees that legal and economic arrangements have a crucial role to play in permitting people to develop their innate human capacities.

Smith's work thus stands at a critical juncture in the tradition. It applies the tradition's insights about human dignity in a way that newly recognizes the material underpinnings of human functioning. Smith argues that most of the salient differences among human beings are the product of habit and education. Because these influences affect the development of human powers, Smith cannot accept the Stoic idea that economic and political differences are irrelevant to true well-being. Instead, we must view it as a matter of the greatest significance that a being who is human is, frequently, given a life in which human abilities are "mutilated and deformed."

Although, to be sure, Smith develops these ideas via controversial claims about free markets and free trade, his argument begins from a keenly observed sympathy with the simple working man and a respect for that person's human potential. And although the argument of *WN* emphasizes the efficiency of the arrangements Smith favors, including the free movement of labor, the end of apprenticeship, and the freedom of trade, he argues for these arrangements in a way that separates issues of justice from issues of efficiency. Particularly salient is Smith's attention to public education as essential to developing powers of mind and citizenship. And although much of Smith's work is concerned with the internal legal arrangements of each society, there are also valuable proposals that develop the tradition's concept of transnational obligation: a critique of colonialism and a defense of political autonomy for colonies; a defense of free trade and the free movement of labor; a critique of irrational patriotism together with an account of local loyalty that links the nation to cosmopolitan ends. All in all, I shall argue, Smith's work paves the way for my "Capabilities Approach" that my final chapter will present as the best contemporary substitute for the cosmopolitan tradition.[4]

There are problems, however, in relating the insights of Smith's two greatest works. In an ironic reversal of common perceptions, it is *WN*, a work commonly reputed as callous, that understands with keen sympathy the depth to which human abilities stand in need of material goods and institutional arrangements. But the (allegedly) softer and more humane *TMS* retains a deep attachment to some problematic Stoic doctrines. While *TMS* contains many ingredients of the picture that Smith develops in *WN*, these elements do not decisively shape Smith's overall argument, which insists on some elements of Stoic doctrine that are problematic from the point of view of *WN*: a strong distinction between justice and beneficence; a conception of harm that denies that the withholding of material support is harmful; and, finally, an endorsement of the Stoic doctrine of the indifference of "external goods" for true well-being.

Smith's endorsement of these doctrines is revised to some extent in the last (sixth) edition of the work, the only one incorporating major changes that postdates *WN*.[5] But there is not as much pulling away from Stoicism as some recent critics suggest. In place of the general Stoic doctrine of the indifference of (all) externals for (everyone's) well-being, Smith introduces an odd asymmetry thesis: we should care about the misfortunes of people close to us, rejecting Stoicism where their losses are concerned, and yet we should not think that *our own* losses are bad—we should retain a strict Stoicism toward personal misfortunes. In connection with this thesis Smith either adds or retains some problematic claims about the alleged equivalence among different "permanent situations" of human life, contradicting some of the best insights of *WN*. His position is made yet less satisfactory by his residual attachment to Stoic Providence.[6]

Is this incoherence caused simply by illness and haste? I believe that the tension between the two works shows us something more interesting: it shows us the intuitive power of the Stoic doctrines, at least in connection with some very traditional and deep-rooted ideas of masculine virtue that are often closely linked to ideas of human dignity. Thus the problems in Smith's account will show us that we need to think critically about those ideals of manliness if we are to succeed in forging a coherent politics of human dignity that makes ample space for the recognition of material need. This will even mean reconceptualizing human dignity itself, to free it from a type of "macho" exhibitionism of fortitude that has infected the ideal, perhaps ever since Cato stood in the Forum, undisturbed as his enemy's spit ran down his fore-head.[7] *The Wealth of Nations* gives us great help as we attempt this difficult task.

II. The Dignity of Exchange

In both of his major works, Smith endorses the main outlines of the Ciceronian tradition, depicting human beings as worthy of respect, and equal respect, on account of their capacity for practical reason, persuasion, and "self-command." This equal dignity gives rise both to forms of reciprocity that are at the core of social life and to duties of justice that involve respect for the rights of the individual. Nature has given all human beings capacities for reasoning, self-control, and a type of impartiality that is at the heart of respect for others: even "the most vulgar education" teaches impartiality between self and other as the key to our conduct (*TMS* 139). A society can endure without love: but none can endure without the mutual respect and regard that consist in constraining one's own conduct by rules of justice (*TMS* 86).

Thus the core of morality is given, for Smith, by "that great stoical maxim, that for one man to deprive another unjustly of any thing, or unjustly to promote his own advantage by the loss or disadvantage of another, is more contrary to nature, than death, than poverty, than pain, than all the misfortunes which can affect him, either in his body, or in his external circumstances" (*TMS* 138, paraphrasing *De Officiis* III.21). We are social creatures who need one another and are highly vulnerable to injury (*TMS* 85). Therefore it is crucial that we learn to regulate our conduct by assuming the perspective of a spectator of that conduct. This perspective, which is advanced by Smith as a model of conscience, the "man in the breast," shows us how we must limit our own pursuit of our interests if we are to live in community with others on terms of reciprocity and mutual respect. Self-command, closely connected with the spectatorial perspective, becomes the key virtue in Smith's ethics.

Conscience and the virtue of self-command are closely linked by Smith to the idea of human dignity: the man who commits injustice against another enrages us above all by "that absurd self-love, by which he seems to imagine, that other people *may* be sacrificed at any time, to his conveniency" (TMS 96).[8] By contrast, when we assume the spectatorial perspective we temper the "arrogance of self-love" (83), seeing that we are "but one of the multitude, in no respect better than any other in it" (TMS 137).[9] Thus the overreacher goes wrong by using people as mere means; acting in accordance with conscience, we both recognize the equal dignity of others and cultivate our own.

In a passage added to the sixth edition of TMS that may have been inspired by reflection on the French Revolution, Smith uses these ideas of self-command and reciprocity to criticize idealistic political schemes that show deficient respect for individual choice and autonomy. A "man of humanity and benevolence," he writes, will respect "the established powers and privileges even of individuals" (233), and will use "reason and persuasion" to correct social ills, never imposing any system of laws, however good, that he cannot persuade the people to accept. By contrast, the "man of system"—a utopian politician who resembles some French revolutionaries[10]—is so enamored by the "supposed beauty of his ideal plan of government" that he is unwilling to compromise at all with popular sentiment, and simply goes on to impose it, "completely and in all its parts." In so doing, he treats his fellow citizens as pieces on a chess board that he can arrange as he likes. "He does not consider that the pieces upon the chess-board have no other principle of motion besides that which the hand impresses upon them; but that, in the great chess-board of human society, every single piece has a principle of motion of its own."

Smith's political thought thus takes its start from this moral norm of respect for each person's powers of choice. A good society would be one in which people learn to be self-commanding, and their individual powers of agency and self-command are respected by the institutions within which they live. (Kant admired Smith's work, and his form of liberalism is clearly influenced by it.) Thus it is a great mistake, by now amply corrected in the literature, to read Smith as the apostle of mere self-interest. His account of each individual's pursuit of his interests is woven into his moral account of self-command, and his account of society, built upon this foundation, lies at a great remove from that of Hobbes, or even Locke.[11] For Smith, as for the Stoics, morality does not simply limit self-interest, protecting all from the overreacher; it expresses what is most human about each person. Institutionalizing the moral norms recommended by conscience is good because such institutions permit all to live together on terms of mutual respect; and such institutions themselves express respect for the human dignity of each person.

This same combination of respect for human dignity with moral egalitarianism is present in WN, and lies at the basis of its vision of society. For Smith, the relations of contract and exchange are paradigm cases of human reciprocity, displaying vividly the difference between human life and animal life. At the very opening of WN, Smith introduces a typical Stoic contrast between human beings and animals in order to make this point. The "propensity to truck, barter, and exchange one thing for another," Smith suggests, is an aspect or consequence of and inviolable" form of property. It is that in us that permits us to express ourselves toward others on terms of mutual respect and reciprocity, bargaining like dignified human beings rather than fawning like dogs. Therefore, the fact that workmen under actual conditions are in many ways prevented from using their labor power in the way they want is not only a paradigmatic violation of property rights, it is also an insult to their humanity, thus a violation of basic justice:

> The property which every man has in his own labour, as it is the original foundation of all other property, so it is the most sacred and inviolable. The patrimony of a poor man lies in the strength and dexterity of his hands; and to hinder him from employing this strength and dexterity in what manner he thinks proper without injury to his neighbour, is a plain violation of this most sacred property. It is a manifest encroachment upon the just liberty both of the workman, and of those who might be disposed to employ him. (138)

Smith's target in this passage is mandatory apprenticeship, which restricts entry into trades and sets up barriers against young people's using their abilities as they choose. Another contemporary target concerning which he makes similar points is the practice of parish registration, which prevents working men from moving from place to place in search of suitable employment. And finally, he uses such observations to object to restrictive trade practices, particularly those connected with colonial monopolies, which prevent colonists from making the deals they want to make with those who want to buy their goods.

Smith is saying, then, that although human beings begin life with a dignity that is equal, societies typically conspire in many ways to

"the faculties of reason and speech" (25). It is "common to all men, and to be found in no other race of animals, which seem to know neither this nor any other species of contracts" (25). Dogs may seem to cooperate, but they do not make contracts with one another. In consequence, they have no way of getting what they want from another but by a servile form of fawning.

> Nobody ever saw a dog make a fair and deliberate exchange of one bone for another with another dog. Nobody ever saw one animal by its gestures and natural cries signify to another, this is mine, that yours; I am willing to give this for that. When an animal wants to obtain something either of a man or of another animal, it has no other means of persuasion but to gain the favour of those whose service it requires. A puppy fawns upon its dam, and a spaniel endeavours by a thousand attractions to engage the attention of its master who is at dinner, when it wants to be fed by him. (26)

In a way that closely follows Cicero and other Stoic texts, and using the dog, their ubiquitous example of animal behavior, to make his point, Smith suggests that non-human animals, lacking reason and language, have available to them only a very reduced form of connection, both with one another and with humans. All they can do is to fawn in a "servile" way on the person or animal they want to please, in the hope that they will get what they want. They have no way of forming projects that involve reciprocity or a recognition of equality. Human beings, having language and reason, can use persuasion to get what they want, and one characteristic expression of that capacity is the making of contracts and the establishment of exchange relations.

The famous passage that follows is usually read out of context. "It is not from the benevolence of the butcher, the brewer, or the baker, that we expect our dinner, but from their regard to their own interest," writes Smith. But he is not claiming that all human behavior is motivated by self-interest, something *TMS* spends seven hundred pages denying and something *WN* has just denied. Smith is saying, instead, that there is something particularly dignified and human about these forms of exchange and deal-making, something that makes them expressive of our humanity. "Nobody but a beggar," he continues, "chuses to depend chiefly upon the benevolence of his fellow-citizens" (27).

Moreover, lest we think that some human beings are intrinsically above others with respect to the key elements of human dignity, Smith immediately insists that this is not the case. The "difference of natural talents in different men is, in reality, much less than we are aware of" (28). The differences we observe among men are the effect, rather than the cause, of the division of labor:

> The difference between the most dissimilar characters, be-
> tween a philosopher and a common street porter, for ex-
> ample, seems to arise not so much from nature, as from
> habit, custom, and education. When they came into the
> world, and for the first six or eight years of their existence,
> they were, perhaps, very much alike, and neither their parents
> nor play-fellows could perceive any remarkable difference.
> About that age, or soon after, they come to be employed in
> very different occupations The difference of talents comes
> then to be taken notice of, and widens by degrees, till at last
> the vanity of the philosopher is willing to acknowledge
> scarce any resemblance. (28–29)

The idea that all human beings are profoundly equal with respect basic capacities that are the seat of human dignity, and that distinctic of class and rank are artificial, is a familiar Stoic idea. But Smith gi them a new twist, in two significant ways. First, he emphasizes the portance of work and the influence of occupation on one's hur abilities, something that did not particularly interest the Stoics. Sec he shows that different conditions of life do not merely create diffe classes and ranks of people in the eyes of those who are foolish enc to care about such things; they actually form the person, directl fecting the development of human abilities. To this crucial clair shall return in section III.

Thus *WN* sets itself squarely in the Stoic tradition: human di consists of a set of capacities for rational and reciprocal relations. Smith adds to that tradition is, however, profound: for he sees relationships of contract and exchange—which ancient Greeks, leisured gentlemen, typically devalued—an expression of core d values. Material relations are not low, as the Greeks typically th (and thus they assigned them to slaves and women, rather tha born gentlemen). Instead, they are, or at least can be, forms of ally respecting rationality.

This being the case, Smith also holds throughout *WN* that t version of these relations is no small matter, but a deformatior entire humanity of a person. There are, of course, many form change, just as there are many types of property. But the prop each man in his own labor[12] is, for Smith, the "original foundatic other property" (138), the core form of property from which a forms derive; this claim is closely linked to the claim that labo real measure of the exchangeable value of all commoditi Because this is so, each man's property in his labor is "the mo:

"the faculties of reason and speech" (25). It is "common to all men, and to be found in no other race of animals, which seem to know neither this nor any other species of contracts" (25). Dogs may seem to cooperate, but they do not make contracts with one another. In consequence, they have no way of getting what they want from another but by a servile form of fawning.

> Nobody ever saw a dog make a fair and deliberate exchange of one bone for another with another dog. Nobody ever saw one animal by its gestures and natural cries signify to another, this is mine, that yours; I am willing to give this for that. When an animal wants to obtain something either of a man or of another animal, it has no other means of persuasion but to gain the favour of those whose service it requires. A puppy fawns upon its dam, and a spaniel endeavours by a thousand attractions to engage the attention of its master who is at dinner, when it wants to be fed by him. (26)

In a way that closely follows Cicero and other Stoic texts, and using the dog, their ubiquitous example of animal behavior, to make his point, Smith suggests that non-human animals, lacking reason and language, have available to them only a very reduced form of connection, both with one another and with humans. All they can do is to fawn in a "servile" way on the person or animal they want to please, in the hope that they will get what they want. They have no way of forming projects that involve reciprocity or a recognition of equality. Human beings, having language and reason, can use persuasion to get what they want, and one characteristic expression of that capacity is the making of contracts and the establishment of exchange relations.

The famous passage that follows is usually read out of context. "It is not from the benevolence of the butcher, the brewer, or the baker, that we expect our dinner, but from their regard to their own interest," writes Smith. But he is not claiming that all human behavior is motivated by self-interest, something *TMS* spends seven hundred pages denying and something *WN* has just denied. Smith is saying, instead, that there is something particularly dignified and human about these forms of exchange and deal-making, something that makes them expressive of our humanity. "Nobody but a beggar," he continues, "chuses to depend chiefly upon the benevolence of his fellow-citizens" (27).

Moreover, lest we think that some human beings are intrinsically above others with respect to the key elements of human dignity, Smith immediately insists that this is not the case. The "difference of natural talents in different men is, in reality, much less than we are aware of" (28). The differences we observe among men are the effect, rather than the cause, of the division of labor:

> The difference between the most dissimilar characters, be-tween a philosopher and a common street porter, for ex-ample, seems to arise not so much from nature, as from habit, custom, and education. When they came into the world, and for the first six or eight years of their existence, they were, perhaps, very much alike, and neither their parents nor play-fellows could perceive any remarkable difference. About that age, or soon after, they come to be employed in very different occupations The difference of talents comes then to be taken notice of, and widens by degrees, till at last the vanity of the philosopher is willing to acknowledge scarce any resemblance. (28–29)

The idea that all human beings are profoundly equal with respect to basic capacities that are the seat of human dignity, and that distinctions of class and rank are artificial, is a familiar Stoic idea. But Smith gives them a new twist, in two significant ways. First, he emphasizes the importance of work and the influence of occupation on one's human abilities, something that did not particularly interest the Stoics. Second, he shows that different conditions of life do not merely create different classes and ranks of people in the eyes of those who are foolish enough to care about such things; they actually form the person, directly affecting the development of human abilities. To this crucial claim we shall return in section III.

Thus *WN* sets itself squarely in the Stoic tradition: human dignity consists of a set of capacities for rational and reciprocal relations. What Smith adds to that tradition is, however, profound: for he sees in the relationships of contract and exchange—which ancient Greeks, being leisured gentlemen, typically devalued—an expression of core dignity values. Material relations are not low, as the Greeks typically thought (and thus they assigned them to slaves and women, rather than free-born gentlemen). Instead, they are, or at least can be, forms of mutually respecting rationality.

This being the case, Smith also holds throughout *WN* that the perversion of these relations is no small matter, but a deformation of the entire humanity of a person. There are, of course, many forms of exchange, just as there are many types of property. But the property of each man in his own labor[12] is, for Smith, the "original foundation of all other property" (138), the core form of property from which all other forms derive; this claim is closely linked to the claim that labor is "the real measure of the exchangeable value of all commodities" (47). Because this is so, each man's property in his labor is "the most sacred

and inviolable" form of property. It is that in us that permits us to express ourselves toward others on terms of mutual respect and reciprocity, bargaining like dignified human beings rather than fawning
like dogs. Therefore, the fact that workmen under actual conditions
are in many ways prevented from using their labor power in the way
they want is not only a paradigmatic violation of property rights, it is
also an insult to their humanity, thus a violation of basic justice:

> The property which every man has in his own labour, as it
> is the original foundation of all other property, so it is the
> most sacred and inviolable. The patrimony of a poor man lies
> in the strength and dexterity of his hands; and to hinder him
> from employing this strength and dexterity in what manner
> he thinks proper without injury to his neighbour, is a plain
> violation of this most sacred property. It is a manifest en-
> croachment upon the just liberty both of the workman, and
> of those who might be disposed to employ him. (138)

Smith's target in this passage is mandatory apprenticeship, which
restricts entry into trades and sets up barriers against young people's
using their abilities as they choose. Another contemporary target concerning which he makes similar points is the practice of parish registration, which prevents working men from moving from place to place
in search of suitable employment. And finally, he uses such observations to object to restrictive trade practices, particularly those connected with colonial monopolies, which prevent colonists from making
the deals they want to make with those who want to buy their goods.

Smith is saying, then, that although human beings begin life with a
dignity that is equal, societies typically conspire in many ways to

prevent that natural equality from developing freely. The free choice of occupation and freedom of travel and association seem to him key human entitlements demanded by the idea of human dignity itself; and yet these freedoms are every day violated.

What is the source of these violations? Throughout the work—as Rothschild and Fleischacker effectively document—Smith refuses to pin blame on workers for their sad condition. He shows great sympathy and respect for workers, and for the rationality of the decisions that they would make if they were allowed room to exercise choice. And as we have seen, he mocks the pretensions of those who claim an inequality of talent from birth: these differences are manufactured by differences of education and habit. Smith does suggest that, just as the characteristic vices of the rich are "avarice and ambition," so too the poor have some characteristic vices, namely "the hatred of labour and the love of present ease and enjoyment" (709). On the whole, however, he holds that the poor are basically thrifty and hard-working—when they are treated decently. "Where wages are high, accordingly, we shall always find the workmen more active, diligent, and expeditious, than when they are low" (99).

The real source of the abuses Smith documents is to be sought in the imbalance of power between masters and workers, in combination with the fact that government, held hostage to wealth, supports the masters against the workers. Given the asymmetry of power:

> It is not . . . difficult to foresee which of the two parties must, upon all ordinary occasions, have the advantage in the dispute, and force the other into a compliance with their terms. The masters, being fewer in number, can combine much more easily; and the law, besides, authorises, or at

THE COSMOPOLITAN TRADITION

least does not prohibit their combinations, while it prohibits those of the workmen. We have no acts of parliament against combining to lower the price of work; but many against combining to raise it. (83–84)

Smith imagines the objection that we don't actually hear much about these conspiracies among masters, whereas we hear a lot about conspiracies among workers. He scoffs, "[W]hoever imagines, upon this account, that masters rarely combine, is as ignorant of the world as of the subject. Masters are always and every where in a sort of tacit, but constant and uniform combination, not to raise the wages of labour above their actual rate" (84). Moreover, when masters get together to fix wages deliberately, their dealings "are always conducted with the utmost silence and secrecy"; when workmen yield without resistance, as they usually do, although their situation is "severely felt by them" it is simply "never heard of by other people" (84).

One of Smith's constant concerns is the undue influence of masters, especially large manufacturers, on government. Discussing the disastrous influence of manufacturers on foreign trade through the practice of monopoly, Smith compares manufacturers to "an overgrown standing army" that has "become formidable to the government, and upon many occasions intimidate the legislature" (471). Any member of Parliament who votes with the manufacturers finds his future assured, through "great popularity and influence with an order of men whose numbers and wealth render them of great importance" (471). It thus comes about that "[w]henever the legislature attempts to regulate the differences between masters and their workmen, its counsellors are always the masters" (157). Smith infers from this fact the following striking conclusion: when the resulting regulation favors the workmen, "it is always just and equitable"—presumably because only an extremely clear and even flagrant violation of justice would ever be voted down by legislators so placed. When the resulting legislation favors the masters, however, "it is sometimes otherwise," says Smith with ironic understatement (157–158). The desirable state of things would be that the legislature's deliberations be directed "not by the clamorous importunity of partial interests, but by an extensive view of the general good" (472). This state of affairs is, however, very far from being realized.

Smith is clearly after a society that respects human dignity and "natural liberty," in which each person is able to contract and exchange, particularly with respect to his own laboring power, without intrusions that reduce his condition to that of a fawning and servile animal. His key addition to the Stoic tradition is the insight that economic arrangements are critical to the full expression of human dignity, making our social relations either mutually respectful and reciprocal, or fawning and deformed. Respect for human dignity requires an ample measure of liberty for workers, including free choice of occupation and free movement from place to place.

Is a "hands-off" state part of Smith's picture of what political morality requires? Many have thought so. But Smith is no simple advocate of an inactive state in his account of how societies ought to secure his basic goals. Indeed, his analysis of the politics of his own time calls into question the very distinction between state action and inaction: for the fact that legislatures do not regulate the practice of monopoly is in one way inaction; but it is plainly also action, the deliberate choice of legislators to favor the interests of the manufacturers in whose sway they are. Smith plainly thinks that there are a number of areas in which states should be more active, in the conventional sense of passing interventionist laws, than they currently are. He holds that law should regulate monopolies and the practice of colonial domination. He favors the abolition of the slave trade, and indeed campaigned on behalf of this cause. He shows sympathy with wage regulations that favor workmen: all workmen should be guaranteed that "lowest rate that is consistent with common humanity" (91), which means enough to maintain a household with a wife and enough children to guarantee that two survive to adulthood.[13] And as we shall see, he gives the state a very large job in the area of education. What he objects to most about the current behavior of the state is not that it is active, but that it is active in the wrong way, held hostage to monied interests, rather than deliberating in light of an "extensive view of the common good."

The Wealth of Nations is famous above all for its efficiency arguments, and these are indeed of great interest. Smith does not try to persuade his audience to make the changes he favors for moral reasons alone. Therefore he devotes much of the work to arguing that monopolies, trade restrictions, apprenticeship, and restrictions on the free movement of labor are actually inefficient. Those arguments, besides being intrinsically important, themselves have moral significance. For Smith holds that "no society can be flourishing and happy, of which the far greater part of the members are poor and miserable" (96); the state that is going to flourish must, then, find ways to produce economic growth, at least up to the point where it can support all its citizens at a decent level. "[I]t is in the progressive state . . . that the condition of the labouring poor, of the great body of the people, seems to be the happiest and the most comfortable . . . The progressive state is in reality the chearful and the hearty state to all the different orders of the society" (99). For this reason people who believe that a good living standard for the poor is a moral imperative should be interested in efficiency.

But Smith also has arguments for his concrete proposals based on justice and independent of efficiency.[14] His critique of the apprenticeship system is based on the "manifest" injustice of violating a person's "sacred and inviolable property" in his own labor (138). Similarly, to remove a man from a parish in which he chooses to reside is, for Smith, "an evident violation of natural liberty and justice" (157). In the colonies, Smith holds, the joint stock companies operate inefficiently—but also "unjustly, capriciously, cruelly," taxing the subject people for "worthless purposes" to support the bad and wasteful behavior of their own employees. Similarly, although Smith holds that slavery is inefficient (99, 386–389), he also clearly holds that it is unjust, proceeding from a "tyranic disposition" (*LJ* [B] 132, cf. *TMS* 206–207, discussed later). In general, Smith observes in *WN*'s discussion of slavery, "The pride of man makes him love to domineer, and nothing mortifies him so much as to be obliged to condescend to persuade his inferiors" (388). Indeed, the desire to lord it over others in ways that fail to recognize their human dignity is Smith's explanation for the persistence, and virtual ubiquity, of a manifestly inefficient institution. Legal regulations favoring workmen, we recall, are "always just and equitable" (*WN* 157–158), whereas those that favor masters are not. His arguments for reducing working hours to allow some leisure and relaxation allude to efficiency issues, but also to the "dictates of reason and humanity" that ought to prompt masters, in any case, to support the workers' natural need for rest (100).[15] His argument for decent living wages, while it does stress that workmen actually work better when well paid, also alludes to justice, as a separate consideration: "It is but equity, besides, that they who feed, cloath and lodge the whole body of the people, should have such a share of the produce of their own labor as to be themselves tolerably well fed, cloathed, and lodged" (96). Finally, Smith's argument for the need to spend money improving institutions that administer justice makes much of the flagrant injustices occasioned by inequalities of property (709–710), as well as the "insecurity" that such injustices produce.

For Smith, societies are to be assessed not by some quality they possess as organic wholes, but by what they do for the individuals in them. In this he is a major forerunner of the liberal tradition. This being the case, it is no surprise that even economic growth is regularly assessed for the contribution it makes to human happiness, and in a way that factors distribution into account: "No society can surely be flourishing and happy, of which the far greater part of the members are poor and miserable."[16] But Smith goes beyond even this general observation, pointing out that the working classes have a claim based in justice to decent living conditions and basic liberties of employment and association.

III. The Material Foundations of Human Abilities

Smith has agreed with the Stoics that human dignity deserves respect. We have moral duties to respect the dignity of our fellow citizens, forming relations with them that are based on reciprocity rather than force or deception. In all of this Smith is Ciceronian. But he modifies the Ciceronian argument in two very productive ways.

First of all, as we have seen by now, Smith does not interpret the ideas of justice and respect as narrowly as do Cicero and the Stoics. He sees that a life worthy of human dignity requires more than the absence of aggression, torture, and theft. It requires, as well, certain conditions of labor, because it is in the sphere of labor that a person's humanity is deeply and fundamentally expressed. The freedom to contract for one's own labor, the freedom of movement, and the free choice of occupation are all essential to a life in which one can "barter and exchange" like a human, rather than fawning like an animal. More-over, a life worthy of human dignity also requires the wherewithal to raise a family and bring up children to adulthood, thus a decent living wage; spaces for rest and recreation; and a political life in which laws are made for the good of all, not by pressure of the rich on a captive legislature. Unlike the Stoics, who asked for decent treatment of slaves while holding that the institution itself was a matter of indifference, Smith sees that institutions matter for a life worthy of human dignity and that slavery, colonial domination, and certain forms of domination by the rich over the poor are violations of basic justice. Smith's argument thus strikingly anticipates similar arguments made by proponents of the Capabilities Approach today.

Smith, then, rather than departing radically from the Stoic tradition, removes a gross inconsistency in Stoic thought. For it is inconsistent to deny the importance of external goods in the context of material dis-tribution, but to insist so strongly on their importance in the context of aggression and respect. Thinking more deeply about labor than the Greek and Roman authors did helps Smith to correct this mistake, and thus to realize the potential of the Stoic doctrine more fully.

But another issue lurks in the background: and it is on this issue that Smith makes his most creative contribution to the tradition. The Stoic doctrine of the indifference of "external goods" causes us to underrate the importance of external goods in a life in which practical reason and moral choice are already operative. This is the thread of Smith's cri-tique that we have followed up until now, as he emphasizes the self-command and rationality of poor workmen. But the doctrine also causes us to miss the fact that deprivation of external goods can damage the development of parts of the personality essential for a life worthy of human dignity: rationality, moral choice, the will. This failure of Stoicism Smith now insightfully corrects.

Many of the workers mentioned in WN have tolerably decent lives, and Smith emphasizes that these workers are worthy of respect for their self-command, intelligence, and capacity for choice. But he also emphasizes, as we have seen, the fact that habit and education play a profound role in shaping human abilities: the philosopher and the street porter differ in education, not by nature, although the "vanity" of the former supposes otherwise. Much of WN is accordingly dedicated to documenting the many factors that can cause key human abilities to fail to develop. Some of these factors are straightforwardly physical. Poverty is unfavorable to life and health. Some nations are so poor that they are forced to practice infanticide, and to leave the elderly and sick to be devoured by wild beasts (10). Even in Britain, however, high child mortality is characteristic of the working, and not the more prosperous, classes. "[P]overty, though it does not prevent the generation, is extremely unfavourable to the rearing of children. The tender plant is produced, but in so cold a soil and so severe a climate, soon withers and dies" (97).[17] In the Scottish Highlands, it is common for a woman to bear twenty children and yet to have fewer than two alive. "In some places one half the children born die before they are four years of age; in many places before they are seven; and in almost all places before they are nine or ten" (97)—this among the working classes, who cannot afford to give children what they need. Elsewhere, Smith generalizes the point: any class that cannot support itself from wages will be afflicted with "want, famine, and mortality" (91).[18]

These points seem obvious enough, but they already put the Stoic project in trouble. For they remind us that human dignity is not some-

thing rock hard. It is, rather, a "tender plant"[19] that will wither if it en-
counters a severe climate. This means that we cannot hold that the
distribution of material goods is irrelevant to human dignity: for dignity requires, at the very least, life,[20] and the lives of children are in
the hands of these material arrangements. The Stoics may have thought
it possible to ignore this point because, along with most of their society,
they simply did not think that very young children were fully human:
they had no more right to continue living than non-human animals.[21]
Or they may simply have thought that there was little societies could
do to affect infant mortality. Both of these thoughts were and are in-
correct. Smith's close attention to people's actual economic circumstances and his awareness that infant mortality is linked to poverty
enable him to attain a simple but neglected insight: if human dignity
ought to be respected, then we had better arrange things so that
children can live to adulthood.

But it is in his lengthy discussion of education that Smith develops
most fully his ideas about the fragility of human dignity. The question
he faces is whether the state ought to take responsibility for the education of its people, and, if so, in what way. Recall that Smith has already
argued that habit and education go very deep, forming more or less the
entire difference between the philosopher and the street porter. He
now observes that the division of labor, combined with a lack of general education, has a very pernicious effect on human abilities:

> The man whose whole life is spent in performing a few
> simple operations, of which the effects too are, perhaps, al-
> ways the same, or very nearly the same, has no occasion to
> exert his understanding, or to exercise his invention in
> finding out expedients for removing difficulties which never

occur. He naturally loses, therefore, the habit of such exertion, and generally becomes as stupid and ignorant as it is possible for a human creature to become. The torpor of his mind renders him, not only incapable of relishing or bearing a part in any rational conversation, but of conceiving any generous, noble, or tender sentiment, and consequently of forming any just judgment concerning many even of the ordinary duties of private life. Of the great and extensive interests of his country, he is altogether incapable of judging; and unless very particular pains have been taken to render him otherwise, he is equally incapable of defending his country in war. The uniformity of his stationary life naturally corrupts the courage of his mind, and makes him regard with abhorrence the irregular, uncertain, and adventurous life of a soldier. It corrupts even the activity of his body, and renders him incapable of exerting his strength with vigour and perseverance, in any other employment than that to which he has been bred. His dexterity at his own particular trade seems, in this manner, to be acquired at the expence of his intellectual, social, and martial virtues. But in every improved and civilized society this is the state into which the labouring poor, that is, the great body of the people, must necessarily fall, unless government takes some pains to prevent it. (782)

It is otherwise, Smith continues, in "barbarous" societies, because in such societies each person has to perform a variety of tasks, and minds are kept on the alert. Everyone has to be a warrior, a statesman, a judge, and so on. "Every man does, or is capable of doing, almost everything which any other man does, or is capable of doing" (783), and people thus attain a well-rounded development of their faculties. A high level of development, by contrast, brings with it great dangers for the human faculties. Those whose privilege permits a contemplative role have a lot to contemplate, and their minds may become developed "in an extraordinary degree." But these are the exceptions: "Notwithstanding the great abilities of those few, all the nobler parts of the human character may be, in a great measure, obliterated and extinguished in the great body of the people" (784).

The danger, Smith continues, is not great where we are dealing with "people of some rank and fortune." For even when the children of these people are not bound for a contemplative life, they are typically given an expensive and well-rounded education before they go into the trade they will eventually pursue. If they don't profit by it, it is seldom for want of parental investment. Moreover, the rich usually don't work as many hours as the poor do: so they can keep some part of their day to "perfect themselves" in some branch of knowledge or activity other than that of their trade. The public sphere does not need to worry much about their loss of human capacities.

It is otherwise with the common people. They have little time to spare for education. Their parents can scarce afford to maintain them even in infancy. As soon as they are able to work, they must apply to some trade by which they can earn their subsistence. That trade too is generally so simple and uniform as to give little exercise to the understanding; while, at the same time, their labour is both so constant and so severe, that it leaves them little leisure and less inclination to apply to, or even to think of any thing else. (784–785)

Smith now argues that this situation is not inevitable. No state can guarantee all citizens as extensive an education as the rich currently receive at their parents' expense. But it can (as Scotland typically does) provide all with "the most essential parts of education," by requiring them to learn reading, writing, and accounting before they are permitted to take on paid employment. He goes on to describe a scheme for low-cost[22] compulsory education in parish schools.

Smith now inserts a historical digression: the compulsory gymnastic exercises of ancient Greece and Rome, in an analogous way, maintained a citizenry all of whose members were ready to defend their state and its liberty. Extolling the virtues of a citizen army drawn from all classes of society, he notes that a person who is not capable of defending himself and his society "is as much mutilated and deformed in his mind, as another is in his body, who is either deprived of some of its most essential members, or has lost the use of them" (787). And he is worse off than the physically disabled person, to the extent that mental aspects of happiness are more central than the physical. He now applies this insight to the question of the laboring poor:

> The same thing may be said of the gross ignorance and stupidity which, in a civilized society, seem so frequently to benumb the understandings of all the inferior ranks of people. A man, without the proper use of the intellectual faculties of a man, is, if possible, more contemptible than even a coward, and seems to be mutilated and deformed in a still more essential part of the character of human nature. Though the state was to derive no advantage from the instruction of the inferior ranks of people, it would still deserve its attention that they should not be altogether uninstructed. (788)

Smith has a deep insight in this fascinating discussion. It is that human abilities come into the world in a nascent or undeveloped form, and require support from the environment—including support for physical health and especially, here, for mental development—if they are to mature in a way that is worthy of innate human dignity. Smith clearly believes that all normal human beings are capable of developing the more mature or advanced capabilities that would make their lives fully human, not "mutilated and deformed." His discussion of the philosopher and the street porter has already made the point that the differences among men that bulk large in society are the work of habit. But he breaks from the Stoics in insisting that what the world does to the basic innate abilities of humans really matters. We simply do not have a life worthy of our dignity if we stunt powers of mind that are crucial for a life of active choice and citizenship.[23]

This insight is not altogether new: Smith himself finds precedent for his ideas in ancient Greece and Rome. But of course those societies did not pursue the education of the laboring classes very far, if at all; for Aristotle, the fact that some people have to labor all the time simply means that they cannot get the education provided by the city, and thus cannot be full participating citizens.[24] Closer to Smith's own time, universal education was certainly being discussed on the continent,[25] but I know of no discussion that connects its absence to human deformity or mutilation; in Britain he is clearly a pioneer. Even Wollstonecraft's later proposals, though more ambitious in including women, are less emphatic about the duty of the state not to permit the waste of human abilities. It was only with the work of T. H. Green late in the nineteenth century that a concrete political movement for compulsory education would receive developed philosophical backing.[26]

Marx's *Economic and Philosophic Manuscripts of 1844*, with their famous discussions of true human functioning, are in some respects the best parallel to Smith's argument here, and Smith anticipates that argument in striking ways. But Marx does not emphasize the key importance of education to the development of human abilities: he focuses on the workers' material conditions and their lack of control over their work lives and what they produce. Smith's emphasis on education and on the free choice of occupation takes us in a direction that is much more productive for contemporary thought.

Smith, we can now see, is developing a two-stage politics: a politics that commits itself to supporting and developing human abilities through an adequate living standard and the public provision of education; then allows those abilities room to become active, creating spaces in which workers may live according to their own powers of thought and self-command.

Instead of saying, with the Stoics, that all human beings simply have full human dignity no matter what the world has done to them, Smith's argument fulfills Chapter 3's demand for a threefold distinction: between *basic capabilities* and developed *internal capabilities,* and between both of these and *combined capabilities* to choose related functionings. The workers described by Smith are still worthy of respect as human beings, because there is that in them (the basic capabilities) which might have been transformed (although by the time they are adults it may not be possible to bring about this transformation). Similarly, Marx's workers are still human beings, although they are given a "merely animal" mode of existence. We do not take the full measure of the damages that poverty and ignorance can do, unless we understand clearly that ignorance can at least sometimes stunt core mental and moral faculties.

IV. Sketches of a Transnational Politics

WN is primarily concerned with the internal economic affairs of nations, but it is far from indifferent to global issues. Because of his topic, Smith does not address the classic Ciceronian topics of just war, humanitarian intervention, and other "duties of justice." He does, however, show concern that all the world's people should have the chance to develop the abilities of intelligence and self-command that he prizes (internal capabilities), and should then be put in a position to govern themselves (combined capabilities). The point of his contrast between "progressive" and "declining" nations is to give all nations some pointers about how their citizens may become better off. To some extent, this job is the job of each nation, but Smith also acknowledges that relations between nations have a considerable impact on the likelihood that any given nation will achieve success. From his remarks about international affairs we may extract at least a sketch of a transnational politics of human capability, containing the following elements:

I. FREE TRADE. Famously and influentially, Smith defends the role of markets in promoting the prosperity of all nations, and argues that prosperity is very much impeded by protectionistic policies, however appealing they seem in the short run. Despite the fact that he earned his living working in the Customs House, he denounces the mercantile system vigorously, in favor of a far more open international regime.

In this regard, Smith might seem to be the direct ancestor of free trade proponents of the present day, and of such international movements as the World Trade Organization. Caution, however, is necessary. Smith is perfectly aware that free trade means more than simply removing protectionistic tariffs. Genuinely free trade is impeded constantly by monopolistic practices, both within nations and in deals struck across national boundaries: what Smith calls the "mean and malignant expedients of the mercantile system" (610). Ancestors of modern multinational corporations were already known to him, in the form of the East India Company and other joint stock companies.[27] His account of their operations is devastating. He argues that they disrupt both the internal economies of the nations involved (particularly the poor colonized nations) and the healthy relations of trade that might emerge between nations, because they adopt policies designed above all to perpetuate their own power and profit, not the power and profit of the nations in which they do business. When they operate in a colony, they protect the indolence and bad behavior of their employees. The real interests of the home country, if only people understood this, are in harmony with that of the colony. "But the real interest of the servants [that is, the colonial authorities] is by no means the same with that of the country, and the most perfect information would not necessarily put an end to their oppressions" (640). Thus the correction of these abuses cannot be achieved by inaction alone.

Smith insists that these monopolistic practices are bad for both the colony and the home country. How, then, did they come about? Once again, his answer is to point to the influence of manufacturers on the political process:

> To found a great empire for the sole purpose of raising up a people of customers, may at first sight appear a project fit only for a nation of shopkeepers. It is, however, a project altogether unfit for a nation of shopkeepers; but extremely fit for a nation whose government is influenced by shopkeepers.

Such statesmen, and such statesmen only, are capable of fancying that they will find some advantage in employing the blood and treasure of their fellow citizens, to found and to maintain such an empire. (613)

Here as before, his arguments focus on efficiency issues, but he also makes it amply clear that colonial monopolies of trade are "oppressions," and "unjust" (628), "a manifest violation of the most sacred rights of mankind" (582).

2. AN END TO COLONIAL EXPLOITATION: SELF-RULE IN EVERY NATION, THE COMMUNICATION OF KNOWLEDGE. More generally, Smith is appalled by the whole practice of setting up colonies and running them from afar. "Folly and injustice seem to have been the principles which presided over and directed the first project of establishing those colonies; the folly of hunting after gold and silver mines, and the injustice of coveting the possession of a country whose harmless natives, far from having ever injured the people of Europe, had received the first adventurers with every mark of kindness and hospitality" (588). Smith exempts to some extent the North American colonies, whose settlers were fleeing from religious persecution, motives "more reasonable and more laudable" (589). Even here, however, he insists that the settlements are no credit to Europe: for if injustice in Europe was not the direct motive for founding the colony, it was an indirect cause. In short, "Upon all these different occasions it was, not the wisdom and policy, but the disorder and injustice of the European governments, which peopled and cultivated America" (589). And as we shall see further, he is keenly sensible of the wrong done to the native inhabitants of America as well

as of the other more directly exploitative enterprises: he speaks here of the "cruel destruction of the natives which followed the conquest" (568).

Smith's overall view is that no colonies ever should have existed. But since they exist, he also recognizes that it is utopian to expect that the European nations will simply give them up all at once: that would be "to propose such a measure as never was, and never will be adopted, by any nation in the world" (616). At least, however, they ought to follow the example of the English and give the colonists as much self-rule as possible—"[p]lenty of good land, and liberty to manage their own affairs their own way" (572). Smith points to the domestic representative assemblies of the American colonies, their self-command and civil liberty that is "in every respect equal to that of their fellow-citizens at home" (584–585).

Moreover, we should and can support the communication of knowledge and technology from Europe to the colonies, which over time will help to correct the imbalance of power. Here Smith allows himself to foresee a future in which all nations will have the resources to maintain genuine national sovereignty, winning protection for their rights and developing the human powers of their inhabitants:

> At the particular time when these discoveries were made, the superiority of force happened to be so great on the side of the Europeans, that they were enabled to commit with impunity every sort of injustice in the remote countries. Hereafter, perhaps, the natives of those countries may grow stronger, or those of Europe may grow weaker, and the inhabitants of all the different quarters of the world may arrive at that equality of courage and force which, by inspiring

mutual fear, can alone overawe the injustice of independent nations into some sort of respect for the rights of one another. But nothing seems more likely to establish this equality of force than that mutual communication of knowledge and of all sorts of improvements which an extensive commerce from all countries to all countries naturally, or rather necessarily, carries along with it. (626–627)

This far-sighted paragraph is still of significance to public policy in a nominally post-colonial era. One can have little doubt that Smith would favor policies that support education in all nations, at least through technology transfer and other forms of intellectual exchange. But most likely, in light of his attacks on the behavior of the employees of the East India Company, he would also urge multinational corporations, and their employees, to devote some of their resources to the education of the working people in places where they do business. As usual, he would probably support this policy as both efficient and equitable.

3. MIGRATION: A GAP IN SMITH'S ACCOUNT. Smith's account of trade questions the salience of national boundaries. Just as barriers between regions, and monopolistic practices, within a nation are bad, so too are barriers between nations that impede the operations of a genuinely free (monopoly-free) market. The other side of the coin might seem to be support for free movement of peoples across national boundaries. Just as the free choice of occupation, and free movement to secure work, are linchpins of his program in the domestic case, so too, one might conjecture, they ought to be in the transnational case. But Smith does not say this, and to that extent there is a large gap in his account.

If indeed Smith does not support fully open borders, a reason may be found in his strong interest in democratic self-government within each nation. Obviously enough, national self-government is at least threatened when there is too rapid and uncontrolled a movement of citizens in and out of the country. Citizenship needs to continue to exist and to mean something, if voting and representation are to have the weight Smith believes they should. Nonetheless, Smith should favor liberal immigration into richer nations as both efficient for the richer nation and a key source of human liberty for the worker.

4. A CRITICAL PATRIOTISM. The general sense conveyed by WN that Smith favors a diminished salience for national boundaries is very much borne out by his highly critical discussion of patriotism and nationalism in TMS book VI (added for the sixth edition). Smith does not favor assuming a detached perspective from which we always strive to maximize the good of all humanity. We ought to perform our moral obligations within our own context, and to see our connections from our own internal point of view. In book VI, Smith recapitulates and expands on some well-known Ciceronian arguments for special duties to our family, friends, and local context. Like Cicero, he seems to think these attachments have intrinsic value and are not simply delegations from the whole.

Smith follows Cicero in thinking that our own state should receive a particularly large measure of our concern, for reasons of both accountability and motivational psychology. The nation-state is typically the largest unit over which we can have much influence (227). It is typically the home of all the people we most love. "It is by nature, therefore, endeared to us, not only by all our selfish, but by all our private benevolent affections" (227). Because of this connection, we are inclined, as well, to feel proud of it and to compare it favorably with other nations. We think that its warriors, poets, philosophers, statesmen, are better than those of other nations; "we are disposed to view [them][28] with the most partial admiration, and to rank them (sometimes most unjustly) above those of all other nations" (228). Smith goes on to say that this love of one's country shows the "wisdom which contrived the system of human affections" (229). It includes two principles: respect and reverence for the established constitution, and "an earnest desire to render the condition of our fellow-citizens as safe, respectable, and happy as we can" (231).

Already in characterizing the permissible and even laudable sort of patriotism, however, Smith could not resist inserting a criticism: our overestimation of our own is often "unjust." He shortly expands on this point, saying that patriotism often veers over into a mean-spirited denigration of other nations: "The love of our own nation often disposes us to view, with the most malignant jealousy and envy, the prosperity and aggrandisement of any other neighboring nation" (228). For this reason, too, nations often treat one another immorally, showing contempt for international law. "From the smallest interest, upon the slightest provocation, we see these rules every day, either evaded or directly violated without shame and remorse . . . and the mean principle of national prejudice is often founded upon the noble one of love of our own country" (228). Smith reproves the elder Cato for ending every speech with the famous words, "It is my opinion likewise that Carthage ought to be destroyed," calling this the "savage patriotism of a strong but coarse mind." Scipio's opposite, anti-aggressive posture was "the liberal expression of a more enlarged and enlightened mind" (228).

In general, then, Smith finds patriotism unacceptable when it leads nations to violate international law, and also when it leads them to hate the prosperity of other nations. He now turns to current events:

> France and England may each of them have some reason to dread the increase of the naval and military power of the other; but for either of them to envy the internal happiness and prosperity of the other, the cultivation of its lands, the advancement of its manufactures, the increase of its commerce, the security and number of its ports and harbours, its proficiency in all the liberal arts and sciences, is surely beneath the dignity of two such great nations. These are all real improvements of the world we live in. Mankind are benefited, human nature is ennobled by them. In such improvements each nation ought, not only to endeavour itself to excel, but from the love of mankind, to promote, instead of obstructing the excellence of its neighbors. These are all proper objects of national emulation, not of national prejudice or envy.
>
> The love of our own country seems not to be derived from the love of mankind. The former sentiment is altogether independent of the latter, and seems sometimes even to dispose us to act inconsistently with it. (229)

Smith urges us to identify with the good of all humanity, while remaining devoted to our own nation. While we prepare to ward off unjust aggression, as the law of nations permits, we should also take pride in, and even actively foster, the prosperity and cultural achievement of human beings, no matter where they are.

Smith's sketch of a cosmopolitan world order is a mere sketch; and yet it has some valuable ideas that appear nowhere else in the Stoic internationalist tradition. Characteristically, Smith sees the economic issues involved in global justice with a sharpness that most philosophers writing in the tradition do not. Even where he is pessimistic about achieving a stably just world society, his diagnosis of the difficulty is itself a major step forward.

V. Stoicism in *Theory of Moral Sentiments*: Justice and Beneficence

We have now seen Smith's great innovations. But the story is not at an end, because we must now see how the Stoic tradition continues to exert its hold on his thinking, causing him to turn away from some of his best insights. As we can see, TMS to some extent agrees with WN in advancing the basis for a cosmopolitan politics based on universal regard for humanity. But the reader of TMS will search in vain for WN's insightful recognition that duties of justice *include* duties of material aid and support for human capacities. To a surprising extent, given the innovations of WN, TMS remains thoroughly in the grip of a Ciceronian politics that bisects our duties into two categories, one strict and one less strict, and enjoins self-command to those who are deprived of material support. In one important respect, TMS lags well behind Cicero, denying the existence of "passive injustice."

An obvious Ciceronian feature of TMS, present unchanged in all six editions, is its strong distinction between justice and beneficence in II.ii.1 (78–82). Beneficence, Smith argues, is meritorious, but it is "always free": it cannot and should not be enforced by law. The reason he gives for this is that the absence of beneficence "tends to do no real positive evil" (78). The person who lacks beneficence may incur moral criticism, but, nonetheless, "he does no positive hurt to any body. He only does not do that good which in propriety he ought to have done" (79). When the person's failure is a failure to pay back a specific benefactor, the failure approaches "nearest to what is called a perfect and complete obligation." Nonetheless, however, it does not fully qualify as a perfect obligation. To force such a person to perform what "gratitude" morally implies that he ought to perform "would, if possible, be still more improper than his neglecting to perform it" (79). Duties of beneficence to friends, relations, and strangers are even further from perfect obligation. Even when parents fail to support their children, and children their parents, nobody supposes that the law has any right to extort performance of a moral duty by force (81).

It is otherwise with justice. Duties of justice are fully enforceable, because a violation of justice involves "injury: it does real and positive hurt to sòme particular persons" (79). (Smith's examples, very Ciceronian, are assault, robbery, and murder.) The obligation to act according to justice is strict and may be enforced by law.

Smith now qualifies his distinction: for he recognizes that in fact the laws "of all civilized nations" do in fact "oblige parents to support their children, and children to maintain their parents, and impose upon men many other duties of beneficence" (81). Public officials are not in fact limited to punishing violations of justice; up to a point they "command mutual good offices." But Smith skates rapidly over this issue, simply saying that the lawgiver has a very delicate task here, and had better watch out that he does not push it to excess. "To neglect it [this task of enjoining material support] altogether exposes the commonwealth to many gross disorders and shocking enormities, and to push it too far is destructive of all liberty, security, and justice."

Apart from this brief and cryptic paragraph, Smith appears to buy the whole Ciceronian package, justifying it with reference to the by then conventional distinction between perfect and imperfect duties. But we have seen that this distinction is not very helpful in defending the distinction: for duties of beneficence may be seen as very strict and fully enforceable, without being seen as duties to a particular assignable individual—for example, in connection with a public system of taxation. And this point is too obvious to escape Smith. The qualifying paragraph begins with duties to assignable individuals that are legally enforced (parents and children); but it ends by alluding to a wide range of duties to prevent "gross disorders and shocking enormities." Presumably the lawgiver handles these in exactly the way that *WN* elaborates, through taxation of various types.

What is odd about this section is its half-baked character. Smith endorses a distinction, then introduces considerations that are fatal to what he has just said, then drops those considerations and goes back to the original distinction. Nor, in revising the work, does he see fit to develop the qualifying paragraph by reference to the insights of *WN*. One would suppose that the provision of free public education would be an instance of preventing "shocking enormities" through state action that would have to be supported by taxation. Such an example could easily have been given; but it is not. More generally, Smith's entire *WN* discussion of how the public sector raises money to support its operations is highly relevant here, as is his nuanced account of different types of taxation, some more morally appropriate than others.

The failure of the *TMS* passage is not merely, however, a failure to expand in light of new insights. For the new insights actually cut against any form of the distinction between justice and beneficence. Smith has insisted repeatedly that justice itself requires good treatment of laborers, whose productivity supports national prosperity; that it is a gross miscarriage of justice not to institute public education; that interference with the free movement of labor is a violation of "the most sacred and inviolable" property rights (WN 138); and so forth. In other words, the workers have a claim grounded in justice to a certain type of treatment, which is fully a claim of justice and even involves notions of property and violation that are at home in the discourse of justice; the remaining question can only be, who has the duties correlated with these just claims, and what, precisely, is the content of these duties? This, of course, is a massive and difficult question, which we still do not understand very well (see Chapter 7). But Smith has said quite a lot in WN that helps us to answer it. At the very least, we know that he believes states, and their citizens, have the following duties: to maintain a system of free public education; to adopt economic policies that allow the free movement of labor and free trade; to constrain monopolies; to raise money for support of the public sector through a reasonably equitable system of taxation that focuses on consumption and avoids taxing the necessities of life; to prevent manufacturers from unduly influencing the political process; to give complete political autonomy to such colonies as a nation has founded; to abolish the slave trade. The violation of any of these duties is a violation of basic justice. That means that the individual violator (say, a monopolist, a slave trader, a tax delinquent) can be penalized by law. It also means that where laws themselves are defective, political reform must intervene to make these violations punishable offenses.

Here is one place where the revision of TMS looks especially slipshod: for the qualifying paragraph shows that Smith already sees problems in his argument, problems that *WN* exposed fully. Far from dropping the Ciceronian distinction as unhelpful, however, Smith actually takes Cicero's unhelpful distinction even further than Cicero did. For he insists that justice is "but a negative virtue, and only hinders us from hurting our neighbor" (82). It enjoins no positive action. "We may often fulfil all the rules of justice by sitting still and doing nothing" (82).

Why does Smith reject the doctrine of "passive injustice," one of the most subtle and interesting features of Cicero's doctrine? Presumably it is because he understands that this Ciceronian doctrine (as I argued) actually blurs in a fatal way the boundary line between justice and beneficence by enjoining, in the name of justice, active projects of assistance and rescue that typically involve expenditure that would normally be construed as a type of beneficence. Moreover, the doctrine of passive injustice confuses the issue where perfect and imperfect duties are concerned. If I have a duty of justice to intervene to prevent other people from getting attacked or killed, then duties of justice begin to look very unlike "perfect duties" to assignable individuals, and far more like "imperfect" duties of beneficence where individuals may have some latitude to select the particular object of their efforts. But Smith appears determined to maintain the Ciceronian distinction of duties in a strong form; therefore he rejects the doctrine of passive injustice.

VI. Stoicism in *Theory of Moral Sentiments:* External Goods and Self-Command

These problems are serious, but one can imagine solving them in a way that incorporates Smith's best insights about social justice from *WN.*

A much thornier problem is created by Smith's appropriation of Stoic attitudes to external goods. In the early editions of *TMS*, he more or less consistently endorses the Stoic line that a virtuous person will not attach any importance to external goods, or consider their loss any serious loss. He will cultivate an attitude of virtuous self-command that rises above the blows of fortune. Smith uses the Stoic sage as a moral norm, and at several points alludes to the Stoic doctrine of *oikeiôsis* for his own account of the way in which each of us is properly qualified to care for himself.

It is well known that in the sixth edition of *TMS* Smith distances himself to some extent from this Stoic view. He criticizes the Stoic attitudes of detachment and *apatheia* (freedom from passion). For Charles Griswold, who offers a detailed and in some ways extremely helpful account of the shift, Stoicism now "supplies Smith with a case study of how natural moral sentiments become distorted when pressed philosophically."[29] For Rothschild, similarly, Stoic "apathy and indifference" is "odious to Smith, and especially so when it impinges on the 'private and domestic affections.' Richardson, Marivaux, and Riccoboni, he says, are here 'much better instructors than Zeno, Chrysippus, or Epictetus.'"[30]

All of this is true up to a point: Smith does distance himself in some ways from Stoicism and does criticize Stoic *apatheia* as a guide to the "domestic affections." But neither author spends enough time distinguishing what is criticized from what is retained. Such an effort pays off: for Smith's actual doctrine is far odder than the relaxed and sympathetic one they impute to him.

In the revised sections, Smith makes two criticisms of Stoicism. First, he makes the valuable point that the perspective of utter detachment, especially when we combine it with a Stoic doctrine of Providence, makes the urgency of moral distinctions impossible to grasp. By "endeavouring, not merely to moderate, but to eradicate all our private, partial, and selfish affections, by suffering us to feel for whatever can befall ourselves, our friends, our country, not even the sympathetic and reduced passions of the impartial spectator," Stoicism produces an indifference to "every thing which Nature has prescribed to us as the proper business and occupation of our lives" (293). Smith argues that the doctrine of extreme detachment is not only incompatible with the right sort of concern about virtue and vice in this world; it is also in many ways at odds with the aims of Stoicism, which are "to animate [people] to actions of the most heroic magnanimity and most extensive benevolence" (293). Nature, unlike Stoicism, "has not prescribed to us this sublime contemplation as the great business and occupation of our lives" (292). We should station ourselves within the network of our human concerns, including concerns for those near and dear to us. These criticisms are valuable: the Stoic sage is indeed likely to prove an oddly sluggish agent in a world of wrongdoing, both because he has removed local attachments in favor of complete impartiality (our "problem of watery motivation") and because he lacks the sort of attachment to external goods that is required to give justice and courage their point.[31] Stoicism, he argues, gives us a good way of correcting for what is unbalanced and partial in our passions, through the device of the spectator. But it carries detachment too far, in a way that is both wrongheaded and self-defeating. This is the critique I proposed in Chapter 3.

Smith makes a further criticism of *apatheia* in the crucial newly added chapter, "Of the Influence and Authority of Conscience" (*TMS*

III.iii). And it is here that closer attention to the text shows a tension in his own account. Stoicism, he argues, urges us to think of ourselves "not as something separated and detached, but as a citizen of the world, a member of the vast commonwealth of nature" (140). Thus we should regard our own immediate concerns as no more important than any other part of this large system. When a calamity befalls us, or our friends and relations, we should view it in the same way that we view a calamity befalling any other citizen of the world. (He cites a lengthy passage of Epictetus to make the point [141].)

Smith now introduces a crucial distinction, and it is this that commentators typically miss. There are, he says, two sorts of personal calamities that might prompt us to an excessive reaction. One sort affects us "only indirectly, by affecting, in the first place, some other persons who are particularly dear to us; such as our parents, our children, our brothers and sisters, our intimate friends" (142). (Note that spouses are absent, here as in Smith's own life.) The other sort affects us directly, either in body or in reputation. The distinction proves fundamental to Smith's critique of Stoicism. For the critique applies only to the first sort of calamity: "The man who should feel no more for the death or distress of his own father, or son, than for those of any other man's father or son, would appear neither a good son nor a good father. Such unnatural indifference, far from exciting our applause, would incur our highest disapprobation" (142). Smith elaborates this point at some length, stressing the importance of filial piety and other such "natural" sentiments in human life. Excessive sentiments in such cases are viewed indulgently; defective sentiments are "always peculiarly odious" (143). And it is here that Smith arrives at the conclusion to which Rothschild alludes, that the poets and novelists are better guides in such cases than Stoic philosophers:

The stoical apathy is, in such cases, never agreeable, and all the metaphysical sophisms by which it is supported can seldom serve any other purpose than to blow up the hard insensibility of a coxcomb to ten times its native impertinence. The poets and romance writers, who best point the refinements and delicacies of love and friendship, and of all other private and domestic affections, Racine and Voltaire; Richardson,[32] Maurivaux, and Riccoboni; are, in such cases, much better instructors than Zeno, Chrysippus, or Epictetus. (143)

In other words, Smith criticizes Stoic apathy only with regard to the first class of misfortunes, those that affect us by affecting our friends and relations. His concern is that the sentiments that bind families and friendships together are very valuable; Stoicism undercuts too much by undercutting this.

Smith now turns to the second class of misfortunes, making it immediately clear that his treatment of these will be different: "It is otherwise in the misfortunes which affect ourselves immediately and directly." Here, he argues, it is the excess that is odious, and defect of reaction is not odious. Indeed, "there are but very few cases in which we can approach too near to the stoical apathy and indifference" (143). Even that qualified utterance is dropped in what follows, as Smith strongly urges us to have contempt for people who are oppressed by their own personal calamities. A young child, he argues, may be pardoned if it is inconstant, for it has just entered "the great school of self-command." An adult of some firmness tries to distance himself from his misfortunes by thinking about how a spectator would view his situation, thinking of the admiration that all must feel for him "when he thus preserves his tranquillity" (146). Sometimes he gives way, however, "to all the weakness of excessive sorrow" (146). Finally, we arrive at the description of the person Smith wants each one of us to be:

> The man of real constancy and firmness, the wise and just man who has been thoroughly bred in the great school of self-command, in the bustle and business of the world, exposed, perhaps, to the violence and injustice of faction, and to the hardships and hazards of war, maintains this control of his passive feelings upon all occasions; and whether in solitude or in society, wears nearly the same countenance, and is affected very nearly in the same manner. In success and in disappointment, in prosperity and in adversity, before friends and before enemies, he has often been under the necessity of supporting this manhood. He has never dared to forget for one moment the judgment which the impartial spectator would pass upon his sentiments and conduct. He has never dared to suffer the man within the breast to be absent one moment from his attention. With the eyes of this great inmate he has always been accustomed to regard whatever relates to himself. This habit has become perfectly familiar to him. He has been in the constant practice, and, indeed, under the constant necessity, of modelling, or of endeavouring to model, not only his outward conduct and behaviour, but, as much as he can, even his inward sentiments and feelings, according to those of this awful and respectable judge. He does not merely affect the sentiments of the impartial spectator. He really adopts them. He almost identifies himself with, he almost becomes himself that impartial spectator,

and scarce even feels but as that great arbiter of his conduct directs him to feel. (146–147)

This passage needs to be read in its entirety, so that one can see that the detachment of the spectator is recommended as a norm for both feeling and conduct, for this person who has been supporting his "manhood" in all the tumult of life. Moreover, Smith hastens to assure us that the spectator's stance is one of pretty complete *apatheia*. He thoroughly approves himself, and "[m]isery and wretchedness can never enter the breast in which dwells complete self-satisfaction." The Stoics may exaggerate just a little when they say that the happiness of this man is equal to what it could be in completely different circumstances, but they are basically correct (147–148).

Thus Smith's account contains an asymmetry: Stoic apathy is "odious" when a friend or family member is hit by calamity, but it is basically the right attitude to take toward our own misfortunes. Smith's portrait of manly self-command strongly suggests that any other attitude would be unmanly weakness. Nor can we restore symmetry by saying that the asymmetry pertains to behavior only: Smith plainly wants the inner feelings and sentiments of people to be different in the two cases.

Smith's asymmetry thesis is hard to render coherent. For if calamities are bad when they affect others, why are they not really bad when they affect the self? If it is bad for a parent to be ill, why is it not bad to be ill oneself? If death is bad when it happens to a parent or child, why is it not bad when one faces it oneself? And conversely, if calamities should be borne with sublime indifference, why is the parent or child who suffers not an object of criticism or contempt for minding the suffering so much? How can we follow Richardson and weep at Clarissa's rape, and poverty, and death, without concluding that it is a very bad thing to be raped, to be poor, to die oneself? Indeed, the very allusion to literary spectatorship is problematic: Smith standardly uses literary spectatorship as a way of modeling the proper emotions of the judicious spectator;[33] thus it models one's own proper attitude to one's own calamities.

But internal consistency is not Smith's only problem. In the service of making his point about indifference to one's own misfortunes, Smith is led to repudiate some of the best insights of WN about poverty and misery and their effect on the mind. Poverty, he now holds, is nothing very serious:

> The mere want of fortune, mere poverty, excites little compassion. Its complaints are too apt to be the objects rather of contempt than of fellow-feeling. We despise a beggar; and, though his importunities may extort an alms from us, he is scarce ever the object of any serious commiseration. (144)

Smith now adds that the fall from riches to poverty does sometimes excite commiseration on the part of others—even though "in the present state of society, this misfortune can seldom happen without some misconduct, and some very considerable misconduct too, in the sufferer" (144). Despite this alleged fact, friends typically commiserate with this falling person; he himself, however, will be most admired if he accommodates himself "with the greatest ease" to the situation and carries on with firmness.

Several jolting points are made here: first, that a long-term state of poverty is contemptible. Second, that a fall into poverty is (in the present state of society) the fault of the impoverished person. Third, that the poor person should easily adjust to the new situation and view the change as basically insignificant. Smith now elaborates on the third point, arguing that in a very general way the Stoics were right in holding that "between one permanent situation and another, there was, with regards to real happiness, no essential difference: or that, if there were any difference, it was no more than just sufficient to render some of them the objects of simple choice or preference; but not of any earnest or anxious desire"—alluding here to the Stoic doctrine of the "preferred indifferents," worldly goods that a rational person will pursue if nothing impedes, but whose absence should not disturb us (149). Tranquility can be attained in any permanent situation. A man with a wooden leg gets used to it and "soon identifies himself with the ideal man within the breast" (148), realizing that it is no impediment to happiness. Imprisoned in the Bastille, the Count de Lauzun "recovered his tranquillity" (149). In general, "The great source of both the misery and disorders of human life, seems to arise from over-rating the difference between one permanent situation and another" (149): between poverty and riches, bad and good reputation. Anyone who thinks seriously will see "that, in all the ordinary situations of human life, a well-disposed mind may be equally calm, equally cheerful, and equally contented."

These claims are, to say the least, difficult to render consistent with *WN*, which holds that circumstances of life produce all the major differences that we see among men—between the porter and the philosopher, between the person who can't think about anything and the person who can contemplate everything, between the person who is mutilated and the person who is whole. Maybe once adults are already whole—once, that is, they have had a decent education—changes in their situation are less important for the inner life. But in this chapter

Smith is clearly thinking of situations that extend throughout the whole course of life, including a young person's response to misery as well as that of a mature person. So it is hard to avoid the conclusion that he has simply waved aside, or even rejected, for whatever reason, the insights into human formation that he achieved in *WN*.

I have focused on this chapter of *TMS* because it was added in the sixth edition, and thus represents, indubitably, Smith's latest reflections on Stoicism, reflections that postdate *WN*. These final reflections show that Smith has distanced himself from Stoicism only in one respect, and in a way that introduces inconsistency into his account. In other respects he stands squarely with the Stoics: differences in fortune are never properly the object of intense or eager concern. At most they have the status of preferred or dispreferred indifferents—where one's own personal calamities are at issue. Indeed, in another late passage (279–288) Smith goes one step further even than the Stoics, criticizing the Stoic doctrine of suicide as capitulation to weakness on the part of Stoic heroes. "It is only the consciousness of our own weakness, of our own incapacity to support the calamity with proper manhood and firmness, which can drive us to this resolution" (287). Contrast the "savage" of America, who can withstand the most terrible torments with equanimity. "He places his glory in supporting those torments with manhood, and in retorting those insults with tenfold contempt and derision" (288).

Not only did Smith thus add to the sixth edition passages that ally his position with that of the Stoics, where one's own personal calamities are concerned. He also let stand other passages that have exactly this point. Thus, in the discussion of utility in book IV, Smith claims that Providence has not abandoned the poor, even though it looks that way: "In what constitutes the real happiness of human life, they are in no respect inferior to those who would seem so much above them. In ease of body and peace of mind, all the different ranks of life are nearly upon a level, and the beggar, who suns himself by the side of the highway, possesses that security which kings are fighting for" (185). And in book I, after a preliminary and less developed sketch of the asymmetry thesis (we may indulge melancholy passions in the calamities of our friends, 48–49), Smith asserts very strongly that "it is quite otherwise with the person principally concerned" (49). He is "mean and despicable, who is sunk in sorrow and defection upon account of any calamity of his own . . . The weakness of sorrow never appears in any respect agreeable, except when it arises from what we feel for others more than from what we feel for ourselves" (49). A similar catalogue of examples follows, culminating with the shameful behavior of a French duke, the Duc de Biron, who actually wept on the scaffold (49–50). Thus not even the critique of Stoicism embodied in the sixth edition is really new with edition six: the asymmetry thesis is present already, if in a less developed form.

Similarly, in the following chapter, Smith insists that true tranquility can be attained in any station of life: ambitious concern with station is therefore all vain and inappropriate (50). Here Smith explicitly states that the life of the "meanest laborer" is no worse than any other:

What then is the cause of our aversion to his situation, and why should those who have been educated in the higher ranks of life, regard it as worse than death, to be reduced to live, even without labour, upon the same simple fare with him, to dwell under the same lowly roof, and to be clothed in the same humble attire? Do they imagine that their stomach is better, or their sleep sounder in a palace than in a cottage? The contrary has been so often observed, and, indeed is so very obvious, though it had never been observed, that there is nobody ignorant of it. (50)

Once again, these Stoicizing passages (highly reminiscent of Seneca's letters) contradict the subtle insights of *WN,* which knows well that nutrition and health are not equal among the social classes, that though the working classes have more children, far fewer are able to grow up to adulthood.

And as we have already begun to see, the tension between *TMS* and *WN* is not just a normative tension, with *TMS* asking us to disregard as unimportant what *WN* appears to regard as highly important, urgently in need of correction. There are empirical claims in *TMS* that are quite plainly at odds with the more careful empirical work of *WN:* the claim already mentioned that people cannot fall into poverty without considerable fault—which is belied by so many passages about the way monopolies, colonial masters, and other social forces work; the claim made in the passage just cited, that the digestion and sleep of the poor are as good as those of the rich—belied by *WN*'s discussions of nutrition and infant mortality; the claim, immediately before this passage, that the "wages of the meanest laborer can supply" all the "necessities of nature"—belied, again, by discussions of high infant mortality, as well as by the account of education; a claim that in the world as a whole there are twenty people who are happy for everyone who is miserable (140)—belied, it would seem, by so much in *WN* about the operation of colonial masters, slave traders, monopolists, the system of apprenticeship, the absence of public education, as well as by *WN*'s observation that for every one person who is rich there are five hundred who are poor (710); the claim that the rich actually consume about the same amount of resources as the poor, and thus "divide with the poor the produce of all their improvements"—belied by so much in WN about the way in which the rich skew the operations even of government in the direction of their own interests, preventing the poor from having the chance to raise children and to get an education, and, often, taxing the very "necessities" of life in a way that burdens the poor severely;[34] the claim that most misery comes from not knowing that you are well off—belied by WN's stinging indictments of apprenticeship, mercantilism, slavery, and colonialism; and, finally, a claim that "[p]overty may easily be avoided, and the contempt of it therefore almost ceases to be a virtue" (205)—belied, it would seem, by the entire argument of WN concerning the large and ungovernable forces of monopoly, capital, and colonialism that engender and perpetuate much of the worker's poverty. In addition to all these flat-out contradictions (or so they look to me), there is a profound difference of tone in the two works, with TMS speaking scornfully of poverty and even more scornfully of people who mind it, and WN having the keenest interest in and sympathy with the lives of the poor, and respecting their struggles. It is as if TMS was authored—even in the sixth edition—by Epictetus, and WN by someone far more "Italian" or even "feminine," that is to say, keenly interested in the interpenetration between the material conditions of life and salient human abilities.

One last complication in the TMS account must now be addressed: Smith's view of Providence. As we have seen, Smith urges the active agent not to assume the point of view of the universe when he asks what to do and what not to do: moral distinctions, and personal relationships, ought to be seen from within. But it seems to me quite

mistaken to conclude, as does Rothschild, that Smith no longer believes in a providential ordering of nature. References to a Stoic-type
Providence are ubiquitous in the text of *TMS*, and indeed determine its
whole approach to the moral sentiments. Again and again we are told
that "nature" has designed our sentiments in ways that work out well,
even without our conscious good intentions.[35] Nor is this mere
"order without design," as Rothschild would have it: there is clearly a
conception of a divinely ordered universe here, even if the deity in
question is more like Stoic Zeus than like the Christian God. Indeed,
when Rothschild entitles her final chapter "A Fatherless World," suggesting that it is in this world that Smith believes that we live, she
oddly distorts the passage from which she draws the phrase: for right
after asserting the existence of a "great, benevolent, and all-wise
Being," Smith writes, "To this universal benevolence . . . the very
suspicion of a fatherless world, must be the most melancholy of all
reflections" (235).

Thus what is surprising about the occurrence of the phrase "the
invisible hand" in *TMS* is that anything much has been made of it. It is
just a passage like so many others in the work, in which Smith asserts
that an arrangement produces good results without our conscious
participation. The rich contribute to general well-being because "[t]hey
are led by an invisible hand to make nearly the same distribution of
the necessaries of life, which would have been made, had the earth
been divided into equal portions" (184–185). Besides the fact we have
already remarked, namely that the statement is both false and inconsistent with *WN*, there is nothing remarkable about it. It would be
very odd indeed if we could read Providence utterly out of *TMS*, and
bizarre to read all its occurrences as "ironic," as Rothschild believes
the "invisible hand" passage is.[36]

What is true, however, and what no doubt motivates Rothschild's analysis, steeped as it is in *WN* more than *TMS*, is that the whole idea of Providence is much less in evidence in *WN*, and indeed, hardly in evidence at all. In that work, it does appear that Smith is concerned with "order without design," and does not commit himself to any divine plan in the scheme. Thus the one famous occurrence of the phrase "invisible hand"[37] in *WN* might well be regarded as a holdover from Smith's early work, and a vestige of Providence in a work that, as a whole, does not rely on that idea.

Here, then, we have another odd discrepancy, which at least helps to explain the other discrepancies. Given that Providence plays such a large role in the whole analysis of *TMS*, it would be more difficult, at least, for Smith to get upset at the way poverty works, or the way different people have different "permanent situations." He does allow that Nature has directed human beings to correct her own arrangement (168), but that expedient can be used only so often, lest the "order" of the whole look like disorder.

VII. Macho Stoicism and Human Dignity

What accounts for Smith's failure to carry the insights of one work into the other? To begin with, one must point simply to circumstances of composition. *TMS* began as lectures in Smith's courses in Glasgow. He did not give such lectures after 1763. Life in London and France, and then, as a customs official, in Edinburgh, was very different from the academic life, allowing little time for writing, for twenty-five years.

Smith turned to the project of revising *TMS* partly in the awareness of advancing age (he was sixty-five when the revisions got under way, and he died before the edition was released), and partly to head off the unauthorized Dublin edition of 1777, which called itself the "sixth edition" without his permission. Initially he did not plan a very comprehensive or time-consuming revision. Two letters of the period apologize for his tardiness in making the revisions, one saying that "the subject has grown upon me."[38] That way of putting things strongly suggests that he had initially thought the revision a smaller project than it turned out to be—but then he got engrossed in it and decided to do more. At first he went on doing his regular duties at the Customs House, but then he found that he had to take a leave of several months to complete the work. These pressures made comprehensive rethinking impossible.[39] He also complains of weak health.[40] This is a frequent complaint: Smith had a sickly childhood and probably also had many hypochondriacal and psychosomatic ailments.[41] So there is an argument for not taking the complaint at face value. Yet he did actually die a short time after.[42]

I think, however, that there is something more going on than haste and illness. Throughout his work, Smith's Stoicism is strongly colored by an ideal of proper, self-commanding behavior that is strongly gendered. Smith apparently had little close knowledge of women, apart from his mother and Janet Douglas, the unmarried relative who kept house for him and his mother in Edinburgh.[43] At any rate, there is no record of any intimate relationship with a woman in any walk of life, although Dugald Stewart does mention an early infatuation that did not end in marriage.[44] His deep intimacy with and admiration for his mother—an awe-inspiring, rather Stoic and heroic Scottish lady whom he outlived by only ten years, and with whom he lived for most of his adult life, precluded other intimacies, and seems to have led him to disparage other women.[45]

Smith's lack of attention to women is a conspicuous feature of his writings as well. His failure to devote any systematic discussion to women's work, including both the "productive" work of home-based workers (for example, the Highland spinners) and the contribution to the economy made by women's work in the home, is striking even for his time, and has been much criticized, then and now.[46] Nor do his very promising discussions of education contain anything useful about the education of women, a topic that had already generated a very lively contemporary debate, as is evident from Mary Wollstonecraft's *A Vindication of the Rights of Woman* (1792). For Smith, women's education is fine as it stands: their largely practical training fits them for what they actually do in the home, and contains "nothing useless, absurd, or fantastical" (*WN* 781).

In *TMS*, women again play a very small role, but one that has significance for Smith's larger project. On the one hand, seen as objects of male desire, they exemplify temptations that periodically beset men, causing them to lose their self-command, as in the famous discussion of male disgust following intercourse (28) and the equally odd discussion of love as comic and shameful (31–34).[47] Seen as moral subjects, they exemplify excesses of sentiment that are a ridiculous weakness and that would not be found in the man of self-command. Thus, in the revised parts of the sixth edition, even when Smith is in the midst of granting that a man of self-command may "for some time indulge himself in some degree of moderated sorrow" when a friend or child dies (oddly or not so oddly, he does not mention the death of a spouse), he immediately cautions against womanly excess, saying, "An affectionate, but weak woman, is often, upon such occasions, almost perfectly distracted" (*TMS* 151). Similarly, although Smith from time to time praises "humanity," the quality that consists in ready sympathy with others, when the chips are down he ranks this womanish quality below that of "generosity," which is a deliberate and self-commanding character-istic that disposes us to make real sacrifices for others. "Humanity is the virtue of a woman," he announces, "generosity that of a man . . . The most humane actions require no self-denial, no self-command, no great exertion of the sense of propriety." Generosity, by contrast, re-quires deliberation from the point of view of the spectator, and an "ef-fort of magnanimity."[48]

At this point, the picture turns sharply Stoic, as Smith, in order to illustrate the manly virtue of magnanimity and contrast it with femi-nine weakness, provides a catalogue of magnanimous agents who make heroic sacrifices of their own interests, in the process treating their own happiness, or reputation, or even life, as "a trifle":

> The man who gives up his pretensions to an office that was the great object of his ambition, because he imagines that the services of another are better entitled to it; the man who ex-poses his life to defend that of his friend, which he judges to be of more importance . . . The soldier who throws away his life in order to defend that of his officer, would perhaps be but little affected by the death of that officer, if it should happen without any fault of his own . . . But when he endeavours to act so as to deserve applause, and to make the impartial spec-tator enter into the principles of his conduct, he feels, that to every body but himself, his own life is a trifle compared with that of the officer, and that when he sacrifices one to the other, he acts quite properly and agreeably to what would be the natural apprehensions of every impartial bystander. (*TMS* 191)

In this passage the stance of the spectator, which of course is supposed to be a representation of moral conscience, is at the same time highly gendered, exemplifying a norm of the type of manly conduct that excites applause. The contrast with mere womanly "humanity" makes it impossible to miss the extent to which Smith's agents, in seeing themselves from the point of view of the spectator, are also holding themselves up to a macho mark. We may think it a little odd that a man who so deeply loved and honored the only two women he knew well would take such a view of the sex as a whole. But really it is not odd at all, for we can well imagine the very imposing Margaret Douglas (Mrs. Smith) saying just such disparaging things of women who did not have her fortitude.[49] Janet Douglas, too, evidently prided herself on a Stoic demeanor, both calm and mocking in the face of pain and misfortune.[50] Moreover, Smith's friends clearly understand Smith's Stoic demeanor in the face of his own death as exemplifying a male norm: "He wishes to be cheerful; but nature is omnipotent. His body is extremely emaciated . . . But, like a man, he is perfectly patient and resigned."[51]

Now obviously Smith's Stoic ideal is not the machismo of everyday male aggressiveness, which Smith elsewhere repudiates with appeal to the Stoics.[52] It is subtle Stoic machismo, the machismo of self-command and the contempt of adversity. We might even call it Scottish Stoicism. But it is precisely this tendency to treat losses as of no account that mars, I have argued, the portrayal of material conditions in TMS as a whole. The strong man can grieve moderately for others. In his own misfortunes, however, he must be a true Stoic, or he runs the risk of looking womanish and soft.

These same judgments surface in a fascinating way when Smith discusses the relationship between moral character and national circumstances. Immediately following the passage just discussed, Smith asserts that the circumstances that are most conducive to developing the "gentle virtue of humanity" are "by no means the same with those which are best fitted for forming the austere virtue of self-command" (153). Humanity is fostered by ease and security, including "the mild sunshine of undisturbed tranquillity, . . . the calm retirement of undissipated and philosophical leisure." These circumstances, however, do little to form self-command. "Under the boisterous and stormy sky of war and faction, of public tumult and confusion, the sturdy severity of self-command prospers the most, and can be the most successfully cultivated" (153). These situations, however, often produce a neglect of humanity. This whole passage, added in the last edition, may express Smith's sense, now that he has lived both lives, of the difference between academics and men of action. Whatever its source, what it says is deeply disturbing: that the most precious type of moral virtue may actually be incompatible with ease and happiness. Well-being is not only unnecessary for virtue (a claim that already would be much at odds with *WN*), but actually in tension with it. People may indeed become better, with regard to the sort of virtue that matters most (for manliness, but that means matters most in general) if they live in hardship, tumult, and confusion.

This idea is borne out in a fascinating chapter that survives from the first edition to the last, "Of the Influence of Custom and Fashion upon Moral Sentiments" (V.ii, 200–211). Smith begins with a repeat statement[53] of the thesis of book III: ease of life is good for humanity, but rude conditions are good for self-command. What emerges here is that Smith has deep ambivalence toward the type of refined, sensitive, and emotionally open behavior fashionable in France and Italy, and favored, so he argues, by the comfortable, easy, and "civilized" conditions of life in those countries. What begins as a mere description of differing norms soon veers into an implicit critique of the lack of manliness with which French and Italian males approach calamity:

> The emotion and vivacity with which the French and the Italians, the two most polished nations upon the continent, express themselves on occasions that are at all interesting, surprise at first those strangers who happen to be travelling among them, and who, having been educated among a people of duller sensibility, cannot enter into this passionate behaviour, of which they have never seen any example in their own country. A young French nobleman will weep in the presence of the whole court upon being refused a regiment. An Italian, says the abbot Dû Bos, expresses more emotion on being condemned in a fine of twenty shillings, than an Englishman on receiving the sentence of death. (207)

Even that fine Italian Cicero comes in for a drubbing, as the frank emotionality of his orations is pejoratively compared to the imagined "order, gravity, and good judgment" of the Scipios and the elder Cato (208). (And remember Duc de Biron, who disgraced himself by weeping on the scaffold.)

Nor does Smith hesitate to draw the conclusion his discussion in book III seems to entail: rude and difficult circumstances produce characters of heroic magnificence. In one of the most peculiar and revealing passages in this work, Smith devotes a lengthy excursus to praise of the courage and magnanimity of (male) Native American "savages" who learn to rise above distress because in such rude circumstances they cannot expect any sympathy or help from their fellows:

> A savage, therefore, whatever be the nature of his distress, expects no sympathy from those about him, and disdains, upon that account, to expose himself, by allowing the least weakness to escape him. His passions, how furious and violent soever, are never permitted to disturb the serenity of his countenance or the composure of his conduct and behaviour. The savages in North America, we are told, assume upon all occasions the greatest indifference, and would think themselves degraded if they should ever appear in any respect to be overcome, either by love, or grief, or resentment. Their magnanimity and self-command, in this respect, are almost beyond the conception of Europeans . . . The weakness of love, which is so much indulged in ages of humanity and politeness, is regarded among savages as the most unpardonable effeminacy. Even after the marriage, the two parties seem to be ashamed of a connexion which is founded upon so sordid a necessity. (205)

Much more follows, concerning the separate dwelling places of married couples, their evident shame at their sexual connection—all making "savages" look a lot better than the deluded and ridiculous lovers Smith mocks in his own discussions of sex and love.[54] Finally, Smith provides a detailed and lengthy description of the noble indifference of male "savages" to the most gruesome tortures, and their stoical songs and poems, which express cool contempt for death and for their enemies. (Thus, although Smith begins by supposing that the "savages" have intense emotions and just learn not to express them, it seems to be his considered position that they rise above the passions through the force of their self-command.)

Smith dwells at length on the details of the tortures, in which the "savage" is hung over a fire, and then "lacerated in all the most tender and sensible parts of his body for several hours together." Nonetheless, during a brief "respite" from this treatment, he proves able to carry on a lively conversation about many topics, "and seems indifferent about nothing but his own situation." He even sings a "song of death," insulting his tormentors (206).[55] Here Smith closely replicates Roman descriptions of the deaths of Stoic heroes (Seneca, Thrasea Paetus), though with sadomasochistic elements that are all his own. And as we recall, he returns to the example in a passage added for the sixth edition, when he condemns Stoic suicide by contrast to the "manhood" with which the "savage" supports his torments (288).

The reader who compares this passage to what Smith says elsewhere in his own voice about rising above pain and about the ridiculous comedy of love, can have no doubt that Smith's fantasy portrait of distant races expresses an ideal of his own. This is even clearer when we get to Smith's discussion of slavery, a justly famous passage:

> The same contempt of death and torture prevails among all other savage nations. There is not a negro from the coast of Africa who does not, in this respect, possess a degree of magnanimity which the soul of his sordid master is too often scarce capable of conceiving. Fortune never exerted more cruelly her empire over mankind, than when she subjected those nations of heroes to the refuse of the jails of Europe,

to wretches who possess the virtues neither of the countries which they come from, nor of those which they go to, and whose levity, brutality, and baseness, so justly expose them to the contempt of the vanquished.

This heroic and unconquerable firmness, which the custom and education of his country demand of every savage, is not required of those who are brought up to live in civilized societies. (206–207)

Quite apart from his moral condemnation of the slave trade, Smith is evidently fascinated and stirred by the heroism of African males under the most degrading circumstances. He sees in them something that too easily gets lost in comfortable conditions like those of France and Italy. He simply *admires* them more—not only more than their odious captors, but more than the fine French gentleman who will cry at being refused a regiment. It's obvious that Smith here runs together the idea of human nobility and self-respect (whatever is not "fawning" or "servile" the way dogs are, as in *WN* I) with the idea of Stoic indifference, and both with the idea of a true manliness, free from French "effeminacy." No wonder, then, that Smith never fully repudiates Stoic indifference as a correct response to one's own misfortunes. No wonder that he fails to endorse, in *TMS,* the great lesson of *WN,* that good social conditions are required for developed capacities and a life worthy of our human dignity.

We might simply stop here, and say that Smith sticks as close to the Stoics as he does because he is in the grip of a cultural and gendered picture of virtue, one that, in addition, appears to have, for him, a quasi-erotic fascination. All this seems true. But if we do stop at this point we suggest that Smith's conflation of the idea of human dignity with these macho-Stoical elements is a confusion easily set right once one has noticed how it works. We have already seen in Chapter 3, however, that this confusion is not so easily set right. The Cynic tendency to scoff at the "externals" has its roots in a deep idea of what it is to stand on one's own and claim respect. So if we think that it is right to be deeply upset about the absence of externals, both in the life of another and in one's own, we had better have something to say about what the ideal of human dignity actually looks like under this new construal.

Here we might recall the insights of Greek tragedy, which shows us clearly how someone *might* greet a disaster without servility and yet with recognition of its weight. A tragic hero, whether male or female, does not fawn or cringe. Nor does he or she inflict her suffering as a burden on others. He or she bears the blows of fortune with dignity. But at the same time he or she is fully cognizant of the importance of things like citizenship, political liberty, an intact city, the presence and health of loved ones, and one's own bodily integrity and health, for the flourishing human life. Such a hero (whether male or female) cries out in pain, both for others and for herself; but it is not a fawning pain, it is one that asserts, indeed, the great importance of human dignity, and makes a claim on behalf of that dignity, for conditions that honor it. Smith's portrait of the working poor, in *WN*, is in many respects a Greek tragedy. For the Scottish poor (who have some education) are portrayed as having dignity, mental capacity, and self-respect, and yet as having the most important thing of all, their labor power, taken from them by the unjust hand of law and capital.

To portray the lot of the working man as both tragic and unjust would be a fitting way of capturing, in *TMS*, the analysis of *WN*. It would also be fully compatible with Smith's observations about justice and the reactive attitudes in *TMS* (see section II of this chapter). Why, then, does Smith not incorporate such an insight into his account? Clearly, immersed in these reflections about self-command, he finds even the wailing of the tragic hero a kind of undignified effeminacy. He shares that reaction with his beloved Epictetus, who mocked the tragic hero, defining tragedy as "what happens when chance events befall fools." (Only fools care so much about the events of chance.) And he apparently feels that such a position is required if he is to give the Africans and the Native Americans their due. (There would, of course, be another way of characterizing them, which he initially favors: they have intense emotions, but just don't want to give their captors the pleasure of seeing their suffering.)

But there is a further dimension to this issue, which we see when we consider Smith's description of English working men who are described in Smith's arguments on behalf of public education. These men are not like tragic heroes, because they are inarticulate about their own situation. The monotony of their labor has dulled their minds, and "mutilated" their human ability to think about the world. They know little about their country and its affairs. They have no leisure for reflection or conversation. Ground down by repetitive movements and long hours, they do not even take cognizance of what has happened to them. So they cannot be expected to cry out in pain, or to call the universe to witness the injustice that has been done to them.

The tragic working man is already a success story, because one can see in him, and he can see in himself, the developed capacities that have been blunted in his fellow. The heroic slaves and "savages" depicted in *TMS* are bad guides in two ways to what the world's blows can do to people: first, because they apparently do not mind losses that really are serious and severe; but second, and more important, because they retain developed human capacities, abilities, and virtues that some of life's blows may actually deform or extinguish in others. Their (fictional) presence serves to romanticize loss, rather than taking its full measure.

De-Stoicizing the idea of human dignity requires not only giving it, so to speak, a French or Italian, or we might even say a feminine, flavor, permitting the dignified human being to weep at his losses and cry out in anger against injustice. It also requires finding the human dignity in the "mutilated" man, seeing a claim to equal treatment in the human potential itself, the *basic capabilities,* that the absence of public education and other suitable conditions of life is blighting or, even, has already irretrievably blighted. Human dignity has to be seen as not full achievement, in such a way that only those who display virtue and dignity actually have it, but as a lower-level capacity to develop a higher-level set of capabilities for fully human functioning. Human dignity is a basic potential that gave all workers, from the start, a claim to treatment on a basis of equality with others. English workers did not get that treatment, and this is the deepest tragedy that political life offers. They were "mutilated" not by any failure of their own will, but by a government neglectful of its duties and hostage to the "overgrown standing army" of manufacturers, whose "clamorous importunity" prevented the law from pursuing an "extensive view of the general good."

SIX

The Tradition and Today's World

Five Problems

I. The Cosmic City Today

Human beings are social beings. On this basis the tradition we have examined, from the Greek Stoics to Adam Smith, held that we are already citizens of a single world order. The fact that we are capable of interacting with one another through speech and reason, and that we are in a deep sense interdependent and interactive beings, means that we are moral fellow citizens, in the sense that any world citizen's harm can be grasped by any other, and can move another to appropriate action. Ignorance, distance, obtuseness, and various artificial distinctions separate us. But our human capacities are such as to make us members, in principle, of a global moral community. Any child might have been born in any nation and spoken any language. Events in other nations are comprehensible to us as human events, affecting members of our species. Our moral concern, our enthusiasm, and our compassion are frequently, if unevenly, aroused by events in other regions. Each child who is born, is, as Kant says, therefore not just a little worldly being, but also a little world citizen (*Weltbürger*).

But if this was so in Cicero's time, it is true in our time in a much more urgent sense. In our time, the peoples of the world have both communicative and causal links that are far tighter than any even Kant could have imagined. We can be in touch with people in India, Africa, and China at the press of a button. Networks such as the international women's movement may forge closer and more intimate links than many people have with their own relatives, and certainly their fellow citizens. Nor can we comfort ourselves with the thought that our actions have consequences only in a narrow sphere. The gasoline we use affects the common atmosphere; our decisions about childbirth affect global population; our domestic health policies influence the global spread of AIDS and other deadly diseases.

Moreover, national sovereignty around the world is increasingly being eroded by the growing global power of multinational private institutions—especially corporations and nongovernmental organizations—to which we contribute in countless ways through our daily choices as consumers. When I drink a Pepsi, I have an impact, however slight, on the living conditions of workers in Mumbai. When I buy a pair of running shoes, I support factories in other nations that are likely to use child labor. Countless choices I make as a consumer support dictators who get rich from rare natural resources and use their global advantage to tyrannize over their people.[1]

In this world of constant and complex, frequently hidden, causal interactions, there is no posture of moral safety. Even by boycotting all businesses that are involved in child labor abroad (a stratagem that has always seemed to me morally smug and ultimately quite unhelpful), I am having some kind of an impact on the lives of those children. Most often, given the diversity and complexity of corporations and their subdivisions, I will not even see the connections in which I am implicated, and thus I will not be able to steer clear of moral connection even were I to try. Even by taking up a rural life of self-sufficiency and domestic production of all necessities, I would really not be failing to interact with people in other parts of the world. (Had Gandhi's *khadi* movement had widespread success, it would have greatly influenced the Indian economy, and, through that, all of India's trading partners and foreign investors.)

Our connectedness becomes deeper when we consider migration: the floods of people seeking asylum from political disasters in Syria and Latin America, and from human rights violations in many parts of the world; the more chronic flights from poverty and crime in Latin America and Africa. As citizens we participate in the making of policies that affect these people's lives, welcoming them or turning them away. Grotius's radical idea of the earth as common property is not accepted today (even he did not articulate it with any precision), and migration is the source of some of our fiercest political struggles.

Since all this is true, we have far more immediate and compelling moral reasons than Cicero's readers had to endorse his moral starting point: we are fellow citizens, bound by a common set of moral concerns. For it seems that a sufficient condition of moral concern is causal impact: if what I do to B materially affects B, I must consider the morality of these actions. Thus the Ciceronian / Grotian tradition, radical and highly controversial in its own time, has now become the necessary starting point for all reflection about morality in an era of rapid globalization.

The tradition has left us with some deep insights about human dignity and equality, and about the connection between dignity and a policy of treating human beings as ends. Although by itself the term "cosmopolitanism" is now too vague to be useful,[2] designating any number of distinct positions, the philosophical texts I have examined here delineate a distinctive philosophical tradition with distinctive positions and arguments. This tradition has left us the very general idea that in our dealings with human beings anywhere we may not exploit them or use them as mere tools, and we must not even allow them to be so exploited or violated if it is in our power to help them. These vague ideas need to be much more fully specified; but the tradition does further specify them, and by now we have, as I've argued, a good set of alternatives, at any rate, in the area of aggression, torture, and other violations of humanity.

But, as I have also argued, the tradition has left us with some profound problems, both in the area of moral psychology and in the area of normative thought about material aid. In these two concluding essays, I shall comment on how we might face these problems, giving a sketch of what I shall call a *materialist global political liberalism* based on ideas of human capability and functioning.

So, let us assume that we are beginning where Grotius left us, and with Smith's new insights into the effects of material deprivation on human capabilities. What further work do we need to do?

II. Problem One: Moral Psychology

The Stoics had trouble motivating real human beings to care about global justice. At best they could conceive of local and familial attachments as delegations from a general duty of respect for humanity, chosen for efficiency reasons. And given their worries about the divisive impact of partiality, they often discouraged even this sort of local love. Cicero offers a better model, showing how concern for basic principles of respect for human dignity gets sustenance and depth from a variety of more particular attachments, which are also intrinsically valuable—particularly those to family, to friends, and to one's own republic. Those attachments can certainly give rise to tensions with one's pursuit of justice, as Cicero frequently notes in his treatise on friendship and elsewhere. But on balance it seems a risk worth running, since a pursuit of justice denuded of love is pallid and unable to sustain people. Justice is difficult, and to pursue it in a world that is in many respects hostile to our strivings requires sources of energy, attachment, and pleasure that the Stoics rejected. So we must bring them back in, not only urging people to cultivate particularistic attachments but also fashioning a politics that cultivates particularistic love.[3] These attachments help us pursue larger concerns, but they are also valuable in themselves, and a large source of the value of our lives.

There are better and worse ways of doing this, obviously. Here again, Cicero is a valuable guide. He understands that friendship can be fashioned in a way that gives rise to fewer collisions with justice—if one chooses friends who support and complement one's own pursuits, who don't engage in political corruption, and who, even if they disagree about many large things (as did he and Atticus), still disagree within a very general shared ethical framework. Personal loss also threatens to upset duties in the political sphere: if you love a person deeply, you risk deep grief, and Cicero's devastating grief at the death of his daughter Tullia did withdraw him from his urgent political concerns for some time. Asking Atticus to make his apologies, Cicero at the same time asserts that by grieving he is doing what he thinks he ought to do: some attachments simply require a pause in one's useful efforts.[4] And then, of course, he does return to Rome and once again takes up the cause of the republic.

Similarly, there are obviously better and worse ways of loving one's nation, ways that are more and less conducive to global justice. If one imagines the nation as itself striving toward justice and human rights, and built on a commitment to human dignity, this way of loving the country is easy to extend outward, albeit once again with conflict and tension.[5] The tradition recommends this moralized understanding of the nation and does not endorse me-first nationalism. If one sees the history of the United States as built upon a commitment to human equality—as does Abraham Lincoln in the Gettysburg Address (albeit with some historical implausibility)—then it is possible to see this experiment as fostering, as well, respect for human dignity all over the world. Leaders from Lincoln to Franklin Delano Roosevelt and Martin Luther King, Jr.—and Nehru, Gandhi, and Mandela outside the United States—have made this move, refashioning patriotic national loyalty into a loyalty to values that are also keys to a just global order. As with friends and country, so here: there are bound to be difficult tensions. But the balancing act is possible to execute with grace and respect—as would not be the case if one's conception of one's nation were ethnocentric, or based purely upon greed.

Thus far, the cosmopolitan tradition is flawed, but capable of self-correction; and one of its leading exemplars, Cicero, already points the way to a more adequate moral psychology. There remains, however, a psychological problem I have not yet mentioned. To build societies that aspire realistically to global justice and universal respect, we need a realistic understanding of human weaknesses and limits, of the forces in human life that make justice so difficult to achieve. We need, then, accounts of fear, disgust, anger, and envy. We need accounts of group clannishness and group subordination, of misogyny and racism and the manifold other forms of stigma and prejudice. And we need to understand, if we can, how these baneful forces develop, studying the contributions of human evolutionary equipment, of child development, and of culture—all interacting in complicated ways.

This task was not taken on by the Stoics, whose account of bad behavior was unfortunately crude, tracing it all to a selfish partiality that we may overcome by rational work on ourselves. One reason why they could not attain deeper insights is that they lacked altogether a sense of the personality as developing through infancy and childhood, perhaps because they really never studied infants or children, given that males spent virtually no time with their offspring until a much later age. The entirety of Greco-Roman culture lacked the idea that one's individual history in early childhood is a crucial part of what we must understand and confront if we are to live well. Eighteenth-century thinkers such as Rousseau and Kant do have more to say, and Kant at least advances a doctrine of "radical evil"—evil that is endemic to our natures prior to culture. But he understands that evil thinly, as a propensity to rivalrous competition. He never asks where this competition comes from or what it is about.

We need, then, to undertake a project that the Stoics not only ignored, but also would likely have repudiated: the systematic study of infant attachments, as they unfold in constant interaction with cultural norms and perceptions. A kind of anthropological psychoanalysis, if you will. If we don't do this, our high-minded proposals will very likely prove fruitless, inasmuch as they will not be addressed to real people as they are.

This is not the place to advance a proposal in this area. It's what I've been doing throughout my career, in work on disgust, anger, envy, and fear; my views are not easily summarized, since I have changed them over the years, sometimes in important respects.[6] So let us leave a blank at this place, to be filled in elsewhere. It requires, in effect, a large research program in which many nations and traditions should participate, describing the roots of prejudice, stigma, and hate in many times and places and using these insights to form useful policies.[7]

III. Problem Two: Pluralism and Political Liberalism

Like earlier Greco-Roman philosophical traditions, the Ciceronian-Stoic tradition is a skeptical critic of dominant forms of received religious belief and practice. The pre-Socratic philosophers challenged traditional religious accounts of natural phenomena, which invoked the activity of gods in our world, by producing naturalistic causal accounts of how things happen. Socrates was charged with subverting the gods of the city and inventing new gods. Aristotle's god was an abstraction, totally different from the gods that most people worshipped. The Stoics were just as anti-conventional. They viewed god as internal to the natural world, a moral and rational principle immanent in nature and animating the lives of human beings (the view for which Spinoza was later denounced as a heretic by his fellow Jews). Cicero, more anti-conventional still, was a skeptic in matters of epistemology and religion.

Similarly, later followers of these Roman traditions were unorthodox in their beliefs. Grotius, personally a pious man (though in exile for following the Arminian heresy), shocked his culture by portraying his arguments as, in principle, utterly independent of religious backing. Smith, a leading figure of the Scottish Enlightenment, was not an outright atheist like Hume, but he has basically no interest in conventional religion. His view of Providence is Stoic; he is basically a Deist, like many people of his time. Kant was a religious rationalist, holding that we ought to pursue religion "only within the limits of reason." Most of the tradition, then, believed that people should follow religious rationalism, although they typically showed concern for freedom of belief, speech, and practice. Apart from Grotius, they defined their political approach in terms of the rejection of what they termed superstition and idolatry. And, with the exception of Grotius, they advanced their normative views as a fully comprehensive doctrine covering all of human life, not as a partial doctrine endorsed only for political purposes. Cosmopolitan ethics thus replaces traditional religion rather than coexisting with the many religions of the world.

Today philosophers should not think this way. We observe that under conditions of freedom, and indeed wherever there is not brutal repression, people in every part of the world turn to religions for insight, community, meaning, and guidance. Many people reject conventional religion, but many reasonable people do not. Moreover, among the people who consider themselves religious in some regard, there is not much agreement about what that commitment entails.

Some religions are rationalist in the manner of our Stoics and neo-Stoics. Among those I count my own religion, Reform Judaism, which was inspired by the rationalist ideals of Immanuel Kant and Moses Mendelssohn, according to which the core of religion is the moral law.

Those religions have an easy time reconciling their religious commitments with those of secular philosophy. The same is at least in principle true of nontheistic religions such as Buddhism and Taoism. Among the Christian faiths, Roman Catholicism has a profound rationalist aspect, and typically values secular moral philosophy very highly. For example, all the major Catholic universities require extensive preparation in philosophy for all undergraduate students, separate from any requirements they may impose in theology. Still, Catholics also insist that secular philosophy is not a complete guide to life, and would deeply resent any suggestion that religion be subordinated or marginalized. And some religions are made still more deeply uneasy by philosophy's claim to understand the world by reason. Among those I would count most forms of Christian Protestantism, particularly the evangelical forms so common in the United States.

Respecting one's fellow citizens means respecting their choice to live their lives in their own way, by their own doctrines, so long as they do not invade the basic rights of others. This idea of respect, which John Rawls has called the idea of "political liberalism," requires a lot from political institutions.[8] First, it requires extensive protections for freedom of religious belief and practice, wherever that freedom does not violate the rights of others. Saying what those limits are is a very difficult matter; the United States is currently embroiled in struggles over what people may do in the name of religion to express their disapproval of gay, lesbian, or transgender people. Often that disapproval expresses itself in ways that many, including I myself, take to violate those people's fundamental rights. But these disputes are far from settled.

Second, equal respect requires a vigilant opposition to any form of established church—which, even if it does not invade the liberty of non-adherents, does always send signals of hierarchy and exclusion to outsiders. And third, it also requires, in connection with that idea of non-establishment, that basic political principles must be formulated in a neutral language, neither that of any particular religion, nor even taking sides in the larger dispute between religion and non-religion. Principles must be abstemious, expressed in a thin sort of ethical language, not using metaphysical concepts that belong to one tradition rather than another. Otherwise, even if freedom is respected, we get what I have called "expressive subordination," where society announces that one doctrine is preferred and others dispreferred. And in order to respect religious liberty sufficiently, principles must also be narrow, not pronouncing on all matters on which citizens differ.

Political philosophers, then, should operate in that restricted space. They ought to argue for principles that could ultimately prove acceptable to all citizens in a pluralistic society, in what Rawls calls an "overlapping consensus," without requiring them to abandon their religious commitments or to convert to some dominant religion in order to accept the principles. The principles that philosophers propose should not denigrate or marginalize any on grounds of their religion. This will require a practice of political philosophy very different from that of Seneca and Cicero, and more like that of Grotius, who proposes arguments that can be endorsed independently of religious commitment, but makes clear, at the same time, his own adherence to a particular creed. Following that model, philosophers should not propose a fully comprehensive doctrine: they should seek principles that can ultimately be embraced by all citizens who endorse some basic values of equal respect and are willing to respect the good-faith views of others. Basic political principles must be advanced not as a fully comprehensive doctrine, but as what Rawls calls a "module," a partial doctrine that can then be attached to a person's fully comprehensive doctrine as a part of it, whatever it is.

How could such a meeting ground possibly be found? The Stoic tradition already suggested an answer that has proven compelling to the contemporary human rights movement: ethical ideas of human dignity, human equality, and rights—and, I would add (as does Adam Smith), human capabilities. As the framers of the Universal Declaration discovered, these ideas can unite people otherwise different in religion and worldview. Some will interpret the idea of human dignity in connection with a religious doctrine; some will not. But the ethical idea itself all can accept. And religions must agree to accept the constraints of that political idea of equal human dignity.[9]

But why should religious people accept an idea that does not have religion in it? Doesn't this express a skepticism about religion, or willingness to give it a minor role? Not at all. As Catholic thinker Jacques Maritain, one of the framers of the Universal Declaration, wrote, the reason for not including your own religious ideas in a political doctrine that involves other people who don't share your religion is not skepticism or frivolity, it is respect.[10] Respecting other people means respecting their equal freedom to choose a doctrine by which to live, and they will not be fully free if the political core doctrines announce that a particular religion is the preferred basis for the political ideas.

Rawls made his argument for political liberalism within the Western tradition, noting its distinctive features. I have argued that the same considerations that support political liberalism for Western societies also support it for other world societies, both internally, and in the construction of the international society of which Grotius spoke.[11]

For these reasons, as Chapter 7 will further explain, my capabilities list is not a comprehensive account of the worthwhile human life, but, rather, a narrow and non-metaphysical list for political purposes that can ground political entitlements in a pluralistic society. Since cosmopolitanism is usually defined as a comprehensive ethical doctrine, political liberalism means rejecting cosmopolitanism (so conceived) as the basis for our political principles.

IV. Problem Three: Limits of International Human Rights Law

Our next two problems are framed by the normative and practical importance of the nation. Nations, I have argued, should be respected as vehicles for human autonomy and the accountability of law to people. They also have an obvious practical importance, as loci for channeling aid and support. If one disagreed with my normative claim one might try to change this, fashioning international institutions with real teeth. Nations today can be very large: India and the United States are both huge federated nations. But it's a matter of institutional structure, not population size: there is accountability to the people, and people make their own laws.

Some versions of the Stoic tradition are committed to a strong role for international law, especially human rights law. Mine, following Grotius and emphasizing the importance of national sovereignty, is not as deeply committed to this role for law as many other "cosmopolitan" positions are, because it accepts the Grotian normative claim. The picture of international society I have mapped out, following Grotius, holds that the international realm is always moral but not by any means always legal. International law has some useful roles to play, and might be further developed. But one should always beware of leaching away national sovereignty, particularly in favor of an international realm that is not decently accountable to people in each nation through their own political choices and self-given laws.

Many early internationalists were starry-eyed about international law, attributing to it both more efficacy than it appears able to achieve and a bigger normative role than seems compatible with national sovereignty and human autonomy. In recent years, a controversy has emerged over both the practical possibilities of international law and its normative appropriateness.[12] Looking at the operations of the United Nations and assessing the contributions of a variety of international agreements, legal thinker Eric A. Posner has come to a negative conclusion about the practical: nothing much has been achieved. Posner's normative conclusion is more complex: obviously enough there are things that international law might have done that would have been useful, particularly where tyrannical regimes do not meet basic standards of legitimacy. But on the whole, interventions into the affairs of sovereign nations are not well advised.

This controversy cannot be rehearsed in full here, but it is important for the cosmopolitan tradition to confront it. I do not think that Posner's skepticism threatens the core of the tradition, for the simple reason that the cosmic city is not a state or a legal order, but a moral realm, albeit one that should at times use law to effect its ends. International agencies and international documents are in essence normative statements that attempt to persuade the world. As such they may have great value, even if they are not enforced or enforceable as law: they testify to an emerging consensus, and can then be used by protesters in each nation to bring pressure to bear on their governments. This mode of influence is normatively preferable in any case, as more respectful of citizens' autonomy.

A concrete example will illustrate this valuable contribution, while supporting Posner's basic position about law.[13] Women's human rights were long unrecognized by most of the nations of the world—meaning both that the world did not recognize for women the same rights that it did for men (for instance, voting rights, employment rights), and also that concerns urgent for women (sexual violence, domestic abuse, contraception) did not make it onto the world's agenda at all. Today there is great progress around the world on the first issue—even Saudi Arabia gave women the vote in 2015—and at least some progress on the second, with much greater global awareness than at any time in human history of the toll taken by sexual violence, domestic battery, sexual harassment in the workplace, lack of respect for home-based work as work, and lack of control over fertility and childbirth. These issues are now on the world's agenda. Even if there is still a lot of bad behavior, it is already important that it has been named as bad.[14]

How much of this progress is attributable to international agreements such as CEDAW (Convention on the Elimination of All Forms of Discrimination against Women)? I argue that this question is not quite the right question to ask. Basically, international agreements are important parts of international movements, and the moral work that is done in international society is often enormously important, bringing people together around a common set of demands and complaints, and giving them opportunities to meet, exchange ideas, and reinforce one another. The international women's movement (like the disability rights movement, to cite but one additional example) has for years now brought together women from many different countries. Prior to international mobilizing, women were pretty isolated, and had no world fora in which to develop ideas and strategies. The various women's congresses have built a valuable type of solidarity and ferment, and this energy has surely contributed greatly to the progress of women in most nations of the world.

But what about documents? Meetings usually need some conclusion, some piece of writing that expresses what has been agreed. In this case the feminist revolution needed to coalesce around a list of normative claims. Without that, people would not go to the next meeting. They would think that wheels were spinning. Documents propel things forward, give a sense of a progressing common cause. Once that cause produced CEDAW, and that agreement was taken back to the nations of the world and ratified by most of them,[15] the very fact of ratification gave new impetus to domestic political efforts.

CEDAW accomplished little directly. It is also a deeply flawed document, skirting around some of the most important issues, such as access to artificial contraception and counting women's work as work in national income accounts. It has also not altered the relentlessly male-centered perspective of other human-rights documents. As Eleanor Roosevelt warned from the beginning, giving women a separate lobby and a separate document is a double-edged sword, possibly sidelining women's energies, which might have been used to fight in the more inclusive forum. In this case, however, there is no doubt that, despite the efforts of many, the United Nations has always been and remains a profoundly patriarchal institution, hostile to women's equality. Fighting in the more inclusive forum would have been frustrating and probably doomed, whereas the mobilization of women worldwide to create a text that stands before all the world, affirming women's equality, has proved politically and strategically valuable, no matter what the defects of the document and the yet greater defects of its implementation, which basically amounts to a handful of domestic court cases in countries with woman-friendly judiciaries (India and Botswana) in which the fact that the nation ratified the treaty has been used to effect legal change.[16]

In short, in this case and in many others, international documents are not legally enforced and do not amount to a world constitution. That is actually good, according to the Grotian picture I have been developing. It is more appropriate that these documents remain sources of persuasive norms, to be enforced through domestic policies, including constitution-making, legislation, and judicial interpretation—occasionally citing the document itself, but more often influenced by the arguments and the persuasive climate of the international community that led to and received additional impetus from the document. International society remains primarily a moral realm of persuasion, and only becomes a truly political realm occasionally. This does not mean, however, that the process of creating and ratifying documents is useless: it creates solidarity and a sense of common goals, enabling powerful transnational movements to arise and to influence national policies.

V. Problem Four: The Inefficacy and Moral Difficulty of Foreign Aid

Duties of material aid have preoccupied us throughout this analysis, and it might be expected that in applying the insights of the tradition to today's world, I would propose some definite guidelines for their implementation across national borders. In *Frontiers of Justice,* indeed, I tentatively did so, stating that richer nations have a stringent moral duty to give at least 2 percent of GDP to help poorer nations attain a higher living standard. I envisaged the aid as flowing primarily from government to government, and occasionally from governments to NGOs that express the will of the nation's people in an inclusive manner.

Foreign aid seems morally imperative, and yet it is not clear that it does any good. Aid may be divided into two types: official nation-budgeted foreign aid, and aid flowing from individuals through non-governmental organizations (NGOs) or foundations that operate across national lines (or a network of such NGOs). The latter type of aid has been urgently recommended by Peter Singer and other theorists of global justice.[17] It has numerous pitfalls. First, there are collective action problems: each individual has no idea how to maximize effective giving, and the international world of charities is a patchwork that gives little insight as to how one might wisely invest. This problem could potentially be addressed by concentrating giving in the hands of a small number of large charities, and Singer has done his best to steer people in that direction. But even if the large ones are managed as well and efficiently as possible (and assuming that we can trust Singer to monitor this as well as he can, and to steer people in the right direction), such a concentration simply magnifies the second problem, the democracy problem. To the extent that any NGO becomes a powerful policy-maker across the world, the sovereignty of nations is undermined— just as surely as it is undermined by multinational corporations. Large charities typically have beneficent goals, unlike the profit-oriented multinationals. But benevolent paternalism is itself morally problematic: the people of the world have not elected the NGO, or indeed the foundation, and they might quite like to determine their own future.

Moreover, there is much evidence that benevolent paternalism doesn't work, simply because it is paternalistic and far above the ground. Economist William Easterly speaks of the "forgotten rights of the poor," and of a "tyranny of experts" that fails to improve people's lives, in large part because the agents of change are not residents of the country and think, casually and wrongly, that they know all about it.[18]

A further problem about individual aid channeled through NGOs is that NGOs often have a sectarian political or religious agenda that may not be apparent to the well-intentioned donor. Many charities are explicitly linked to a church or churches, and while much of the work these groups do is meritorious, it may also have an exclusionary element, or involve religious tests for receipt of aid. In the worst cases, they may even fund violence against other religions or groups, as is strongly suspected concerning some Hindu charities with ties to the RSS (Rashtriya Swayamsevak Sangh, the leading social organization of the Hindu Right).[19] In this case the difficulty of tracing the money is so great that the American umbrella charity that disperses such funds has retained its 501c3 tax-exempt designation despite lots of attempts to produce evidence to show the illicit purposes it serves over in India. If scholars and activists who spend their entire careers on such tracking can't deliver the goods, it is unreasonable to expect every well-intentioned donor to get enough correct factual information to make an informed decision.

What about country-to-country aid, or aid that is reasonably responsive to priorities that people themselves have established? Here we avoid the democracy problem. But we arrive at a different problem, which makes me skeptical, now, concerning the solution that I advocated in *Frontiers of Justice:* the mounting evidence that foreign aid not only does little or no good, but can often be detrimental. The primary person arguing for this position, and very powerfully, is distinguished health economist Angus Deaton, winner of the Nobel Prize in economics for 2015.[20] Here's how Deaton's argument goes. Aid given to an autocratic government is highly likely to be abused, spent on the whims of the autocrat rather than on the intended improvements in people's lives. Corrupt governments even in democracies create the same problem. But suppose aid reaches its intended recipients: what happens as a result? Deaton argues that the availability of external funds to support, say, health-related services actually weakens the political will of a people to create durable and adequate health institutions through their own efforts, and to elect governments that will make health and other key needs a strong priority. As Deaton then shows with a mountain of empirical evidence, drawn especially from the different Indian states, a stable health infrastructure is the single most important determinant of health outcomes. It is because the people of Tamil Nadu and Kerala have long supported political parties that prioritize health infrastructure that they have been able to achieve outstanding health outcomes. Money channeled from outside would not help things, and it would actually be likely to hurt them.

Deaton's evidence comes primarily from health; he does not even attempt to show that the same thing holds for education, or other important material needs. He also makes an exception: aid targeted at a particular disease, he grants, may possibly be useful.

More generally, although there continues to be great controversy about what makes nations develop well, there is increasing evidence that a, or even the, key role is played by institutions.[21] I have insisted on channeling aid through democratic institutions because of my normative position about accountability and sovereignty. But even those who do not share that normative position need to attend to institutions, simply because they work. I am now persuaded that any use of foreign aid must be keenly responsive to empirical information of the type that Acemoglu and Robinson, and Deaton, offer. We need to learn a lot more: for example, would aid given to education (whether to existing institutions or toward the establishment of new institutions) work better than aid given to health projects? What about aid given to legal services for the poor, whether directed toward government programs or toward democratically responsive NGOs? We need to learn a great deal more about the conditions under which aid from abroad may possibly be productive. What we may no longer do, however, is to fantasize that our duties can be satisfied through aid from a distance in a way that really and stably makes things better without structural and institutional change.

Even the one instance that Deaton singles out as a possible exception—aid targeted at a particular disease—contains a hidden problem: approaching a complex social web one problem at a time is usually a recipe for failure. In his excellent book *The Logic of Failure*, psychologist Dieter Dörner shows that our minds have tendencies, suited no doubt to a simpler earlier time, that lead, unchecked, to disastrous mess-ups when our minds confront complex modern social systems.[22] For our purposes the central such tendency is a tendency to approach social problems one element at a time, failing to look sufficiently at the system as a whole. Using computer simulations, he invites experimental subjects to make a hypothetical developing country better. Typically people begin by identifying one salient evil, say malaria, and eradicating that. But as they do so, they have not thought at all about population growth or agricultural capacity—so their well-intentioned choice produces unanticipated problems, and these problems continue to proliferate as the subjects tackle them one by one, rather than in a coordinated and systemic way.

Dörner's analysis has obvious pertinence to the one development issue for which Deaton thinks foreign aid may possibly help: if people target aid at one illness, but haven't thought about the whole situation, will this aid after all not be likely to produce failure—not for the reasons that Deaton has in mind, but for quite different reasons? Once again there is a connection to my critique of benevolent paternalism: for people who live in a place are typically not focused on one issue only. Through daily experience they see the whole picture (and that, indeed, is one of Dörner's main points). Benevolent paternalists are much more like the subjects in Dörner's experiment: they think that they are doing a great good when they focus on just one thing. Once again, the conclusion seems to be that democratic institutions, which inevitably have the whole picture in view, or at least are constantly barraged by information concerning a wide range of interlocking issues, are indispensable to a wise and lasting solution.

Where does this leave the tradition? Believing that we have moral duties, but also that actually acting on those duties may well be counterproductive, is not a comfortable place to be for morally sensitive people. As Deaton says, giving gives a warm glow to the giver, but that happiness is surely not the main thing one ought to consider. One should respect the agency of poor people themselves, rather than delighting in a beneficence that may be both unwelcome and ineffective. Says Deaton, "It is an illusion that lives can be bought like cars." Deaton's advice to students who come to Princeton to work with him from many nations is simple: go back and get involved in the political processes of your own nation.[23] For those of us in affluent societies, we can remember that our own nation contains huge inequalities, and carrying on the fight against those through the democratic political process is one very good use of our energy and resources.

What about aid that puts cash directly into people's hands, or some valuable resource like mosquito netting? Such proposals still face collective action problems, and even should they prove effective in improving a group of individual lives in the present, there is reason to think, following Deaton's analysis, that they will not give long-term *capability security,* and may undermine the political will to create the institutions on which such security depends.

Do these new findings vindicate the tradition's bifurcation of duties and its relative obtuseness concerning duties of material aid? Not in the least. They didn't know this evidence or have the reasons I have advanced. Apparently they just underrated the importance of material aid for human lives. The most one can say is that they reached a defensible conclusion (that we may be morally justified in confining aid to our own republic) by a wrong route.

There is still a huge amount we can do to promote global material justice. We should continue to search for projects abroad that do not have the problems Deaton convincingly demonstrates for health. And we should also remember that many good actions are available that don't have the downside that Deaton demonstrates. For example, one may write reports, books, and articles, or participate in an intellectual / political movement, that people in many nations can use in their own way, in the context of their own political struggles. Just as Alexander Hamilton used Pufendorf and Grotius, so we may create theoretical paradigms that people can use elsewhere—which is what members of the Human Development and Capability Association (who belong to over eighty nations) attempt to do with the different varieties of the Capabilities Approach. We may share technological advances and pool knowledge in many other ways. As I already noted, the international women's movement, similarly, has made progress possible largely through domestic channels, but in a way that centrally involves the work and consultation of thousands of women who participate in it, craft its mandates, and leave them out there for people to use.

Furthermore, there are insights in the tradition that do not wilt under Deaton's analysis. Smith's critique of colonial domination, as devastating for both the economy and the politics of the dominated nation, remains as true now as it was then, and Smith rightly puts the accent on institutions as central sources of well-being, showing how wrecking self-government wrecks human lives. Grotius's eloquent exploration of the theme of common ownership of the earth has much to offer us as we think about climate change and other environmental issues, which need transnational political solutions and do not depend on simply trying to spread some cash around in a well-meaning fashion. And of course his observations about our common ownership of water and air have by now been incorporated into international laws and treaties, and these agreements are legally enforced. (It is sobering to recall that until relatively recently individual property rights in the air above one's land were thought to exist; we have moved rapidly, and wisely, in a Grotian direction.)

VI. Problem Five: Asylum and Migration

No problems today are more acute, or more politically inflammatory, all over the world, than problems of asylum and migration. They involve human dignity at the most basic level. Asylum, as usually understood, involves threats against safety and bodily integrity as a result of political (or religious or ethnic, or at times gender-related) persecution. But migration may involve human dignity just as urgently, since migrants are often in flight from war, crime, or devastation, and, even when they are not, they are often desperately in want of basic necessities of life.

Grotius understood that the idea of respect for humanity, combined with the basic idea that the world is in some sense the common home of all of us, entailed the most serious attention to these questions, even within a nation-centered framework. His own suggestions were bold in his own time, and they remain important for ours. The basic insight is that respect for humanity requires us to furnish the basic where-withal of human life, somehow, to those in desperate need. If that can be done through aid to another country, this aid must be given. But if people are forced by need or persecution to leave their original country, they have at the very least a right of temporary sojourn in another land. They also have rights to contract a marriage, thus potentially pro-longing their stay. And no ethnic group may be singled out for special positive or negative treatment during this process. Moreover, if rich nations have a surplus and others are suffering, that surplus does not actually belong to them, Grotius holds, but is the rightful property of those who need it.

This is a good beginning on some of the problems posed by migra-tion in the modern world, but it fails to make a number of key distinc-tions: between formal or legal migrants and undocumented migrants; between permanent residency and citizenship, and between both of these and temporary guest-worker status; and, finally, between political asylum and economic migration. By now, all these distinctions are the subjects of an impressive and diverse philosophical literature.[24] To intervene in this literature in a determinate and creative way is beyond the scope of this chapter. What I can do at this point is to map out where the tradition leaves us, and gesture toward what remains to be done.

First of all, given the tradition's strong defense of the nation as a moral home for people's autonomy, nations have the right to defend both their security and their national political culture. This does not mean a right to adopt phobic policies of exclusion that are not justified by empirical evidence or to defend dominant national ethnic or religious traditions from the pluralism and challenge that immigration typically brings. The political culture, as I discussed earlier in this chapter, should be formulated as a set of principles that do not give the nod to any preferred religion or ethnicity. What this means is (a) that it is reasonable to limit the number of immigrants admitted, and (b) that it is reasonable to ask of any who apply for permanent legal status that they express the willingness to live under the rule of law and in accordance with the nation's basic constitutional principles. Beyond this, it is probably also reasonable to limit numbers in accordance with skills and job opportunities, since economic stability is a very important ingredient of national stability.

What it does not mean: (a) it is not reasonable to hold the number of immigrants too low in order to preserve national homogeneity, when the world is full of needy people who could make valuable contributions to national culture and stability, particularly in times of falling population in many wealthy states. Nor is it admissible (b) to refuse entry or to deport people for reasons of ethnicity or religion. In the current panic over Islamic terrorism, this basic truth of liberal democracy (certainly honored more in the breach than in the observance) is at risk. Legitimate evidence about a particular individual is one thing; blanket exclusions of groups based on religion is quite another, as Grotius already insisted. Nor should deportation on grounds of a criminal conviction be applied in a draconian manner, for example, deporting people for drug possession offenses that by now we know to be non-offenses and no threat to public safety, or deporting for a minor offense decades later, after the person has long led a blameless life. Deportation of legal immigrants should be extremely rare, and only for serious crimes.

Beyond this, Grotius explicitly mentions marriage as a legitimate mode of immigration, and this sensible idea is followed by most nations.

So far we have not touched on three particularly divisive issues: illegal migration; asylum; and the morality of guest-worker programs. It is reasonable for nations to limit migration, as I've said, and that means keeping many people out and deporting many people who get in illegally. Yet it is quite another matter when nations summon people, in effect, by employment opportunities, offering them work that Americans are unwilling to do, and then turn around and say that all of those people must be deported. This is the problem that has vexed the United States for thirty years and more. Most employers, and, until very recently, the mainstream part of both parties, can agree that the current situation is best righted by a combination of strong border controls with a path to citizenship for those who have been productive workers, and especially for undocumented students, present since childhood, who have managed to enter higher education. But this solution has been politically rejected time and again, and there is at this point no reasonable chance that the solution will be adopted on a nationwide basis, although cities have expressed the determination to protect their own productive members, and universities their students. The solution that I have called reasonable is strongly in accordance with Grotian principles.

Asylum and emergency migration are the crisis of our time, affecting Europe and to a lesser extent the United States as a result of the humanitarian meltdown in Syria. Here the desire to point fingers at groups rather than individuals is especially tempting, and the wave of Islamic terrorist incidents in Europe is fueling anti-immigration politics in most countries. Good crime control is very difficult, as we can see by the astonishing clumsiness of several European nations. Such incidents, even if very rare, assume a disproportionate salience in the popular mind (the well-known "availability heuristic"), which is then further reinforced by political rhetoric. It's a lot easier to exclude en masse, since that requires no work. But the difficult job of investigation and control is the one that must be undertaken, and the crimes of a small number of radicals should not be laid at the door of peaceful desperate families—any more than the crimes of the IRA were laid at the door of all migrants from Ireland, or, if we were to generalize yet further, at the door of all Christians. Grotius insisted rightly that in a time of emergency our common claim, as human beings, to the wherewithal of life should dictate a liberal asylum policy. Much more could be said, for example about the disgraceful practice of holding juveniles applying for asylum in immigration detention and denying them the right to go to school. The U.S. Supreme Court insisted in *Plyler v. Doe* that even illegal immigrants' children have the right to attend the public schools.[25] That right should be explicitly accorded, without delay, to those whose application for asylum is pending. And need one even comment on the policy of separating the young children of asylum seekers from their families at the border, a policy that the head of the American Academy of Pediatrics called child abuse?

Guest-worker programs, used by many nations, are typically ways of getting jobs done without extending to a class of workers the privileges of legal permanent residency or a path to citizenship. Often these programs forbid spouses and children from entering, in order to ensure that these workers do not overstay (or, in those nations that have birthright citizenship, have citizen children). These programs are clearly a moral anomaly. Citizens who live long portions of their lives in a place, and are subject to its laws, deserve, as Grotius insisted, to be among the makers of those laws. In effect these programs are the creation of a permanent class of disenfranchised second-class people, often segmented from the citizen population by ethnicity or religion, as well as by status, a further moral wrong. They are also denied the right to marry and form a family, a right that Grotius explicitly defends. Nations avoid difficult dilemmas by adopting such programs, but the programs should gradually be replaced by programs allowing for family unity, permanent resident status, and a path to citizenship.

Recently these programs have been defended as highly effective mechanisms of redistribution and welfare enhancement.[26] The thorny issue of how to improve material welfare in the light of Deaton's institutional objection requires us to consider this solution very seriously and to continue debating it. Despite the evident fact that such programs can often greatly improve welfare in poorer countries through remittances, however, their cost in terms of selling basic values short still seems to me, at present, too high a price to pay.

The tradition says nothing that sensitive moral philosophers who have not studied the tradition have not said. It does, however, offer a deeper and more principled rationale for the conclusions that many contemporary ethical arguments have been reaching.

On balance, the tradition does well when confronted with the challenges of today's world. It has deficiencies in moral psychology, but these can be corrected, and were already by Cicero and Smith. It failed to formulate principles as a partial political doctrine, not understanding the drawbacks of asking a plural world to accept its principles as a fully comprehensive moral doctrine—but Grotius already saw beyond this, and pointed the way to political liberalism. In the area of human-rights law, the tradition stands up very well, since it demands exactly what seems most feasible, a world of nation-states bound together by an evolving international morality and some international laws, enforced primarily within each nation. In the area of material aid, the tradition again guides our thought well, since it focuses on republican institutions and their stability, thus alerting us to the importance of avoiding self-righteous paternalism and urging us to consult the best empirical evidence about the efficacy of aid. Finally, in the thorny and critical area of migration, the tradition (and especially Grotius) offer good principles to think with as we confront the most contentious issue of our time.

SEVEN

From Cosmopolitanism to the Capabilities Approach

What constructive approach to global issues does the tradition suggest? In this chapter I juxtapose the tradition with the political approach I have long defended, a version of the "Capabilities Approach" (hereafter CA). I argue that in most respects my version of the CA fleshes out the insights of the tradition, with its emphasis on the priority of individual entitlements, each individual being an end and none a mere means to the ends of other; its strong defense of the moral importance of the nation; and its insistence that the international realm is richly moral. With regard to the problem we have traced throughout this book, the problem of material need, the CA goes to the heart of the matter, insisting that all entitlements have an economic and social aspect, and that there is no coherent way of separating duties of justice from duties of material aid. With respect to the issue of political liberalism, adumbrated by Grotius but undeveloped in the tradition, the CA also supplies what was missing, seeing political liberalism as appropriate both within each nation and in approaching global political morality. With respect to moral psychology, the CA leaves room for a reasonable political psychology that I have developed over the years in an attempt to supply what the tradition lacked.

In one respect, however, the CA departs very radically from the tradition. This departure cannot possibly be represented as a minor course correction, or a way of making the tradition the best it can be. For the tradition is relentlessly anthropocentric. Not only the dignity of the human being but also the alleged uniqueness of human capacities and the lowness of other species' capacities are at the very heart of many of its arguments, as they are of Stoicism generally. This anthropocentrism needs a course correction to admit the equal dignity of human beings with severe cognitive disabilities. But it needs more than a course correction if we want to do justice to the claims of sentient beings of other species. Here the tradition must be rejected, and political thought must look for guidance, if it looks for historical guidance at all, to other schools in antiquity—Epicureanism, Neo-Platonism (the vegetarian works of Porphyry and Plutarch), in some ways Aristotle (although he did not develop the ethical implications of his view that all animals are wonderful), and perhaps the vague ideas of Diogenes the Cynic—that understood that many species are worthy of wonder and awe, and that this wonder generates moral claims.

The CA has many anthropocentrists among its defenders. Indeed its other name is the "Human Development Approach," its international association the Human Development and Capability Association, and its journal the *Journal of Human Development and Capabilities*.

Anthropocentrists can still extend concern to other animals instrumentally. But in developing a version of the view in which non-human animals have intrinsic importance as ends, I am diverging from many of my colleagues.

I. The CA: Motivations and Claims

The CA was first advanced by Amartya Sen as a new account of the proper way to make comparisons of welfare among nations.[1] The standard measure had been gross domestic product (GDP) per capita. Sen argued that this measure neglects distribution, giving high marks to nations that contain large inequalities (including inequalities correlated with race and gender). It also neglects the rich plurality of human life: the things human beings have reason to value are enormously plural, and not commensurable along a single metric. Moreover, their availability does not simply increase as a function of GDP. A nation may increase its GDP without doing anything for political rights and liberties, and it may also increase its GDP in ways not directly related to improvements in health and education. (Sen's comparative field studies of the different Indian states showed this lack of correlation, since health and education are areas left by India's constitution to the states, and they have adopted a range of different approaches—some focusing on increasing GDP, and some focusing, as well, on direct action in those two areas.)

Both Sen and I have also insisted that there are grave deficiencies in the other most common comparative metric for welfare, namely the satisfaction of preferences. That metric has the same two problems as

GDP: for again, distribution is neglected; and preferences, properly understood, are plural and non-commensurable. But it has two additional problems. First, people who are deprived may adjust to their living standard and actually not want the things that life has put out of reach, exhibiting what the literature calls "adaptive preferences." People don't like too much unrealized longing, so they tailor their expectations to what they think they can reasonably hope to achieve. This is all the more true when people belong to a subordinated group for whom definite and limited expectations are decreed from birth: they may not protest the absence of equal conditions if they think that such demands are inappropriate for a "good woman," and so on. Finally, satisfaction is a state of a person. It does not involve activity, and can be present even when the person is not doing anything active at all. Robert Nozick's famous "experience machine" makes the point that we would all prefer to live and act ourselves, rather than to be plugged into a machine that merely gave the satisfactions associated with those doings.

Another common approach is based on the distribution of all-purpose resources such as income and wealth. As Sen has long emphasized, this approach may be somewhat better than the two I have just rejected, if the distribution is adequate, and in many contexts all-purpose resources such as income and wealth can be used by people to achieve many distinct things that they value. But the problem is that people have varying needs for resources if they are to come up to the same level of ability to function. A child needs more protein than an adult. A person belonging to a traditionally deprived group may need more expenditure of resources to achieve the same level of opportunity in a society that imposes obstacles. So while resource-based approaches have a pleasing appearance of neutrality, they bias the approach in favor of those already positioned to use resources without impediment.

Given all this, we have proposed that the best approach focuses on people's substantial freedoms to choose things that they value. The right question to ask is, "What are you able to do and be, in areas of importance in your life?" and the answer to that question is the account of that person's "capabilities." As I recorded in Chapter 3, I have distinguished three different types of capabilities. First, there are *basic capabilities,* the innate equipment that is the basis for further development. Second are *internal capabilities,* abilities of a person developed through care and nurture. Developing internal capabilities already requires social resources. But a person might have these inside, so to speak, and still not be fully capable of choice and action: might, for example, be capable of political speech but denied the chance to act politically. So, the really important type of capability for a decent society is what I call *combined capabilities,* internal capabilities plus external conditions that make choice available.

Thus far, capabilities specify a space of comparison, and that is the main use of the approach in Sen's work, as in the Human Development Reports of the United Nations Development Programme of which he was a leading architect. But in keeping with my interest in theories of justice and in constitution-making, I have gone further, using the idea of capabilities to describe a partial approach to basic justice. For that purpose, of course, we must get definite about content—as users of the approach comparatively do already in their choice of examples. I have proposed a list of ten capabilities that must be secured up to a minimum threshold level, if a nation is to have any claim to justice:

The Central Human Capabilities

I. LIFE. Being able to live to the end of a human life of normal length; not dying prematurely, or before one's life is so reduced as to be not worth living.

2. BODILY HEALTH. Being able to have good health, including reproductive health; to be adequately nourished; to have adequate shelter.

3. BODILY INTEGRITY. Being able to move freely from place to place; to be secure against violent assault, including sexual assault and domestic violence; having opportunities for sexual satisfaction and for choice in matters of reproduction.

4. SENSES, IMAGINATION, AND THOUGHT. Being able to use the senses, to imagine, think, and reason—and to do these things in a "truly human" way, a way informed and cultivated by an adequate education, including, but by no means limited to, literacy and basic mathematical and scientific training. Being able to use imagination and thought in connection with experiencing and producing works and events of one's own choice, religious, literary, musical, and so forth. Being able to use one's mind in ways protected by guarantees of freedom of expression with respect to both political and artistic speech, and freedom of religious exercise. Being able to have pleasurable experiences and to avoid non-beneficial pain.

5. EMOTIONS. Being able to have attachments to things and people outside ourselves; to love those who love and care for us, to grieve at their

absence; in general, to love, to grieve, to experience longing, gratitude, and justified anger.[2] Not having one's emotional development blighted by fear and anxiety. (Supporting this capability means supporting forms of human association that can be shown to be crucial in their development.)

6. PRACTICAL REASON. Being able to form a conception of the good and to engage in critical reflection about the planning of one's life. (This entails protection for the liberty of conscience and religious observance.)

7. AFFILIATION.

A. Being able to live with and toward others, to recognize and show concern for other human beings, to engage in various forms of social interaction; to be able to imagine the situation of another. (Protecting this capability means protecting institutions that constitute and nourish such forms of affiliation, and also protecting the freedom of assembly and political speech.)

B. Having the social bases of self-respect and non-humiliation; being able to be treated as a dignified being whose worth is equal to that of others. This entails provisions of non-discrimination on the basis of race, sex, sexual orientation, ethnicity, caste, religion, national origin.

8. OTHER SPECIES. Being able to live with concern for and in relation to animals, plants, and the world of nature.

9. PLAY. Being able to laugh, to play, to enjoy recreational activities.

10. CONTROL OVER ONE'S ENVIRONMENT.

A. Political. Being able to participate effectively in political choices that govern one's life; having the right of political participation, protections of free speech and association.

B. Material. Being able to hold property (both land and movable goods), and having property rights on an equal basis with others; having the right to seek employment on an equal basis with others; having the freedom from unwarranted search and seizure. In work, being able to work as a human being, exercising practical reason and entering into meaningful relationships of mutual recognition with other workers.

This list, humble and revisable, is an abstract template that can be further specified in accordance with a particular nation's history and material circumstances. It was formulated in part by studying the constitutions of nations such as India and South Africa that have focused intensely on human dignity, and it can be used similarly to ground projects of constitution-making or basic legislation. Thresholds will rightly be set aspirationally, but not so as to demand the impossible. I have also argued, however, that the global community has obligations to help poorer nations meet their capability demands in whatever way is feasible. (Chapter 6 shows how difficult it is to figure this out.)

The threshold for some capabilities (political speech, participation, and so on) is already unitary across the world, in the sense that there is an evolving shared understanding of what these capabilities require. It is to be hoped that the threshold for the more circumstance-dependent ones, such as education and health, can in due course converge, since all are held to be entitlements inherent in the notion of a life worthy of human dignity.

The CA is described as a partial approach to justice both because it is silent about other things a nation needs (national defense and security, for example, and reasonable freedom from corruption), and because it makes no commitments about how inequalities above the (high) threshold will be treated. (Where some capabilities are concerned, the right threshold already requires equality: voting rights, religious liberty, and so forth. Where others are concerned, to aim at complete equality seems to me to fetishize material goods too much, and a generous threshold seems a reasonable target; but we may still feel the need to say more in due course about over-threshold inequalities.[3])

Taking a cue from both Aristotle and Grotius, I argue that practical reason and affiliation are especially central, both pervading and organizing all the others. Thus an adequate diet or health-care system will be one designed to respect choice and the needs of human sociability.

II. Justice and Material Aid: No Bifurcation

One of the CA's most central contentions is that material entitlements—to education, to health care, to bodily integrity—are every bit as important for a life commensurate with human dignity as are the entitlements typically covered under the "duties of justice": rights to freedom of speech, conscience, and association, as well as rights of political participation. The capabilities list mingles the two (alleged) types, making no bifurcation. Thus, although the CA is closely linked to the international human rights movement, it refuses as ill-conceived that tradition's division of entitlements into "civil and political rights" and "economic and social rights," with the former figuring as "first-generation rights," the latter as rights of the "second generation." This bifurcation may betray the residual influence of the less salutary parts of our tradition. Adam Smith already used the language of capabilities to describe the material basis of a flourishing human life, and contemporary capability theorists can draw on his rich insights.

But the CA goes yet further, insisting that all entitlements cost money to convey and protect, and that this dependence upon money renders all entitlements "economic and social." We have to tax people to have a system of liberties, a system of contracts, courts that vindicate freedoms of many sorts. As we've seen, Cicero already insisted that inaction did not fulfill the duties of justice—so he was implicitly authorizing a large money-raising enterprise, although he did not comment on how this enterprise would be carried out. All human functions inherent in the idea of a life commensurate with human dignity cost money. The only question is how to raise the funds fairly, and how to allocate them fairly.

Wherever we end up with respect to global duties of material aid—and Chapter 6 has argued that this is a complicated issue, given problems of paternalism and inefficacy—we must not approach these issues with the erroneous bifurcation of duties. If we follow the CA, we will not do so.

III. The Nation and International Society

The CA is understood to be a template for constitution-making, or for fundamental legislation in nations that lack a written constitution. It prescribes entitlements that are argued to be inherent in the very idea of a life commensurate with human dignity, and it suggests that if the arguments are found sound, every single nation has a reason to implement the list in some form. It is designed to be implemented somewhat differently in different places, in accordance with their histories and economic realities. But at some level, the arguments are about what human dignity requires, and those arguments do not apply more or less in one place or another.

National autonomy is protected primarily by making the implementation of the list a matter of sovereign national choice. The space between nations is full of moral arguments, and the arguments backing the CA are certainly by now prominent in that space; they ought to influence nations, above all through the work of their own citizens. If citizens can be helped in their efforts by pointing to an emerging international consensus, so much the better, as with the international women's movement, discussed in Chapter 6. We may also point out that lots of room is left for nations to specify an abstract capability somewhat differently, and, naturally, to add things that are not on the list. Furthermore, the fact that the list centrally commends the freedoms of speech, conscience, and association gives reason for confidence that the autonomy of citizens making and choosing their own laws will not be eroded by the persuasive power of the approach. Thus it cannot plausibly be described as a paternalistic imposition.

In international society, the CA favors debate and persuasion and opposes paternalistic intervention into the politics of sovereign nations, where these meet a minimum threshold of legitimacy. It thus seeks a Grotian type of international society, in which there is a role for some enforceable agreements, but far more room for moral argument and persuasion, directed at mobilizing citizens to strive internally for justice. The Human Development and Capability Association, which publishes the journal mentioned earlier and holds annual meetings, each year in a different region of the world, is designed as a public forum for persuasive argument on all issues connected to the CA, including refining and contesting it.

IV. Political Liberalism at Home and Abroad

My version of the CA is formulated in terms of political liberalism: it is a partial conception of human welfare, endorsed for political purposes, not a comprehensive doctrine of the good human life.[4] The hope is that in due course the political doctrine can command an overlapping consensus of the many reasonable comprehensive doctrines.

My arguments in favor of political liberalism are a very important part of my overall argument for the CA, since only those arguments will show that the CA can show respect for reasonable citizens, by respecting the space within which they express and live by their comprehensive doctrines, religious or secular.[5]

John Rawls made the case for political liberalism as a good choice for the nations of Europe and North America, since they endured the wars of religion. His hope for an eventual overlapping consensus made reference to this historical specificity. I have argued, however, that the same facts that make political liberalism an attractive choice for Europe and North America also commend it to all nations, since all nations of the world today contain basically the same number and even the same list of comprehensive doctrines that a single large Western nation such as the United States does today. At the margins there may be some differences: thus there might be nations that contain no Jains or Parsis, for example. But since any individual might conceivably migrate to any country, we cannot assume that the parties to the overlapping consensus are different even in these unusual cases. And the very same facts that lead Rawls to commend political liberalism for Europe pertain to non-Western nations as well. All have seen that in the absence of brutal repression many different religious and secular comprehensive doctrines will emerge, and not collapse (as was once envisaged) into a single doctrine. So there is nothing about India or Argentina that makes the arguments for political liberalism work differently from the way they work in Germany or Spain.[6]

When we reach global international society, the same facts hold, and even more so, since global society contains, in addition to the many religious and secular comprehensive doctrines, a plurality of national cultures. So it would be right, for similar reasons, to formulate the operative principles of international society in the free-standing way chosen by Grotius, and later by the framers of the Universal Declaration of Human Rights—not grounding the moral principles in any single comprehensive doctrine, but justifying them internally, from moral premises implicit in the shared global culture, principles that can in principle command, over time, an overlapping consensus. Grotius already saw how crucial this was, and the framers of the Universal Declaration agreed. This abstemiousness is all the more important, given the central role of the nation in our international global conception. Nations must retain political autonomy and self-determination. They may be asked to converge on some essentials of what it takes to respect human dignity—as the international human rights movement does. But the list should remain thin, and, as I argued in Chapter 6, its implementation must belong almost entirely to the nations themselves. The CA is out there in international society, and it can direct persuasive and solidaristic movements aiming at political change. But it would be utterly wrong to use it as a weapon to dragoon recalcitrant nations into obedience—except in the rare Grotian cases of genocide, torture, and gross crimes against humanity.

V. Challenging the Basis: Many Beings, Many Types of Dignity

The tradition is relentlessly anthropocentric, and it typically locates the core of dignity in the possession of moral reasoning and the capacity for choice. These two commitments were connected, since it was the high valuation of moral reasoning power as the key value, and source of the rational order of the universe, that led to the singling out of human beings as the only beings who have this power inside themselves. No doubt it was also special pleading on behalf of humanity that led to the emphasis on moral reasoning, since that seemed to be the distinctive trait of humans.

I have suggested that we need not make this connection, and should not. We may value humanity as an end while not locating all worth in the power of moral reasoning, but instead seeing dignity in a wide range of human abilities and human lives. Since we do not accept Stoic metaphysics, according to which the entire universe is animated by moral choice, we have no metaphysical reason to give that ability priority over others, and we have strong moral reasons not to, in a commitment to respect the dignity, and equal dignity, of people with severe cognitive disabilities. We may conclude, as I do, that at least some human capacities must be present in order for a being to be treated as equal—thus a person in a persistent vegetative state, or perhaps an anencephalic child, would not count. But perception, emotional capacities, and the ability to move are all human capacities, and some cluster of them is sufficient for equal respect.

Thus far, the tradition must be revised but need not be rejected—although respecting the equal dignity of people with disabilities will lead us, as we develop the CA in that direction, to reject some standard approaches rooted in the classical social contract tradition.[7]

Beyond this point, however, we must do more than correcting—at least if we wish to take the CA in the direction in which I have been pushing it.[8] I have argued that dignity can be found in many different varieties.[9] All sentient beings strive to flourish, and all these forms of striving inspire wonder, respect, and awe. Although dignity is, as I believe, a very vague notion, it is closely connected to these moral responses, and it has the vague content of being an end, not a mere means for the ends of others. It seems wrong to see dignity in our own particular type of animal life-form and not in those of other animals. What could the possible basis be for such a judgment? Humans are better at some things, but certainly not at all things. Many animals are stronger and swifter; many have superior vision, hearing, and smell; some have spatial perception vastly superior to our own. There are certainly other creatures who exhibit altruism and even culture. If humans do seem capable of some types of moral evaluation that other creatures don't share, we also commit hideous wrongs against our own kind (war, slavery, systematic rape and torture) in a way unparalleled in the other species. So as far as I can see, if humans have dignity it is in virtue of having complicated capacities for a sentient life that strives for flourishing. But that is true of other animals as well.

The idea of justice thus becomes, so to speak, not just horizontal, extending over the entire globe, but also, so to speak, vertical (though this is something of a misnomer, since no animals are lower or higher than others in the evaluative sense), extending into the depths of the oceans and high up into the air, and embracing many different creatures. The challenge of refashioning justice with the whole world of sentient beings in view is a difficult one, and it takes us away, for the most part, from the Stoics—who thought of animals as "brute beasts"[10]—and toward other schools of thought in antiquity, if we want to search for ancient Greek and Roman sources. The late Platonists developed an elaborate account of our ethical duties to animals, and the *De Abstinentia ab esu animalium* (On abstaining from animal flesh) of Porphyry and the vegetarian works of Plutarch still offer very rich guidance in this area. Another type of guidance is offered by Aristotle, who does not have an account of our ethical duties to animals, but who was one of history's greatest biologists, and who does position humans as a type of animal alongside other animals, sharing with other end-directed creatures a "common explanation" of motion through desire and cognition.[11] His instruction to his students to react with wonder to the complex ordering of all animal lives is the start of my ethical project in the CA.[12] Another fruitful source is the Epicurean tradition, which sees the locus of value as the sentient body, and emphasizes the kinship of all bodies. This tradition did not have an ethics of vegetarianism or good animal treatment, but it did ultimately inspire the first modern advocate of animal rights in the Western tradition, Utilitarian philosopher Jeremy Bentham.

And once again the eclectic philosopher Cicero stands out for his insight and good sense: for he strenuously objected to gladiatorial games employing elephants, approving of and joining a popular protest on the grounds that elephants have a commonality *(societas)* with the human species.[13] Here as elsewhere, Cicero's Stoic affiliations did not stop him from grasping something true; perhaps his allegiance to the Platonic academy, rather than the Stoic school, gave him the requisite freedom of ethical judgment.

Obviously enough, a tradition is a good guide to philosophers of today only if we are alert to its weaknesses and deficiencies. We learn by grappling with it and finding it wanting, as well as by appreciating the insights it continues to offer. I have written this book to try to bring forward the tradition's valuable insights as well as to illustrate its shortcomings. Now, armed with what we have learned, we need to approach the imperiled world of nature with scientific fact and philosophical imagination, and continue our work. The gates of the cosmic city must open to all.

NOTES

REFERENCES

ACKNOWLEDGMENTS

INDEX

NOTES

1. See Nussbaum (2008a).

2. See Waldron (2012).

3. See Nussbaum (2016a).

4. See Ambedkar (2011); ibid.; Nussbaum (2015).

5. See Appiah (1992); also Appiah (2005, 2006).

6. See my discussion of the historical evidence in Nussbaum (2016b), ch. 7.

7. See Maritain (1943).

8. All data in this paragraph are from the *Human Development Report 2016* (United Nations Development Programme 2016). The United States does not have the highest life expectancy at birth, at 79.1 years; Hong Kong does, at 84.0 years. Thirty-five nations have higher figures than the United States. These include some nations usually thought of as less "advanced," such as Greece, Hong Kong, Cyprus, Singapore, Malta, Lebanon, and Costa Rica.

9. See Deaton (2013).

10. See Moyn (2018, 2010).

11. For many years Matthias Lutz-Bachmann at the Goethe University Frankfurt has directed a project involving new editions of medieval and early modern cosmopolitan philosophers, with commentaries.

12. See Nussbaum and Levmore (2017).

13. See Sorabji (1993).

2. DUTIES OF JUSTICE, DUTIES OF MATERIAL AID

1. On Kant's debt to Cicero, see Nussbaum (1997).

2. Most such theories take their start from the classical Utilitarian tradition: see, for example, Singer (1972, 2009, 2015); see also Kagan (1989). On limits to these personal duties of beneficence, see Nagel (1991), Scheffler (1982), and Murphy (2002).

3. A much-discussed example is Rawls (1999). For my own detailed critique of his approach, see Nussbaum (2006), ch. 5.

4. I translate the Latin of the *De Officiis* myself throughout, starting from Michael Winterbottom's excellent Oxford Classical Text (Cicero 44a). The best translation is in the excellent annotated version of the work by Miriam Griffin and Eileen Atkins (Cicero 44b). See also the commentary on the work by Dyck (1996).

5. By count of my research assistant Chad Flanders, there are 90 citations or close paraphrases of *De Officiis* in Grotius's *De Iure Belli ac Pacis* (1625), and 80 in Pufendorf's *De Iure Naturae et Gentium* (1688); most of these citations are to the portions of the work I am about to discuss. Both authors are also extremely fond of Seneca. (*Caveat lector:* some English translations, especially of Grotius, omit many of the citations, feeling that the text is top-heavy with them.) For Grotius's tremendous influence on the foundations of modern international law, see Lauterpacht (1946) and Chapter 4. On Kant's influence, see Tesón (1992). Grotius, and the closely related arguments of Vattel and Bynkershoek, all had a major influence on eighteenth- and nineteenth-century jurisprudence in the United States. A LEXIS search shows 74 U.S. Supreme Court cases that refer to Grotius, 176 that refer to Vattel, and 39 that refer to Bynkershoek, all be-

fore 1900; the reliance on these texts seems to be genuine. (Search of
LEXIS, Genfed Library, US File, January 1998: I owe this information to
Jack Goldsmith, who informs me that a similar reliance is evident in dip-
lomatic correspondence and political argument.)

6. Smith ([1759–1790] 1982), III.3.6: "and who does not inwardly feel the truth
    of that great stoical maxim, that for one man to deprive another unjustly
    of any thing, or unjustly to promote his own advantage by the loss or
    disadvantage of another, is more contrary to nature, than death, than
    poverty, than pain, than all the misfortunes which can affect him, either
    in his body, or in his external circumstances." This, as will be seen, is a
    verbatim citation of Cicero, *De Officiis,* III.21.

7. See Kant (1795): *Perpetual Peace,* "Third Definitive Article of a Perpetual
    Peace: Cosmopolitan Right Shall Be Limited to Conditions of Universal
    Hospitality":

    > "If we compare with this ultimate end the *inhospitable* con-
    > duct of the civilised states of our continent, especially the
    > commercial states, the injustice which they display in *vis-*
    > *iting* foreign countries and peoples (which in their case is
    > the same as *conquering* them) seems appallingly great.
    > America, the negro countries, the Spice Islands, the Cape,
    > etc. were looked upon at the time of their discovery as own-
    > erless territories; for the native inhabitants were counted as
    > nothing. In East India (Hindustan), foreign troops were
    > brought in under the pretext of merely setting up trading
    > posts. This led to oppression of the natives, incitement of
    > the various Indian states to widespread wars, famine, in-
    > surrection, treachery, and the whole litany of evils which
    > can afflict the human race . . . And all this is the work of
    > powers who make endless ado about their piety, and who

wish to be considered as chosen believers while they live on
the fruits of iniquity" (106).

8. Appiah (1996), 23. Appiah actually says "Cicero and the Bible," but in
this context there is only one text by Cicero that is likely to have had this
privileged place.

9. I so translate *iniuria;* one should avoid saying "injustice," so that the defi-
nition does not seem circular, but also avoid saying something morally
neutral, like "provocation," since *iniuria* clearly means something morally inappropriate.

10. There is a textual problem here, and Winterbottom obelizes the first half
of this sentence; but the sense—not the argument!—seems clear.

11. The example of Regulus is very important to Cicero in *De Officiis:* he discusses it at greater length at III.99–111, arguing against various people
who would try to reconcile the conflict between virtue and expediency,
or to urge that Regulus ought to have followed expediency. Marcus
Atilius Regulus, a prominent Roman politician and military leader, was
captured by the Carthaginians in 255 BCE. Later he was sent to Rome to
negotiate a peace (or, in some versions, the return of Carthaginian prisoners); he promised to return after executing his mission. When he arrived, he urged the Senate to decline the peace terms; but he kept his
promise to return. The story goes that he was placed in the sunlight with
his eyelids stapled open, dying an excruciating death by both starvation
and enforced sleeplessness. (Sources characterize the torture in various
ways, but all agree on the exceedingly painful character of the death, *ex-
quisita supplicia,* as Cicero says (*Off.* III.100) and compare the summary
of the lost book 18 of Livy; for other references in Cicero and elsewhere,
see Dyck [1996], 619–620.) Romans considered Regulus's story a salient
example of honorable behavior, definitive of a national norm of virtue
(see Horace, *Odes* 3.5), though modern scholars note that the story may

have been invented to defuse criticism of torture of Carthaginian prisoners at Rome; they follow Polybius in holding that Regulus died in
Carthaginian captivity and never went on an embassy to Rome (see Dyck
[1996], 619). Horace's use of the story is exceedingly colonialistic and chau-
vinistic, with vilification of the *barbarus tortor* and praise of the *virilis
voltus* (manly face) of the hero, which receives chaste kisses of his proper
Roman wife. (The context in which the story is introduced is anxiety
about the dilution of warlike Roman blood by intermarriage with bar-
barian peoples.) Cicero standardly uses the story as an example of the victory of virtue over expediency: see also *De Finibus*, defending the Stoic
ideal of virtue against Epicurean hedonism: "Virtue cries out that, even
while tortured by sleeplessness and hunger, he was happier than Tho-
rius getting drunk on his bed of roses" (II.65). In more recent times the
example, however extreme, still fascinates. Turner's painting *Regulus* is
notorious for containing, it would appear, no representation of the central figure; the reason is that the viewer is placed in the position of Regulus, struck again and again by a hammering, implacable sun.

12. It is quite unclear in what sense death and pain could be said to be contrary to nature; even to a Stoic, for whom the cosmos is thoroughly good,
death itself will therefore have to be understood as a good, when it
occurs. And Stoics energetically opposed the thesis that pain is intrinsically bad. Eric Brown suggests that the Stoics can defuse this problem by
distinguishing two viewpoints: from the point of view of Providence,
nothing is contrary to nature; from a local viewpoint, things like death
are contrary to nature, in the sense that they mean the end of some
natural organism. I'm not sure: for the local perspective is not accurate,
according to a strict Stoic account. Marcus and other writers insist again
and again that we must meditate on the naturalness of our own death.

13. Reich (1939).

14. See Dyck (1996), 529: "The example of Hercules, a pan-Hellenic hero, breaks down the boundaries of individual states and emphasizes the common needs and interests of all human kind." He compares *Tusculan Disputations* 1.28 and *De Finibus* 3.65–66.

15. See Nussbaum (1997).

16. Probably Cicero does not allow quite as much latitude as does Kant: for the requirement that we become *boni ratiocinatores officiorum* suggests that we must learn to perform refined calculations, and that it is not simply up to us how they turn out. (I owe this observation to Eric Brown.)

17. See Nussbaum (2002a).

18. Given that elsewhere Cicero prefers a position that ascribes a tiny bit of value to externals (see *De Finibus,* book V), denying that they are necessary for eudaimonia, but asserting that they may make a life *more eudaimôn,* he may waver in this work between that position (which would make it easier to justify duties of material aid to our fellow citizens) and the stricter Stoic position.

19. Sen. *Ep.* 47, in Seneca (65 CE).

20. See Treggiari (1991). The relevant law is the famous (or infamous) Lex Iulia de Adulteriis, passed by Augustus in the first century in an alleged attempt to restore the pristine mores of former times—although, as Treggiari persuasively argues, it is actually much more severe than either legal or social norms that prevailed during Cicero's lifetime. Even this severe law did not restrict sexual access of male owners to their slaves—and, as Musonius comments, public norms generally endorsed such conduct. Adultery was conceived of as a property offense against the husband or father of the woman in question.

21. See Nussbaum (2002b). I argue that Musonius's position is actually more conservative than Seneca's: it does not claim that the slave has any right to respectful treatment; it treats the sex act as a problem of

overindulgence for the free owner, rather than a problem of disrespect for the slave.

22. See Griffin ([1976] 1992), ch. 8, 256–285.

23. A significant attempt to break down the distinction, in connection with thinking about which duties to others are most urgent, is Shue (1980).

24. See Holmes and Sunstein (1999).

25. See Shue (1980), 107 ff., citing Wassily Leontief's claims about the relatively low cost of providing basic material support.

26. See the interesting discussion of this part of Cicero's view in Shklar (1990).

27. See Seneca *De Ira* I.12, where the interlocutor objects that the non-angry person will not be able to avenge the murder of a father or the rape of a mother, and Seneca hastens to reassure him that these central moral acts can all be done without anger.

28. Compare Seneca's *De Otio*, where he argues that the philosopher who does not enter public life may be able to serve the public better through philosophical insights: "We definitely hold that Zeno and Chrysippus did greater deeds than if they had led armies, won honors, and written laws: they wrote laws not for one nation but for the whole human race" (6). Seneca's position is much more retirement-friendly than Cicero's.

29. See Dauber (2013). Dauber argues that Americans have always been reluctant to give relief unless they believe the person to have been the victim of something like a natural disaster, that comes on them from outside; in a dissertation in progress, she argues that Roosevelt understood this, and used the rhetoric of natural disaster to mobilize aid during the Depression. Even the term "the Depression" positioned an economic catastrophe as a quasi-flood or hurricane.

30. For a related myth used to exemplify this point about the bodily appetites, see Plato's account of the Danaids who had to carry water in a sieve, in *Gorgias,* 494.

31.   *O multa dictu gravia, perpessu aspera,*
       Quae corpore exanclata atque animo pertuli. . . .
       Haec me irretivit veste furiali inscium,
       Quae lateri inhaerens morsu lacerat viscera
       Urguensque graviter pulmonum haurit spiritus:
       Iam decolorem sanginem omnem exsorbuit.
       Sic corpus clade horribili absumptum extabuit.

32.   See Sen (1981).

33.   See Goodin (1988) and Shue (1980), 135ff., 142ff.

34.   For the relevant texts, see Schofield ([1991] 1999).

35.   Cicero, of course, is much worse than Nozick, because he doesn't even require a legitimate starting point, and has no theory of just transfer.

36.   See Smith ([1759–1790] 1982), VI.iii: "Of Universal Benevolence." For a related view, see Goodin (1985).

37.   On Horace's depiction of the Carthaginians, see my earlier remarks on Regulus. Tacitus's *Germania* is a good example of the extremes of this tendency under the Empire, but it was already afoot during the Republic.

38.   See, similarly, Shue (1980), 145ff. Shue notes that general duties of this sort will not be in the strict sense perfect duties, since they will take the form that I have a duty to aid either X or someone relevantly like X. But a duty of this type may nonetheless be highly stringent.

39.   Shue (1980) seems to me correct in his insistence that, although at a deep level all duties are duties of persons to other persons, institutions play a crucial role of mediating those duties, both for reasons of efficiency and for reasons of respite; see also Nagel (1991).

40.   For my own attempt at such a sketch, see Nussbaum (2000, 2006, 2012), and Chapter 7.

3. THE WORTH OF HUMAN DIGNITY

1. I do not focus on Cicero here, having discussed his views in Chapter 2.

2. See Diog. Laert. VI.20. On the story and the new historical evidence for it, see Branham (1996).

3. Here I agree with Branham (1996), though not necessarily with his rather Stoicizing positive suggestion.

4. See the discussion in Chapter 1.

5. Sen. *Ot.* 4.1, as translated in Long and Sedley (1987), 1:431.

6. Plutarch, *On the Fortune of Alexander,* 329A–B, my translation; see Long and Sedley (1987), 2:429; for other relevant texts, see Long and Sedley (1987), 2:429–437.

7. See Schofield ([1991] 1999).

8. On Cicero and Seneca, see Griffin (1989). On Marcus, see Rutherford (1989).

9. I discuss these matters at greater length in Nussbaum (1994), ch. 9.

10. See the Plutarch passage cited earlier; for discussion, see Schofield ([1991] 1999).

11. See also I.14, V.16.

12. See Schofield ([1991] 1999) for an excellent discussion of Stoic attitudes to sex equality.

13. See the good discussion of Stoic impartiality in Annas (1993).

14. Kant's idea of the Kingdom of Ends plays a similar role, and he was almost certainly influenced by these Stoic ideas. See Nussbaum (1997).

15. See Rawls (1971).

16. See Schofield ([1991] 1999), ch. 3.

17. For the Hierocles fragment, see Annas (1993), 267–268, and Long and Sedley (1987), 2:349.

18. See Annas (1993).

19. See Nussbaum ([1986] 2000).

20. See Nussbaum (2002b).

21. On Williams, see Nussbaum (2008b).

22. M. Aur. *Med.* II.1, trans. in G. M. A. Grube, *Marcus Aurelius: Meditations* (Indianapolis: Bobbs-Merrill, 1963). Cf. also VI.6: "The best method of defense is not to become like your enemy."

23. There are many similar images of connected purposes: see, for example, VI.38, XI.8, II.3, III.11, and discussion of Marcus's use of *sun*-compounds in Rutherford (1989), 21 n. 58.

24. Translation from Hadot (1998).

25. Nussbaum (1994), chs. 11 and 12.

26. See Nussbaum and Levmore (2017).

27. Translation from Hadot (1998).

28. Based on ibid., with some modifications.

29. See Nussbaum and Levmore (2017).

30. See Sedley (1997).

31. See Nussbaum ([1986] 2000).

4. GROTIUS

1. Henceforth I shall refer to *De Iure Belli ac Pacis* as *BP*. The excellent translation by Francis W. Kelsey et al., under the editorship of James Brown Scott for the Carnegie Endowment for International Peace (Grotius 1625), will be followed with modifications. For example, I standardly replace "man" as the translation of Latin *homo* with "human being." In other cases I make the renderings consistent with those in my own translations of Cicero in other chapters (thus "fellowship" for *societas*, and so on).

2. *De Iure Praedae* (from which *Mare Liberum* derives) was published in 1604–1605, and *BP* in 1625; Hobbes's *Leviathan* appeared in 1651, after Grotius's death. Grotius is thus not responding to Hobbes's arguments; but he is well aware of positions that insist that relations among states are amoral, and argues extensively against them.

3. See Bull (1977, 1990), Lauterpacht (1946), and, in general, the essays in Bull, Roberts, and Kingsbury (1990).

4. For a good short account of Grotius's life, see van Holk (1983).

5. See Schneewind (1998) for a comprehensive account.

6. The idea had older roots in India, going back to the edicts of Ashoka in the second century BCE, and becoming highly developed in the Moghul Empire. The Ottoman Empire had at least a version of this idea. And the North American colony of Rhode Island practiced a complete toleration of different religions. Grotius clearly has sympathy with this idea, since one of the causes of his imprisonment was his support for the view that local states should have the right to make their own laws with regard to religion.

7. The idea of religious toleration is not altogether alien to the Greek world. In one form, at least, the Greeks had it securely: the idea, namely, that there are many gods, all deserving worship. But the Greeks thought that everyone should honor all the gods: thus Hippolytus, who thought he could leave out Aphrodite and devote himself without tension to Artemis, finds to his distress that this neglect has involved him in impiety. The idea that there might be a plurality of total forms or ways of life under religion, all deserving of respect, is less easy to identify. Certainly there were Greeks who joined cults, for example the Dionysian cult, that took them away from their ordinary religious pursuits. And there was at least a nascent sense that one should not persecute such people.

8. Josephus was typical of an educated group of Hellenized Jews who rose in the Roman hierarchy while still practicing their religion. The Empress Poppaea, wife of Nero, seriously undertook to convert to Judaism, although she probably did not complete the process.

9. Dated December 5, 61 BCE.

10. See Van Holk (1983). Grotius also made a collection of ancient Greek and Latin texts on the subject of free will, which was published posthumously in 1648.

11. Holland was in this sense a province, within the loose federation of the Netherlands.

12. Grotius's view about the right to revolution complicates this picture. For although, like Kant after him, he takes a stern line about its non-permissibility, his position is like that of someone who asserts that there is no right to divorce—but ample grounds for annulment. For he holds that in many different ways it may turn out that the people did not after all effectively give themselves over to the despot in question, and then matters are very different.

13. See Bull (1990), 80–81, for the history of this doctrine, apparently first advanced by Henry of Susa, Bishop of Ostia, in the thirteenth century.

14. See Nussbaum (2008b).

15. For example, one can find this doctrine in Thucydides's Melian Dialogue. But, equally important, one can also find it in the total silence of all the major pre-Stoic ethical thinkers about moral relations that transcend the boundaries of the *polis* (except relations of individual friendship).

16. I put this phrase in quotes because Grotius's views concerning the independence of the moral law from divine law make his views distinctively different from mediaeval natural law doctrines, more similar to Stoic views of natural law and Kant's views of the moral law.

17. This is also the Stoic view: they cited the opinions of poets, but also ordinary language, and even ordinary gesture, in support of their propositions. For this they are roundly mocked by Galen, who thinks that one should cite only eminent philosophical experts. See Nussbaum (1994). But, once again, it would appear that their primary line of argument is more selective: they ask each reader to reflect deeply and

critically about the cultural beliefs that may be deeply habitual for most of us.

18. In one or two cases, it is less permissive than the standard implicit in *ius naturale:* for example, the law of nations holds that one may not use poison in wartime. Grotius says that natural law, by contrast, holds that wherever it is in fact permissible to kill someone, any means may be used.

19. See Nussbaum (1995) on Aristotle's (as I believe) similar use of a normative moral idea of human nature.

20. The obvious problem of free riding, so prominent in discussion of Kant, and clearly a problem to which Kant addresses himself, is apparently not a matter of concern to Grotius: he thinks that once we see that a given institution is part of what "natural law" requires, we will all see that we have reason to honor it.

21. Rape is rejected by *ius gentium* largely on efficiency grounds: unbridled lust undermines military discipline, and it does not contribute either to security or to punishment (III.4.19).

22. "To priests and penitents you may properly add those who direct their energy to literary pursuits, which are honorable and useful to the human race" (III.11.8).

23. The colonization of North America was already under way, and while it had a veneer of legitimacy if one ignored the rights of native inhabitants, even British theorists, for example Roger Williams, did not ignore native rights. Williams goes as far in a Grotian direction as was feasible, in his successful attempt to protect at least some native autonomy and property in his negotiations with Charles II.

24. Cicero, *Letters to Atticus,* IX.7C, quoting Julius Caesar.

25. Bull (1977, 1990) calls it the Kantian position, but, since both he and I hold that this is not the best way to read *Perpetual Peace* (see Bull 1977, 24), I depart from this by now well-established usage.

26. This view seems to be that of Nagel (2005), although he does seem to permit some moral argument (*not* claims of justice) outside the state. See the good critique by Cohen and Rogers (2006). Of course there are yet other alternatives, including views (Hobbesian or other) that simply deny the validity of rights claims.

27. Although, in a typically tortuous and oblique fashion, he also holds that a regime is not legitimate if it can be shown that consent was never validly given in the first instance: as I have mentioned, he allows, so to speak, for lots of annulment, though not for divorce.

28. Plutarch, *On the Fortunes of Alexander,* 328C.

29. Another very odd and unfortunate feature of his discussion in that later section is that, while he forbids intervention against a people who fail to accept one's own religion, he permits it toward people who show impiety toward the god that they themselves believe in (II.20.51): he cites desecration of their sacred objects by the Babylonians, and instances of perjury (as violation of a sacred oath). Obviously this is an absurdly broad principle! Moreover, it seems just the wrong direction for him to go, given his account of sovereignty: for surely the members of the religion in question are the ones who should judge how to deal with violations of its prescriptions.

30. See Risse (2012) for an excellent analysis of this material and its implications for contemporary debates.

31. See Bull (1977), 301.

32. Ibid., 39.

33. See ibid.

34. See Nussbaum ([1986] 2000), ch. 1, the "argument from the good of diversity": I insist, however, that diversity is a good only if it first passes some pretty stringent moral tests. We should not defend domestic vio-

lence on the grounds that a society without it would be homogeneous in a morally tragic way.

35. See Rawls (1999).

36. Bull (1977), ch. 10.

37. Ibid., 254.

38. Ibid., 255.

5. "MUTILATED AND DEFORMED"

1. See Sorabji (1993).

2. The first edition of *TMS* was published in 1759; a second edition, with some revisions, appeared in 1761. Editions 3 (1767), 4 (1774), and 5 (1781) are virtually unchanged from the second edition. Edition 6, published after Smith's death in 1790, incorporates major revisions and additions that I shall discuss later. Nussbaum (2001) contains an extensive discussion of Smith's account of sympathy and its limits, including a discussion of Coase (1976). I shall not replicate those discussions here.

3. First edition 1776, thus seventeen years after the (heavily Stoic) first edition of *TMS*. Subsequent editions of *WN* contain some changes, but nothing that alters doctrine substantially.

4. For related views, see Fleischacker (1999) and Rothschild (2001). See also Griswold (1999), an impressive overview of Smith's philosophical thought that offers an account of Smith's relation to Stoicism that I shall be discussing. Muller (1993) helpfully traces the extent to which Smith institutionalized Stoic notions in the design of the "decent society." And see particularly Darwall (1999), a first-rate philosophical overview of recent literature. Our knowledge of Smith's life has been enhanced by Ross (1995).

5.   Edition two incorporates some serious changes, though not nearly as many as the sixth. But it was published only two years after the first, and fifteen years before *WN*.

6.   Thus I shall be arguing that Rothschild is correct that this doctrine plays a small role in *WN*, though I shall not accept her argument about the phrase "invisible hand" (see section VI of this chapter). It is not possible, however, to argue that Smith repudiated Stoic Providence in any overall or coherent way: the entire argument of *TMS* is built upon the idea that our sentiments are providentially designed to achieve results that are good, even when we do not intend the good; and many passages dwell explicitly on the importance of Providence.

7.   Seneca, *De Ira*, III.38. Cato, as usual, is represented as a paragon of Stoic virtue at the end of a long list of people who endure insult, and either get angry (slavishly and weakly) or fail to react (nobly and heroically).

8.   See Darwall's astute analysis of this passage in Darwall (1999), 144–145.

9.   See the comparison to Kant in ibid., 153.

10. Compare Rothschild (2001), who makes some plausible suggestions about the political content of the passage. Darwall, by contrast, says that the "man of system" is a "bureaucrat" (ibid., 154)—less likely, I think, given the date of composition, and Smith's evident preoccupation with current events in France. Bureaucrats, besides, are not so often inspired by beauty; nor do they usually have the power simply to impose their system "completely and in all its parts." See also the detailed discussion in Ross (1995), 385–394, of Smith's reactions to the unfolding events of the French Revolution. He suggests, tentatively, that at least some of the delay in the publication of edition 6 may be due to Smith's interest in these developing events. He believes that the "man of system" is a type of which Robespierre is a prominent representative, and he suggests, more tendentiously, that Danton is at least one example of the man of humanity (394). Fleis-

chacker, more skeptical about any specific reference to events in France, notes Smith's keen interest in events in America, which he admired, and whose date would better suit the date of the revisions. It is quite possible that Smith was ruminating about political life without any one particular object in view.

11. Even Smith's account of prudence is moralized, since it is built upon the Stoic notion of *oikeiôsis,* the idea that nature has instructed each individual to care for him or herself—up to the limits revealed by the spectator.

12. I shall speak as Smith does, both focusing on what he calls "productive work" (neglecting household labor and even home-based craft labor) and speaking of the laborer as male; but these issues will receive further discussion in section VI.

13. On the need to have a significant number of children because of high child mortality, see *WN* 96–97, which insists that this problem derives from the poor health and nutritional status of the lower classes and does not affect wealthier families. The problem of infant mortality is discussed by several eighteenth-century thinkers, including Rousseau, who uses this fact to explain why, although women in the (apparently healthier) "state of nature" were quite independent and active, they must now stay in the home all their lives, because they have to have "nearly four children" to ensure that two survive (*Emile,* book V, footnote near the opening of the book, p. 362 in the Bloom translation). Rousseau does not find a class dimension to this problem, and indeed his argument for confining all women to the home requires, as a premise, that this problem exists in all families.

14. See also Rothschild (2001), who brings out this aspect of the argument very well.

15. Smith's moving discussion of the enervating consequences of constant work of any sort, "either of mind or of body" (100) derives special force

from his own history, in which periods of intense application were typically followed by a breakdown of some sort: see Ross (1995).

16. On this point see also Rothschild (2001) and Fleischacker (1999).

17. See also *LJ* 193: "A child is a very delicate plant, one that requires a great deal of care and attendance, and attention to the rearing"—followed by a discussion of infant mortality similar to that of *WN*.

18. His topic here is unemployment produced by general economic decline.

19. This image was used by Pindar in *Nemean VIII* to illustrate the fragility of human excellence and its need for support from the surrounding environment: see Nussbaum ([1986] 2000), ch. 1. Did Smith have this particular text in mind? There is no way of telling, although his classical learning was clearly wide and deep. It is such a natural image to anyone who thinks, that we could just as easily say that he and Pindar express a similar insight using a similar metaphor. And of course we can already see that Smith is rethinking the metaphor, in a characteristically Scottish way: for the threats to the plant come from the cold, whereas Pindar's "vine tree" appears to be threatened by absence of "green dew."

20. For the Stoics, life was an "external good" just like money, power, and so on. This was always odd: for the idea that life is not necessary for human dignity could be sustained, perhaps, by a Platonist believer in the immortal soul, but the Stoics held that the soul is bodily and dies with the person.

21. One clear exception is Musonius Rufus, a Roman Stoic of Seneca's time, who wrote a little treatise called "That One Should Raise All the Children Who Are Born," opposing the common practice of infanticide on ethical grounds.

22. Not free, because Smith thinks that if the salary of teachers were paid entirely by the state there would be too little parental oversight. Instead, he suggests a fee "so moderate, that even a common labourer may af-

ford it," combined with state payments (including payments for prizes for students who excel). Obviously the problem of oversight that he elsewhere scathingly documents needs to be handled in some way, though whether making the poor pay tuition is the best way may be doubted.

23. See also *LJ* 539–540, discussed in Rothschild (2001), 97: "When a person's whole attention is bestowed on the 17th part of a pin," it is hardly surprising that people are "exceedingly stupid." Smith contrasts England, where boys are sent to work at age six or seven, unfavorably with Scotland, where "even the meanest porter can read and write."

24. See Nussbaum (1988).

25. See Rothschild (2001) on Condorcet; Montesquieu has some seeds of this view.

26. Smith's views, however, appear to have influenced developments in America, where Benjamin Rush's proposal for public schools in Pennsylvania in 1786 resembles Smith's, or at least takes Scottish schools as its model in a similar way; Jefferson's proposals in 1818 also resemble Smith's, and both Rush and Jefferson were enthusiasts for Smith's work.

27. A crucial difference, however, is that the joint stock companies were directly chartered by the government, and given by the government a monopoly over their areas of trade. So in calling for an end to such practices Smith is actually calling for the removal of a certain type of government intervention. This, I think, does not alter the general point that he is well aware that monopolistic practices cannot be effectively limited without some form of government action.

28. There seems to be a misprint in the text at this point.

29. Griswold (1999), 320.

30. Rothschild (2001), 132.

31. See my development of this point with reference to Seneca in Nussbaum (1994), chs. 11 and 12.

32. It seems a little odd to cite Richardson as a source for "the refinements and delicacies of . . . private and domestic affections," given that Clarissa's family is one of the most "peculiarly odious," in its lack of love, in all of Western literature. But perhaps it is precisely the odiousness of this absence that makes the novel of interest to Smith—as Ross (1995, 384) argues.

33. See "Steerforth's Arm" in Nussbaum (1990).

34. This is the sentence that immediately precedes the one occurrence in *TMS* of the phrase "the invisible hand," on which more later.

35. For example "man . . . was fitted by nature to that situation for which he was made" (85); "Nature has implanted in the human breast that consciousness of ill-desert" (86); we suppose that in our conduct to be the invention of man, "which in reality is the wisdom of God" (97); "Nature, however, when she implanted the seeds of this irregularity in the a breast, seems, as upon all other occasions, to have intended the happiness and perfection of the species" (105); "Nature, when she formed man for society, endowed him with an original desire to please" (116); "Since these, therefore, were plainly intended to be the governing principles of human nature, the rules which they prescribe are to be regarded as the commands and laws of the Deity" (165); "the original purpose intended by the Author of nature" (166); "This universal benevolence . . . can be the source of no solid happiness to any man who is not thoroughly convinced that all the inhabitants of the universe . . . are under the immediate care and protection of that great, benevolent, and all-wise Being, who directs all the movements of nature" (235–236); and so on.

36. Rothschild (2001), ch. 5. Granted, the phrase occurs in the early *Astronomy* in a skeptical vein, as Smith uses it to allude to what primitive people believed about the actions of Jupiter. But for this discrepancy the best account is probably Macfie's in the introduction to Smith (1759–1790)

1982, that he just liked the phrase and used it again, later, in a very different way. Rothschild's other evidence that the phrase cannot connote a sincere allegiance to Providence is its use in two works of literature, Shakespeare's *Macbeth* and Ovid's *Metamorphoses,* that Smith must have known. But in both of these texts the phrase is actually sinister, not light-hearted or ironic, so her argument proves the wrong thing if anything. Clearly, whatever we say about *TMS* 185, we cannot say that the operations of the "hand" are sinister. And I don't see any way in which we can read all the allusions to Nature's providential structure away as non-serious.

37. "He is in this, as in many other cases, led by an invisible hand to promote an end which was no part of his intention" (*WN* 471).

38. Adam Smith to Thomas Cadell, March 31, 1789: see Ross (1995), 382–383.

39. Adam Smith to Thomas Cadell, March 15, 1788: "I am a slow a very slow workman, who do and undo everything I write at least half a dozen of times before I can be tolerably pleased with it." And again on March 31, 1789: "I am very much ashamed of this delay." See Ross (1995), 382–383.

40. Smith to Cadell, March 15, 1788: "The weak state of my health and my atendance at the Custom house, occupied me so much after my return to Scotland, that tho' I gave as much application to study as these circumstances would permit, yet that application was neither very great, nor very steady, so that my progress was not very great."

41. See Ross (1995), passim.

42. The central locus of pain was his stomach, and by his death he was very emaciated because, in the words of a friend, "his stomach cannot admit of sufficient nourishment" (ibid., 404).

43. See ibid.

44. Ibid., 402. Later in life he encountered the woman at a party, and did not recognize her. Ross also mentions an infatuation, while in France, with

an Englishwoman named Mrs. Nicol, but concludes that "he seems to have been entirely content with his existence as a bachelor" (402).

45. In a letter of June 10, 1779, shortly after her death, Smith writes to Strahan: "I should immediately have acknowledged the receipt of the fair sheets; but I had just then come from performing the last duty to my poor old Mother; and tho' the death of a person in her ninetieth year of her age was no doubt an event most agreable to the course of nature; and, therefore, to be foreseen and prepared for; yet I must say to you, what I have said to other people, that the final separation from a person who certainly loved me more than any other person ever did or ever will love me; and whom I certainly loved and respected more than I ever shall either love or respect any other person, I cannot help feeling, even at this hour, as a very heavy stroke upon me." After her death, Janet Douglas to some extent filled the void, until her own death in 1788. Smith writes of her impending death, "She will leave me one of the most destitute and helpless men in Scotland" (September 23, 1788; see Ross [1995], 401).

46. See Sutherland (1995) for a comprehensive discussion, including references to Smith's contemporary critics. Among these was Patricia Wakefield (*Reflections on the Present Condition of the Female Sex; with Suggestions for Its Improvement*, 1798), who argued that the free-market economy favored by Smith denies women access to dignified and well-paid work, pushing them into poverty and prostitution.

47. See especially *TMS* 28: "When we have dined, we order the covers to be removed." I discuss both passages in "Steerforth's Arm" in Nussbaum (1990), and the former in Nussbaum (2001), ch. 9.

48. Compare for example *TMS* 37, where Smith holds that "[w]omen, and men of weak nerves," fear the expression of anger in others.

49. Commenting on her character, as revealed in the one surviving portrait (which he reproduces on p. 310), Ross says, "When Smith writes in *WN* of the two systems of morality, on the one hand the *liberal* and on the other the *strict and austere,* it is perhaps appropriate to think of his mother as upholding the values of the second" (Ross 1995).

50. See letter of September 23, 1788: despite being in pain and "reduced . . . to a shadow," probably by colon cancer, unable to leave her bed and barely able to move, she "still, however, continues to direct the affairs of her family with her usual distinctness and attention; and waits for the great change, which she knows is very near, without any impatience, without any fear, and without much regret. Her humour and raillery are the same as usual."

51. William Smellie to Patrick Clason, June 27, 1790 (Ross [1995], 404).

52. The discussion of anger on 37–38 is a close paraphrase of sections of Seneca's *De Ira;* although Seneca is not named, the audience could be expected to catch the echoes.

53. Of course this characterization fits the sixth edition, and is anachronistic for editions 1–5.

54. One cannot help wondering whether this is not the sort of marriage, if any, that Smith's mother would have wished him to have.

55. Ross (1995) finds two sources for Smith's account of the Native Americans, both by French Jesuits. Pierre-François Xavier de Charlevoix's *Histoire et description générale de la Nouvelle France* (1744) was definitely in Smith's library; it describes the magnanimity and self-command of the Indians (169). But his knowledge of the "song of death" must have derived, Ross argues, from another source, the influential *Moeurs des sauvages ameriquains, comparées aux moeurs des premiers temps* (1724), by Joseph-François Lafitau; Ross finds that Smith's discussion closely echoes

Lafitau's. Ross (170) reproduces two plates from Lafitau illustrating the torture of the Indian prisoners and the song of death, and one is struck immediately by their sado-erotic character, as the muscular and mostly naked Indians are tortured in a hideous manner.

6. THE TRADITION AND TODAY'S WORLD

1. See Wenar (2015).

2. Here I agree with Risse (2012).

3. See Nussbaum (2013).

4. See Nussbaum and Levmore (2017).

5. See Nussbaum (2013).

6. See, most recently, Nussbaum (2018).

7. See Hasan, Huq, Nussbaum, and Verma (2019).

8. See Rawls (1986). I endorse and clarify Rawls's view in Nussbaum (2011).

9. See Maritain (1943, 1951).

10. See Maritain (1957).

11. See Comim and Nussbaum (2014), introduction.

12. The skeptical and indeed deeply pessimistic view was presented in Posner (2014); for one intervention on the other side, see Ohlin (2015).

13. See Nussbaum (2016c).

14. For a parallel to Kant's remark about the transformation in perceptions wrought by the French Revolution, see ibid.

15. CEDAW has been ratified by 187 out of 194 nations. The exceptions are Iran, Somalia, Sudan, Palau, Tonga, and the United States.

16. See Nussbaum (2016c).

17. Singer (2015).

18. Easterly (2013).

19. See Nussbaum (2007), ch. 10.

20. See Deaton (2013).

21. See Acemoglu and Robinson (2012).

22. Dörner (1997).

23. Deaton (2015).

24. A fine overview is Wellman (2015). For some leading interventions, see Blake (2003, 2013), Carens (2013), Hosein (2013, 2014), Miller (2014), Walzer (1983), and Wellman (2008, 2015).

25. 457 U.S. 202 (1982).

26. Posner and Weyl (2018).

7. FROM COSMOPOLITANISM TO THE CAPABILITIES APPROACH

1. See Nussbaum (2012) for this history and for the relationship between Sen's project and Nussbaum's. This book also contains a comprehensive bibliography of writing by both Sen and Nussbaum relating to the CA.

2. I would now like to alter this in accordance with the critique of anger in Nussbaum (2016b); I would prefer "and emotions of justified protest."

3. See Nussbaum (2006), ch. 5.

4. See ibid.; Nussbaum (2012).

5. Nussbaum (2011).

6. See ibid.

7. See Nussbaum (2006).

8. See ibid.

9. Ibid.; Nussbaum (2008a).

10. See Sorabji (1993).

11. See Nussbaum (1988).

12. See Nussbaum (2006), ch. 6.

13. See Sorabji (1993); ibid.

REFERENCES

Acemoglu, Daron, and James A. Robinson. 2012. *Why Nations Fail: The Origins of Power, Prosperity, and Poverty*. New York: Crown.

Ambedkar, B. R. (1957) 2011. *The Buddha and His Dhamma (A Critical Edition)*. Delhi: Oxford University Press.

Annas, Julia. 1993. *The Morality of Happiness*. New York: Oxford University Press.

Appiah, Kwame Anthony. 1992. *In My Father's House: Africa in the Philosophy of Culture*. New York: Oxford University Press.

———. 1996. "Cosmopolitan Patriots." In *For Love of Country: Debating the Limits of Patriotism*, edited by Martha C. Nussbaum and Joshua Cohen, 22–29. Boston: Beacon.

———. 2005. *The Ethics of Identity*. Princeton, N.J.: Princeton University Press.

———. 2006. *Cosmopolitanism: Ethics in a World of Strangers*. New York: Norton, 2006.

Beitz, Charles. 1979. *Political Theory and International Relations*. Princeton, N.J.: Princeton University Press.

Blake, Michael. 2003. "Immigration." In *A Companion to Applied Ethics*, edited by R. Frey and C. Wellman, 224–237. Malden, Mass.: Blackwell.

———. 2013. "Immigration, Jurisdiction, and Exclusion." *Philosophy and Public Affairs* 41 (2): 103–130.

Branham, R. Bracht. 1996. "Defacing the Currency: Diogenes' Rhetoric and the Invention of Cynicism." In *The Cynics*, edited by R. Bracht Branham and Marie-Odile Goulet-Cazé, 81–104. Berkeley: University of California Press.

Bull, Hedley. 1977. *The Anarchical Society: A Study of Order in World Politics*. New York: Columbia University Press.

———. 1990. "The Importance of Grotius in the Study of International Relations." In *Hugo Grotius and International Relations,* edited by Hedley Bull, Adam Roberts, and Benedict Kingsbury, ch. 2. Oxford, Eng.: Oxford University Press.

Bull, Hedley, Adam Roberts, and Benedict Kingsbury, eds. 1990. *Hugo Grotius and International Relations*. Oxford, Eng.: Oxford University Press.

Carens, Joseph. 2013. *The Ethics of Immigration*. Oxford, Eng.: Oxford University Press.

Cicero, Marcus Tullius. 44 BCEa. *De Officiis*. Oxford Classical Text, edited by Michael Winterbottom. Oxford, Eng.: Clarendon Press, 1994.

———. 44 BCEb. *On Duties*. Edited and translated by Miriam Griffin and Eileen Atkins. Cambridge, Eng.: Cambridge University Press, 1991.

Coase, R. H. 1976. "Adam Smith's View of Man." *Journal of Law and Economics* 19: 529–546.

Cohen, Joshua, and Joel Rogers. 2006. "Extra Rem Publicam Nulla Justitia?" *Philosophy and Public Affairs* 34: 147–175.

Comim, Flavio, and Martha C. Nussbaum. 2014. *Capabilities, Gender, Equality: Towards Fundamental Entitlements*. Cambridge, Eng.: Cambridge University Press.

Darwall, Stephen. 1999. "Sympathetic Liberalism: Recent Work on Adam Smith." *Philosophy and Public Affairs* 28: 139–164.

Dauber, Michele Landis. 2013. *The Sympathetic State: Disaster Relief and the Origins of the American Welfare State*. Chicago: University of Chicago Press.

Deaton, Angus. 2013. *The Great Escape: Health, Wealth, and the Origins of Inequality*. Princeton, N.J.: Princeton University Press.

———. 2015. "Response to Effective Altruism." *Boston Review,* July 1.

Dörner, Dieter. 1997. *The Logic of Failure: Recognizing and Avoiding Error in Complex Situations*. Revised edition. New York: Basic Books.

Dyck, Andrew R. 1996. *A Commentary on Cicero, "De Officiis."* Ann Arbor: University of Michigan Press.

Easterly, William. 2013. *The Tyranny of Experts: Economists, Dictators, and the Forgotten Rights of the Poor*. New York: Basic Books.

Fitzgibbons, Athol. 1995. *Adam Smith's System of Liberty, Wealth, and Virtue*. Oxford, Eng.: Clarendon Press.

Fleischacker, Samuel. 1999. *A Third Concept of Liberty: Judgment and Freedom in Kant and Adam Smith*. Princeton, N.J.: Princeton University Press.

———. 2005. *On Adam Smith's Wealth of Nations: A Philosophical Companion*. Princeton, N.J.: Princeton University Press.

Goodin, Robert. 1985. *Protecting the Vulnerable*. Chicago: University of Chicago Press.

———. 1988. "What Is so Special about Our Fellow Countrymen?" *Ethics* 98: 663–686.

Griffin, Miriam. (1976) 1992. *Seneca: A Philosopher in Politics*, second edition. Oxford, Eng.: Clarendon Press.

———. 1989. "Philosophy, Politics, and Politicians at Rome." In *Philosophia Togata*, edited by M. Griffin and J. Barnes, 1–37. Oxford, Eng.: Clarendon Press.

Griswold, Charles L., Jr. 1999. *Adam Smith and the Virtues of Enlightenment*. New York: Cambridge University Press.

Grotius, Hugo. 1625. *De Iure Belli ac Pacis*. Paris.

———. 1925. *The Law of War and Peace*. Translated by Francis Kelsey. Carnegie Fund edition.

———. 2005. *The Rights of War and Peace*, book 1. Translated by Richard Tuck. Indianapolis: Liberty.

Hadot, Pierre. 1998. *The Inner Citadel: The Meditations of Marcus Aurelius*. Translated by Michael Chase. Cambridge: Harvard University Press.

Hasan, Zoya, Aziz Huq, Martha C. Nussbaum, and Vidhu Verma. 2019. *The Empire of Disgust: Prejudice, Stigma, and Policy in India and the U.S.* Delhi: Oxford University Press.

Holmes, Stephen, and Cass R. Sunstein. 1999. *The Cost of Rights: Why Liberty Depends on Taxes*. New York: W. W. Norton.

Hosein, Adam. 2013. "Immigration and Freedom of Movement." *Ethics and Global Politics* 6: 25–37.

———. 2014. "Immigration: The Case for Legalization." *Social Theory and Practice* 40: 609–630.

Kagan, Shelly. 1989. *The Limits of Morality*. Oxford, Eng.: Clarendon Press.

Kant, Immanuel. 1795. *Perpetual Peace*. In *Kant: Political Writings*, edited by Hans Reiss. Cambridge, Eng.: Cambridge University Press, 1991.

Lauterpacht, Hersh. 1946. "The Grotian Tradition in International Law." *British Year Book of International Law* 23: 1–53.

Long, A. A., and D. N. Sedley. 1987. *The Hellenistic Philosophers*. 2 volumes. Cambridge, Eng.: Cambridge University Press.

Maritain, Jacques. 1943. *The Rights of Man and Natural Law*. Translated by Doris C. Anson. New York: Charles Scribner's Sons.

———. 1951. *Man and the State*. Chicago: University of Chicago Press.

———. 1957. *Truth and Human Fellowship*. Princeton, N.J.: Princeton University Press.

Miller, David. 2014. "Immigration: The Case for Limits." In *Contemporary Debates in Applied Ethics*, second edition, edited by A. Cohen and C. Wellman, 363–375. Malden, Mass.: John Wiley & Sons.

Moyn, Samuel. 2010. *The Last Utopia: Human Rights in History*. Cambridge: Harvard University Press.

———. 2018. *Not Enough: Human Rights in an Unequal World*. Cambridge: Harvard University Press.

Muller, Jerry Z. 1993. *Adam Smith in His Time and Ours: Designing the Decent Society*. New York: Free Press. Reprinted in 1995 by Princeton University Press.

Murphy, Liam. 2002. *Moral Demands in Nonideal Theory*. New York: Oxford University Press.

Nagel, Thomas. 1991. *Equality and Partiality*. New York: Oxford University Press.

———. 2005. "The Idea of Global Justice." *Philosophy and Public Affairs* 33: 113–147.

Nussbaum, Martha C. (1986) 2000. *The Fragility of Goodness: Luck and Ethics in Greek Tragedy and Philosophy*. Updated edition. Cambridge, Eng.: Cambridge University Press.

———. 1988. "Nature, Function, and Capability: Aristotle on Political Distribution." *Oxford Studies in Ancient Philosophy, Supplementary Volume I*: 145–184.

———. 1990. *Love's Knowledge: Essays on Philosophy and Literature*. New York: Oxford University Press.

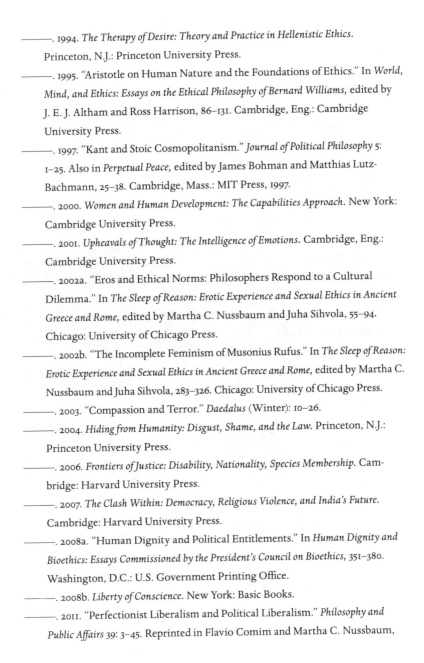

———. 1994. *The Therapy of Desire: Theory and Practice in Hellenistic Ethics.* Princeton, N.J.: Princeton University Press.

———. 1995. "Aristotle on Human Nature and the Foundations of Ethics." In *World, Mind, and Ethics: Essays on the Ethical Philosophy of Bernard Williams,* edited by J. E. J. Altham and Ross Harrison, 86–131. Cambridge, Eng.: Cambridge University Press.

———. 1997. "Kant and Stoic Cosmopolitanism." *Journal of Political Philosophy* 5: 1–25. Also in *Perpetual Peace,* edited by James Bohman and Matthias Lutz-Bachmann, 25–38. Cambridge, Mass.: MIT Press, 1997.

———. 2000. *Women and Human Development: The Capabilities Approach.* New York: Cambridge University Press.

———. 2001. *Upheavals of Thought: The Intelligence of Emotions.* Cambridge, Eng.: Cambridge University Press.

———. 2002a. "Eros and Ethical Norms: Philosophers Respond to a Cultural Dilemma." In *The Sleep of Reason: Erotic Experience and Sexual Ethics in Ancient Greece and Rome,* edited by Martha C. Nussbaum and Juha Sihvola, 55–94. Chicago: University of Chicago Press.

———. 2002b. "The Incomplete Feminism of Musonius Rufus." In *The Sleep of Reason: Erotic Experience and Sexual Ethics in Ancient Greece and Rome,* edited by Martha C. Nussbaum and Juha Sihvola, 283–326. Chicago: University of Chicago Press.

———. 2003. "Compassion and Terror." *Daedalus* (Winter): 10–26.

———. 2004. *Hiding from Humanity: Disgust, Shame, and the Law.* Princeton, N.J.: Princeton University Press.

———. 2006. *Frontiers of Justice: Disability, Nationality, Species Membership.* Cambridge: Harvard University Press.

———. 2007. *The Clash Within: Democracy, Religious Violence, and India's Future.* Cambridge: Harvard University Press.

———. 2008a. "Human Dignity and Political Entitlements." In *Human Dignity and Bioethics: Essays Commissioned by the President's Council on Bioethics,* 351–380. Washington, D.C.: U.S. Government Printing Office.

———. 2008b. *Liberty of Conscience.* New York: Basic Books.

———. 2011. "Perfectionist Liberalism and Political Liberalism." *Philosophy and Public Affairs* 39: 3–45. Reprinted in Flavio Comim and Martha C. Nussbaum,

Capabilities, Gender, Equality: Towards Fundamental Entitlements. Cambridge, Eng.: Cambridge University Press, 2014.

———. 2012. *Creating Capabilities: The Human Development Approach.* Cambridge: Harvard University Press.

———. 2013. *Political Emotions: Why Love Matters for Justice.* Cambridge: Harvard University Press.

———. 2015. "Untouchable." Review of B. R. Ambedkar, *Annihilation of Caste,* edited and annotated by S. Anand. *New Rambler Review,* August 19.

———. 2016a. "Ambedkar's Constitution: Promoting Inclusion, Opposing Majority Tyranny." In *Assessing Constitutional Performance,* edited by Tom Ginsburg and Aziz Huq, 295–336. Cambridge, Eng.: Cambridge University Press.

———. 2016b. *Anger and Forgiveness: Resentment, Generosity, Justice.* New York: Oxford University Press.

———. 2016c. "Women's Progress and Women's Human Rights." *Human Rights Quarterly* 38 (3): 589–622.

———. 2018. *The Monarchy of Fear: A Philosopher Looks at Our Political Crisis.* New York: Simon and Schuster.

Nussbaum, Martha C., and Joshua Cohen, eds. 1996. *For Love of Country: Debating the Limits of Patriotism.* Boston: Beacon.

Nussbaum, Martha C., and Saul Levmore. 2017. *Aging Thoughtfully.* New York: Oxford University Press.

Ohlin, Jens David. 2015. *The Assault on International Law.* New York: Oxford University Press.

Posner, Eric A. 2014. *The Twilight of Human Rights Law.* New York: Oxford University Press.

Posner, Eric A., and E. Glenn Weyl. 2018. *Radical Markets: Uprooting Capitalism and Democracy for a Just Society.* Princeton, N.J.: Princeton University Press.

Rawls, John. 1971. *A Theory of Justice.* Cambridge: Harvard University Press. Original edition.

———. 1986. *Political Liberalism.* New York: Columbia University Press. Expanded paper edition.

———. 1999. *The Law of Peoples.* Cambridge: Harvard University Press.

Reich, Klaus. 1939. "Kant and Greek Ethics." *Mind* 48: 338–354, 446–463.

Risse, Mathias. 2012. *On Global Justice*. Princeton, N.J.: Princeton University Press.

Ross, Ian Simpson. 1995. *The Life of Adam Smith*. Oxford, Eng.: Clarendon Press.

Rothschild, Emma. 2001. *Economic Sentiments: Adam Smith, Condorcet, and the Enlightenment*. Cambridge: Harvard University Press.

Rutherford, R. B. 1989. *The Meditations of Marcus Aurelius: A Study*. Oxford, Eng.: Clarendon Press.

Scheffler, Samuel. 1982. *The Rejection of Consequentialism*. Oxford, Eng.: Clarendon Press.

Schneewind, J. B. 1998. *The Invention of Autonomy*. Cambridge, Eng.: Cambridge University Press.

Schofield, Malcolm. (1991) 1999. *The Stoic Idea of the City*. Cambridge, Eng.: Cambridge University Press. Reissued with a new preface by Martha C. Nussbaum.

Sedley, David N. 1997. "The Ethics of Brutus and Cassius." *Journal of Roman Studies* 87: 41–53.

Sen, Amartya. 1981. *Poverty and Famines*. Oxford, Eng.: Clarendon Press.

Seneca, Lucius Annaeus. (65 CE) 1965. *Ad Lucilium Epistulae Morales*. Oxford Classical Texts, 2 volumes, edited by L. Reynolds. Oxford, Eng.: Clarendon Press.

Shklar, Judith. 1990. *The Faces of Injustice*. New Haven, Conn.: Yale University Press.

Shue, Henry. 1980. *Basic Rights: Subsistence, Affluence, and U.S. Foreign Policy*. Princeton, N.J.: Princeton University Press.

Singer, Peter. 1972. "Famine, Affluence, and Morality." *Philosophy and Public Affairs* 1: 229–243.

———. 2009. *The Life You Can Save: How to Do Your Part to End World Poverty*. New York: Random House.

———. 2015. *The Most Good You Can Do: How Effective Altruism Is Changing Ideas about Living Morally*. New Haven, Conn.: Yale University Press.

Smith, Adam. (1759–1790) 1982. *A Theory of Moral Sentiments*, edited by D. D. Raphael and A. L. Macfie. Indianapolis: Liberty.

———. (1776) 1981. *The Wealth of Nations*, edited by R. H. Campbell and A. S. Skinner. Indianapolis: Liberty.

Sorabji, Richard. 1993. *Animal Minds and Human Morals: The Origins of the Western Debate*. Ithaca, N.Y.: Cornell University Press.

Sutherland, Kathryn. 1995. "Adam Smith's Master Narrative: Women and the *Wealth of Nations.*" In *Adam Smith's Wealth of Nations: New Interdisciplinary Essays,* edited by Stephen Copley and Kathryn Sutherland, 97–121. Manchester, Eng.: Manchester University Press.

Tesón, Fernando R. 1992. "The Kantian Theory of International Law." *Columbia Law Review* 92: 53–102.

Treggiari, Susan. 1991. *Roman Marriage: Iusti Coniuges from the Time of Cicero to the Time of Ulpian.* Oxford, Eng.: Clarendon Press.

United Nations Development Programme. 2016. *Human Development Report 2016.* New York: UNDP.

Van Holk, L. E. 1983. "Hugo Grotius, 1583–1645, A Biographical Sketch." In *Grotius Reader: A Reader for Students of International Law and Legal History,* edited by L. E. van Holk and C. G. Roelofsen, 23–44. The Hague: T.M.C. Asser Instituut.

Van Holk, L. E., and C. G. Roelofsen, eds. 1983. *Grotius Reader: A Reader for Students of International Law and Legal History.* The Hague: T.M.C. Asser Instituut.

Waldron, Jeremy. 2012. *Dignity, Rank, and Rights.* New York: Oxford University Press.

Walzer, Michael. 1983. *Spheres of Justice.* Princeton, N.J.: Princeton University Press.

Wellman, Christopher H. 2008. "Immigration and Freedom of Association." *Ethics* 199: 109–141.

———. 2015. "Immigration." *Stanford Encyclopedia of Philosophy.* Stanford, Calif.: Metaphysics Research Lab, Center for the Study of Language and Information, Stanford University.

Wenar, Leif. 2015. *Blood Oil: Tyrants, Violence, and the Rules That Run the World.* New York: Oxford University Press.

ACKNOWLEDGMENTS

This book began life as the Castle Lectures at Yale University in 2000. (Only Chapters 2 and 3 were presented in that lecture series, however.) The material on Grotius and Smith was written later. All chapters were thoroughly rewritten, and Chapters 1, 6, and 7 were newly written, in 2016–2018. I am therefore in the position of having many debts of gratitude that I can barely remember. I want to thank my Yale hosts for the splendid occasion for exchange; Samuel Fleischacker and Chad Flanders for help with the Smith material; David Weisbach and students in our co-taught class on Global Inequality for helpful discussion of Grotius; and students in several classes on Cicero for their input into my understanding of his contribution. When I presented a draft of Chapter 3 at Saint Andrews University, I was helped by the comments of the late Sir Kenneth Dover, John Haldane, and Stephen Halliwell. Robert Goodin gave me valuable comments on the Cicero material when he edited it for the *Journal of Political Philosophy*. The Adam Smith chapter was presented at the Hume Society in Toronto in 2005, and I thank David Owen, Kate Abramson, and others for their comments on that occasion; it was also presented at Indiana University, and I am grateful to Marcia Baron for her comments then, and to Sam Fleischacker for other comments. In the penultimate stage of revision I was greatly helped by comments from

Nethanel Lipshitz, Eric Posner, and other participants at a Work-in-Progress workshop at the University of Chicago Law School.

A version of Chapter 3 was published in 2002 in a festschrift volume in honor of Miriam Griffin, whose work has been an inspiration to all of us who believe that Roman thought has a great deal to offer to the history of philosophy. Griffin's pathbreaking work (for example in her *Seneca: A Philosopher in Politics*, 1976, second edition 1991) shows how important it is not to treat Roman thinkers simply as sources for an abstract picture of "Hellenistic philosophy." Thinkers in their own right, they are also creative participants in their political context, and their contributions need to be appreciated in that historical setting. My chapter in her festschrift, being that of a political philosopher, lacks the historical richness that distinguishes Griffin's work, and is in that sense an unworthy tribute. But it was offered, nonetheless, with the greatest gratitude for the illumination of her work, and the pleasure of her friendship. Over the years since the festschrift, my admiration for her work has only increased, as I have read more of her articles and edited her translation of Seneca's *De Beneficiis* for the University of Chicago Press Seneca series. Her work on that treatise culminated in her monumental commentary *On Benefits: Seneca on Society* (Oxford University Press, 2013). Being able to see Miriam and her husband, Jasper, as I gave the John Locke Lectures in Oxford in 2014 made that whole experience richer and more fun. (Miriam certainly understood, as few have done so well, how to balance the claims of scholarship with love for her husband, her three daughters, her friends, and for Somerville College, Oxford, to which she devoted so much energy as a leader.) The conference at Somerville celebrating her eightieth birthday, in May 2015, which I was lucky to be able to attend, was a true delight. Unfortunately, I was unable to attend the celebration of the release of her collected papers on April 28, 2018 (*Politics and Philosophy at Rome: Collected Papers*, Oxford University Press). But in correspondence with her about that occasion I told her of my plan to dedicate the present book to her, and she was pleased. In our last email exchange we made a plan to meet in November 2018, my next visit to Oxford. Very sadly indeed, she died shortly after the celebration, on May 16, 2018. In sadness and with love, I dedicate this book to her.

Portions of Chapter 2 were first published as "Duties of Justice, Duties of Material Aid: Cicero's Problematic Legacy" in the *Journal of Political Philosophy* 8, no. 2 (2000): 176–206. Chapter 3 reprints sections of text first published in 2002 as "The Worth of Human Dignity: Two Tensions in Stoic Cosmopolitanism" in *Philosophy and Power in the Graeco-Roman World: Essays in Honour of Miriam Griffin*, edited by Gillian Clark and Tessa Rajak. Since publication of these pieces my views have fundamentally changed, and these chapters include important and extensive revisions that lead to new conclusions.

INDEX

accountability, 59–61, 122, 127, 140, 172, 218, 225

Acemoglu, Daron, 226

Africa, 4, 58, 201, 207, 208

agency, 16, 148, 227

Alexander the Great, 2, 5, 65, 71, 125

Ambedkar, B. R., 4

Anarchical Society, The (Bull), 97

anger, 34, 43, 84, 117, 212, 213; attachment to externals and, 92; against injustice, 205; justified, 242; particularistic passions and, 92; removal of, 81; retributive, 89

animals, non-human, 3, 140, 142, 242; capabilities of, 250; contract and exchange alien to, 148–149; cosmopolitan tradition extended to, 17; ethical duties toward, 251;

human worth versus "brute beasts," 16–17, 251; reason and choice absent from, 69

anthropocentrism, 237–238

Appiah, Joe, 4, 22

Appiah, Kwame Anthony, 4, 22, 258n8

apprenticeship, 144, 156, 190, 191

Aquinas, Thomas, 19

Aristotle, 8, 84, 93, 165, 213, 237, 251

Arminian heresy, 101, 103, 214

association, freedom of, 19

asylum seekers, 16, 130–131, 137, 208, 229–230, 233–234. *See also* migration / migrants

Atticus (friend of Cicero), 10, 90, 91, 102, 210–211

Augustus Caesar, 260n20

human rights (*continued*)
first- and second-generation rights,
7; "human dignity" and, 70;
international society and, 248;
political liberalism and, 14; seen as
prepolitical, 121; transcendent
moral truths and, 106; violated
throughout the world, 208; world
government and, 120, 139
human rights law, international, 14,
15, 30, 218–222, 235. *See also* law,
international
hunger, 7, 41, 49–51, 89

identity, national, 16
imprisonment, 83, 86
incest, prohibition of, 125, 126
inclusion, 89, 133, 142
India, 3–4, 59, 208, 218, 221; constitution of, 4, 238, 243; health infrastructure, 225; Hindu Right in,
224; literacy in, 6; political
liberalism and, 248
individuals, rights of, 118–128
iniuria (wrong, injury), 49, 50, 258n9
injustice, passive, 46–48, 50–51, 175,
179
institutions, 65, 87, 112, 113, 158, 229,
262n39; accountability and, 60;

affiliation and, 242; democratic,
225, 227, 228; dignity and, 148;
duties of justice and, 14, 42;
education, 225; human dignity
and, 148, 159; international, 41, 135,
218; material aid and, 14, 235;
mediation of duties and, 62,
262n39; national sovereignty and,
207; political liberalism and, 215; of
republican Rome, 23, 33, 90, 96;
shared, 32, 59; thick fellowship
and, 58
international community, 109, 127,
222; idea of international society,
134–140; transnational duties of, 18
Italy, 137
ius gentium (law of nations), 100,
109–110, 112; law of war and,
113–118, 267n21; natural law
beyond, 121. *See also* law,
international
iustitia (justice), 24

Jefferson, Thomas, 273n26
joint stock companies, 157, 168,
273n27
Josephus, 265n8
Judaism, Reform, 214
Julius Caesar, 25, 43

moral psychology, 10, 66, 209, 210–213, 235; Capabilities Approach and, 237; Cicero and, 13; Smith and, 12

Moral Rights position, 119, 122, 135

Muller, Jerry Z., 269n4

Musonius Rufus, 37, 78, 79, 260nn20–21, 272n21

national security, 98, 120, 136

nations: ability to maintain public safety, 41; international society and, 245–247; on just and unjust war, 19; just transfer between, 62; as largest vehicle of human autonomy, 14; material aid across national borders, 50; material transfers between, 19; migration and, 234; moral obligations of, 11, 47; nation-states, 98, 135–136, 138–139, 172, 235; perpetual peace among, 94; right of self-defense by, 115; role in moral life of human beings, 98; unequal wealth between, 16; wartime duties of, 18

native North Americans, 169–170, 188, 200–201, 204, 277–278n55

NATO (North Atlantic Treaty Organization), 41

natural law *(ius naturale)*, 99, 103, 117, 125, 267n18. *See also* moral law

nature, 28, 92, 213, 242, 252, 259n12; assaults of non-human origin, 48–50; binary understanding of, 69; cosmopolitan tradition extended to, 17; human dignity and, 53, 146; law of, 29–30, 75; Stoic *apatheia* doctrine and, 181; Stoic doctrine of Providence and, 192, 274n35

Nehru, Jawaharlal, 4, 211

Nemean VIII (Pindar), 272n19

Neo-Platonism, 237

"new medievalism," 137–140

NGOs (non-governmental organizations), 223–224, 226

Niger, 6

Nigeria, 6

Nozick, Robert, 239, 262n35

On the Law of War and Peace [*De Iure Belli ac Paci,* or *BP*] (Grotius, 1625), 11, 30, 140, 264n1; on fellowship, 97; on natural law, 109–110; Prolegomena to, 103; on property rights, 133–134; on rights of passage, 128–129

Stoics / Stoicism (*continued*)
89–92; Smith's lectures on, 12; in
Smith's *Theory of Moral Sentiments*,
175–193. *See also* Providence, Stoic
doctrine of
Suarez, Francisco, 19
suicide, Stoic view of, 188, 201
Supreme Court, U.S., 233, 256n5
Swaziland, life expectancy in, 5
Syria, asylum seekers from, 208,
233

Tacitus, 262n37
Taoism, 215
taxation, 13, 40, 61, 178; foreign aid
and, 60; public education and, 177;
redistribution and, 132–133; rights
of passage and, 129
technology transfer, 171
terrorism, 126, 231, 233
Thailand, 6
Theory of Moral Sentiments, A [*TMS*]
(Smith, 1759, 1790), 12, 21–22;
editions of, 143, 147, 180, 194,
269nn2–3; on external goods and
self-command, 179–193; on the
"invisible hand," 192, 274n34,
274–275n36; on justice and beneficence, 175–179; on Providence,

191–193; Smith's revisions of,
193–194; Stoicism and, 144, 146
Theseus, 124
Thirty Years' War, 101
Thrasea Paetus, 201
Thucydides, 266n15
toleration, 100, 102, 103, 122,
265nn6–7
torture, 7, 19, 40, 82, 158, 250; ban on,
5; inner freedom and, 36; opposed
through international politics, 83;
refraining from, 42; of Regulus,
258–259n11; as violence to human
dignity, 30
Trachiniai (Sophocles), 49
tragic dramas, 83
transgender people, rights of, 215
transnational duties, 11, 18, 62, 64
Tullia (daughter of Cicero), 90, 211
Tusculan Disputations (Cicero), 34, 49

ubuntu, African idea of, 4
United Kingdom, 138
United Nations, 136, 137, 219, 221, 240
United States, 218, 247; life expec-
tancy in, 5, 255n8; migration
issues, 232
Universal Declaration of Human
Rights, 4–5, 217, 248